'THIS IS A BASTARD OF A PLACE...'

said a soldier on the Anzio beachhead. This was the bitter truth. What started as an easy victory turned abruptly into a massacre. Over 18,000 Allied soldiers were wounded and 4,400 killed in the early months of 1944.

This book, by a man who was there to the very end, tells the whole, shocking story.

"Explains in vivid detail ... what the soldiers ... and one general can be proud of and what other generals need to explain."—LIFE

ANZIO *was originally published at $5.00 by Holt, Rinehart and Winston, Inc.*

ABOUT THE AUTHOR

WYNFORD VAUGHAN-THOMAS is one of the best and most popular BBC correspondents. During the war, a young lady who worked as a censor in the British Office of War Information was so impressed with the author's Anzio reports that she kept copies of them all. After the war, she met the writer and urged him to set down his impressions in book form. The book became ANZIO—and the young lady became the author's wife. They live in London with their son David.

ABOUT THE BOOK

IN THE AUTHOR'S WORDS: "I was on the beachhead from the first moment to the last . . . I had always felt that justice had not been done to the men, American and British, who fought there . . . At Anzio, American and British leaders *had* to learn how to work together or perish. This theme is not without its lesson today."

ANZIO

Wynford Vaughan-Thomas

POPULAR LIBRARY • NEW YORK

Ned L. Pines · President

Frank P. Lualdi · Publisher

POPULAR LIBRARY EDITION
Published in September, 1962
Copyright © 1961 by Wynford Vaughan-Thomas
Library of Congress Catalog Card Number: 61-5210

Published by arrangement with Holt, Rinehart & Winston, Inc.
Holt, Rinehart & Winston edition published in August, 1961
Three printings

ACKNOWLEDGMENTS
The publishers and author are indebted to the following for permission to reproduce copyright material:
William Blackwood & Sons, Ltd., for an extract from the article "With a Casualty Clearing Station at Anzio," by J.A.R. (Major J. A. Ross), from *Blackwood's Magazine*, May, 1946; Houghton Mifflin Company for material from *The Second World War*, Vol. 5, "Closing the Ring," by Sir Winston Churchill; E. P. Dutton & Co., Inc., New York, for extracts from *Command Missions* by General Lucien K. Truscott; Major D. L. Fitzmaurice and Gale & Polden, Ltd., for extracts from *History of the Irish Guards in the Second World War*; Harper & Brothers, New York, for material from *Calculated Risk* by General Mark Clark; William Morrow & Co., Inc., New York, for extracts from *Kesselring: A Soldier's Record*.

DEDICATION:

*To the ordinary soldiers
—British and American—
who, by their valour, held the beachhead*

AUTHOR'S NOTE
This story could not have been told without the help and encouragement of Major-General Sir Ronald Penney, KBE, CD, DSO, MC, who commanded the British 1st Division at Anzio and who has allowed me full use of his private papers. I am also indebted to Major-General J.S.M. Pasley, CB, CBE, MVO, who has given me the benefit of his advice on all matters concerning the artillery on the Beachhead.

My thanks are also due to Miss R.E.B. Coombs of the Imperial War Museum and Mr. W. G. Williams of the War Office Library.

Military and political personalities in my text are given the title and rank held at the time of the events described.

—W. V.-T.

Contents

A SHORT GLOSSARY OF
SOME MILITARY AND NAVAL TERMS

AMG — *Allied Military Government.*

DUKWS — *Amphibious Motor-lorries.*

G2 — *In the British Army, an abbreviation of GSO2 (General Staff Officer, Second Grade). In the American Army, G-2 is the Intelligence section or officer of a formation staff.*

LCA — *Landing Craft (Assault).*

LCI — *Landing Craft (Infantry).*

LCT — *Landing Craft (Tank).*

LSI — *Landing Ship (Infantry).*

LST — *Landing Ship (Tank).*

OKW — *Oberkommando der Wehrmacht — High Command of the German Armed Forces.*

Overlord — *Code name for the invasion of North-west Europe, 1944.*

RAP — *Regimental Aid Post.*

RCT — *Regimental Combat Team—American equivalent of a British brigade.*

REME — *Royal Electrical and Mechanical Engineers, British Army.*

Recce — *Reconnaissance (Regiment).*

Shingle — *Code name for the Anzio Landing operation.*

SP gun — *Self-propelled gun.*

TD — *Self-propelled gun designed specially as a tank destroyer.*

1

Prologue

The time—the small, cold hours after midnight on 22 January 1944; the place—the deck of a landing craft out to sea from the sleeping port of Anzio, thirty miles south of Rome; for me, and for thousands of Allied soldiers, the most uncomfortable yet surprising moment in the whole of World War II.

For we were about to invade Hitler's European fortress six months before D-Day in Normandy. This was to be one of the most daring moves yet carried out by the High Command; we were to fling ourselves boldly ashore in the darkness far behind the German lines. We had been briefed in numerous 'pep-talks' about the vital importance of our mission. We were going to break the dismal deadlock which had gripped the Italian front through the winter of 1943. We would outflank the formidable defences of the Gustav Line, 'roll back the Boche'. Rome in ten days! And then, who could count the glittering prizes which might fall into our hands—the Germans flung back to the Apennines, the Balkan front ablaze, the whole course of the war triumphantly altered? So the bright visions played over our expedition and over Allied Headquarters far behind us at Naples and Algiers.

But for us, watching the minutes tick on to Zero Hour, the world had now shrunk to one precise danger-point—the dark line to the east that marked the shore. Soon, far too soon for most of us, the orders would be given. Quietly we would heave ourselves down slippery ladders into the waiting boats. Then, full speed ahead, we would race towards the beaches. What would happen? Were we five minutes away from another Salerno?

The men in this invasion had bitter memories of Salerno

and the way the Germans had waited for them to come close inshore. Then the storm of bullets and shellfire and all the hell of a contested landing!

We couldn't banish it from our minds as we waited for 2 a.m., the scheduled time for our assault. I was sailing in the headquarters craft which carried the splendidly named naval officer entitled SNOL (Senior Naval Officer Landings) and the HQ company of the 2nd Brigade of the British 1st Infantry Division. I took comfort from this roll-call of naval and military designations; it made me feel that I was part of the great fighting machine of the invasion even though I had no control over the working of it.

I was the BBC's war correspondent for the landing. My only weapon of war was the new, cumbersome portable recorder which I was to be the first to take into action—a gramophone type affair which had to be cranked up every few minutes and used discs instead of tape. It sounds a creaking antique now, but it was a revolutionary invention in 1944. On it I hoped to capture the strange, tense atmosphere of a landing at night from the sea.

The shore remained a vague, dark line on the surface of the waters somewhere out to the east, but the night now started to fill with little local sounds—the faint creak of the davits as the assault craft were swung out, the quiet thud of the screws of the LSTs moving closer to the beaches. Some of these sounds must have been carried eastwards by the night breeze, but there was still no sign of life from the land. It did not seem possible that the enemy was still unaware that a vast armada of ships—cruisers, destroyers, troop-carriers, minesweepers, landing craft of all shapes and sizes—was now lying silent only two miles out to sea.

0153 hours; the uncanny silence of the night was torn apart with sudden brutality, the whole sky to port seemed to flare into fire and a crashing explosion rocked the anchorage as if an ammunition ship had gone up. For a moment we could see the long line of assault craft poised like race-horses at the starting gate. Out to seaward the whole great fleet was silhouetted against the glare.

It was the rocket ship going into action—792 5-inch rockets hurtling onto the beach, all exploding within ninety seconds. The ground must have heaved under them like an earthquake. No minefield or any German near it could possibly have survived.

8

A muffled figure on the bridge at my side muttered, 'That's shaken them. Now we're in for it.' I braced myself for the shock of the searchlights stabbing out from the shore, followed by the tracers pouring over the waters. But again a silence more intense than ever held the whole area as the assault craft crept in.

0200, Zero Hour itself, and suddenly the radio on board began to crackle. The first wave had touched down, and not a shot had been fired. The incredible had happened. We had got the one thing we had never bargained for, utter and complete surprise. The reports poured in and our Brigadier stood with SNOL in the tiny blacked-out cabin where the maps of the beaches had been laid out under hooded lights. The first news was that the beaches were awkward—there was trouble with sandbanks offshore, and mines had been found on the dunes and in the pine woods beyond.

'We must take a risk,' a helpful officer declared. 'We ought to get the troops to push on.' (The appropriate comment on this suggestion appeared in the official report after the landing: 'It must be realized that no amount of shouting through loud hailers will induce troops to advance through a minefield.')

But gradually the position became clearer, and a feeling of quiet optimism pervaded the cabin. The first elements were through the pine woods; they were crossing the coast road, probing carefully forward in the darkness and had met nothing.

Now the sky was beginning to lighten, and it was our turn to land. SNOL came down from the bridge to see us off into the small craft which was to take us onto the beach. He was a man with many cares on his mind, but he still felt that, in keeping with the long tradition of the Royal Navy, he should give a formal farewell to his guests.

He looked down on the little huddled group in khaki now gathered in the well of the LCA. 'Good-bye,' he shouted, 'and good . . .' But his farewell stopped in mid-career. The steersman of the landing craft had allowed it to scrape the immaculate topsides of the headquarters ship. SNOL seized his loud-hailer and roared, 'You there! Don't stand about like a half-plucked fowl. Cast off!'

Propelled by the force of SNOL's farewell we made for the shore, wading through the chill water to reach the beach. Our steps were clogged as, heavily loaded, we struggled through the sands and muffled voices warned us of minefields. Our little party picked its way carefully along the lines of white tape and stumbled out into the woodlands.

Overhead came an unpleasant whine followed by a crash and the faint smell of high explosive. It was the first shell from a German self-propelled gun. Instinctively the men cringed and ducked. The Brigadier, now outlined in clearcut profile against the growing light in the east, looked neither right nor left but issued the crisp order 'Forward, Brigade' and led us onward like the headmaster leading a school 'crocodile,' while the antennae of the pack radio carried by his signaller shook against the dawn.

And as the light strengthened so did our surprise and relief at the fantastic ease of our landing. Dawn was fine and chill, and not an enemy in sight!

There before us were the long line of marching troops entering the woodlands behind Anzio, the first guns coming ashore and the tanks lumbering after them. Still no enemy —only an odd shell from somewhere out ahead. Nothing to worry about. We had achieved utter and complete surprise.

The only Germans we saw were a forlorn group standing under guard at a farmhouse door. They had been fast asleep when we landed, and clad in pyjamas had jumped into their car, driven it out through the door of the barn and had been rounded up before they had gone a hundred yards.

The sun strengthened and we pushed on to the main road running out of Anzio towards Rome. We could see the smiling countryside ahead untouched by war and, in the distance, the graceful, welcoming outline of the Alban Hills. Beyond lay Rome, and there was nothing to stop us driving straight down the road to the Eternal City.

'Bliss was it at that dawn to be alive.' The peasants crowded around the jeeps and pointed excitedly down the road. 'Niente Tedeschi?' we asked in our broken Italian. 'Nobody, nothing. A Roma, pronto!' came the reply.

Time for a quick 'brew up' and then, surely, the orders would arrive to push on at all speed, to occupy the Alban Hills and reconnoitre to the very gates of Rome. We held the whole world in our hands on that clear morning of January 1944.

So we waited for the orders to advance.

We went on waiting . . . the hours passed . . . the sun

became warm . . . the road stretched invitingly ahead . . . but still no instructions reached us to get into our jeeps. 'Well,' said the sergeant who was with us, 'that's that, lads. It doesn't look as if we'll be moving before night. Better kip down where we are and get ready for an early start. They're bound to push us up that road soon.'

Four months later British soldiers were still halted at the same spot, but the landscape around them had undergone a violent change. The farmhouses were heaps of rubble, the trees mere shell-torn skeletons, and the fields churned by tanks into a sodden morass. A complicated trench-system zigzagged across the tortured countryside.

At night the star-shells soared up over shell-holes and barbed wire while the guns rumbled and flashed far to the rear. Just before dawn in late April a British sentry in a forward trench cocked his Bren gun and peered into the darkness. A deep voice suddenly said, 'Good evening.' The startled sentry crouching in his slot in the ground, jerked his head back in time to see a German officer looking down on him.

'Hullo, Tommy,' said the officer in perfect English, 'are you still there?' And before the soldier could swing his Bren round the German disappeared.

The adventurous officer was given no chance to repeat his exploit, but his question went on puzzling his opponents during the weary, frustrating months they spent at Anzio. It has continued to puzzle them ever since.

After all, this was 1944 not 1917!

What, indeed, were the Tommy and his comrade-in-arms the American GI doing in malodorous slots in the ground, fighting for the only time in World War II a battle which, for long weary months, seemed to belong to the trench warfare of World War I; a struggle in the mud, complete with duckboards, trench-raids and patrols in no-man's-land, a miniature Passchendaele in the era of the *Blitzkrieg*?

What went wrong with one of the boldest and most adventurous strokes planned by the Allies in the whole of the 1939-45 war?

The passage of time brings an order and clarity into battles which was never apparent to the men who did the actual fighting. Today, after the generals and the war leaders have published their memoirs, we can see only too clearly why

Anzio failed to fulfil its first bright promise. The answer to the problem is simply this—the adventure was launched under divided counsels and against the inner conviction of one of the partners. The men in Britain who were responsible for the higher conduct of the war believed in Anzio; their American colleagues did not. When Allies disagree they have to compromise, but compromise never won a battle yet. No wonder that the general selected to lead the troops into battle muttered as he left the final conference, 'This is going to be worse than Gallipoli!'

A battle, even a campaign as important as that of Normandy, is only an incident in the great sweep of events that goes to make a world war. The compromise over Anzio, the disagreement amongst the Allies and the agony and final triumph of the Beachhead can be understood only when they are seen as part of the wider picture. There is no need here to go into the details of that picture. It will be enough for our purpose if we give a brief outline of the position of the Allies in 1943 and their discord over the presence of Anglo-American armies on the soil of Italy. From this basic disagreement over the conduct of the Italian campaign the difficulties of the troops at Anzio flowed with the inevitability of a law of nature.

The early months of 1943 marked a turning-point in the fortunes of the Allies. The Germans had been cleared out of North Africa, their armies were reeling back from Stalingrad, and the Japanese had been decisively checked in their Pacific advance. Hitler had been sealed into his stronghold of Fortress Europe.

It was clear that the Allies could hardly lose the war, but it was equally clear that they had not yet won it. To do this they must break into Hitler's fortress. The great debate raged amongst the leaders of Britain and America as to how this break-in could best be achieved.

The Chiefs of Staff at Washington felt that the right way to end the war was by a powerful blow to the heart—'Overlord', the landing in Normandy. Everything should be subordinated to this. Said one general discussing the problems ahead, 'In America we don't solve our problems, we overwhelm them!'

The British, while agreeing that 'Overlord' was essential, favoured a more indirect approach. A campaign in the Mediterranean would do two things—draw the German reserves south away from the Normandy front and open up a rewarding second front. Where else but in the Mediterranean could the Allies fight the enemy while they waited for the launching of 'Overlord'?

Reluctantly the Americans allowed themselves to be persuaded.

The Allies occupied Sicily. In September they advanced into the mainland of Italy. The British Eighth Army under General Montgomery pushed up the east coast along the Adriatic while the American Fifth Army under General Mark Clark took Naples and drove forward on the western side of the peninsula. These two armies formed the 15th Army Group commanded by General Sir Harold Alexander.

Back at Algiers, General Eisenhower as Commander-in-Chief Allied Expeditionary Forces in the Mediterranean presided happily over the whole scene.

Well might Mr. Churchill chuckle: 'It is true, I suppose, that the Americans consider that we have led them up the garden path in the Mediterranean, but what a beautiful path it has proved to be. They have picked peaches here and nectarines there. How grateful they should be.' [1]

But as the summer of 1943 faded a chill wind began to blow through the Italian garden, and the gratitude of the Americans became less obvious. The Allies' advance was slowing down. They were coming up against the basic facts of Italian geography, fighting their way through a tangled mass of high mountains where every river seemed to flow the wrong way. The troops had been committed to what General Fuller described as a five-hundred-mile steeplechase 'with each fence a river, a ridge, a ravine. . . . In such a campaign of what use are your tanks, your guns, your men, for what you want is an army of bullet-proof kangaroos!'

No wonder that a curious malaise, a sense of waste and futility, began to envelop the Italian scene. For many this malaise was deepened by the very setting of the battle. This war was being fought through one of the most beautiful landscapes in the world, towards cities and towns that were rare monuments to Man's achievement over long centuries. Driving an army through such a country was like driving a tank through the British Museum. Our generals were no Philistines and they did their best in most difficult circum-

---

[1] Kennedy, *The Business of War*.

stances to save what they could without too great a sacrifice of their men, but there was irony in the wit of the French General de Montsabert as he contemplated the problem:

This campaign is becoming difficult. It is not the Art of War any more but the War of Art. The fifteenth century? I must not attack but must make an outflanking movement. The sixteenth? Then I permit myself a little machine-gun fire. The seventeenth? Ah! now we can have artillery support. The eighteenth means tanks and for the nineteenth, monsieur, I have no hesitation in calling in the air. If only Italy had all been built in the twentieth century we should be on the Alps by now! [2]

But in late October 1943 the Allies' front was very far from the Alps or even the Northern Apennines. It was in fact a bare seventy miles north of Salerno, where they had landed in September, and General Alexander and General Eisenhower had other things to occupy their minds than the preservation of works of art. They began to realize a little ruefully that they had underestimated the power that the very structure of the country gave to the defence. On the east coast the coastal plain was narrow and all the rivers ran straight across it to the sea, thus forming a series of perfect anti-tank ditches. The central mountains were frankly impossible, and already the first snows of winter were beginning to whiten their 6,000-foot summits, bringing a sinister threat of what might happen at low levels **as** the year wasted to an end.

Worse still, the signs multiplied that the Germans had built a formidable defence line right across the peninsula from the Adriatic to the western sea. This Gustav Line was a masterpiece of fortification, bristling with traps, concrete gun-emplacements and barbed wire. Its pivot was the mountain mass of Cassino, which completely dominated the only valley that led through the lines towards Rome. High over this Liri valley brooded the gaunt, fortress-like monastery of Monte Cassino, which seemed to grow out of the rock and mark the barrier beyond which the Allied soldiers dared not pass.

Slowly and stubbornly, General Kesselring, the German C-in-C South-West, fell back towards his defences. This redoubtable and resourceful soldier could be relied on to hold

[2] Spoken to the author.

the Gustav Line to the last man if need be.

As yet the Allied intelligence had no details of the new fortifications, but they sensed that there was something of the sort ahead. General Eisenhower and General Alexander realized that unless they acted soon and with resolution their painful advance up the long ridge of Italy might soon be blocked for ever. But need that advance always be a slow, remorseless slogging match among mountains that gave every trick to the defenders? Why not go round them? A sea-borne landing behind the German defences would solve the problem. The quick stab in the side can be more deadly than the bludgeon blow from the front.

The Higher Command determined to try it. General Alexander issued a new directive to his army commanders for a two-pronged advance up the east and west coasts of Italy. The Eighth Army was to strike first at the end of November and try to advance to the port of Pescara on the Adriatic, where it would be in a position to cut one of the few good roads that led across the mountains westward to Rome. Then at the beginning of December the Fifth Army would push into the Liri valley to the neighbourhood of Frosinone. This small town lay a good thirty miles beyond the rocky jaws of Cassino and within striking distance of the capital. Once Frosinone was secured a sea-borne landing would be launched on the coast thirty miles south of Rome.

In the light of our later knowledge of the German strength and intentions this plan looks amazingly optimistic; the spearheads of the advance thrust onwards over mountains and rivers as boldly as the arrows drawn on newspaper maps. But at the time no one knew for certain that the Germans were determined to stand south of Rome or that the Gustav Line was such a formidable barrier. It seemed sensible to act on the principle outlined for mountaineers by Captain Farrar of the Alpine Club, 'Never say a climb will not "go" until you have rubbed your nose in it.'

The landing was to be an affair of one division and paratroops. The planners carefully emphasized that it could take place only after the Fifth Army had broken through to Frosinone and was in a position to make a quick link-up with the invaders. It was to be the last blow which would finish off the tottering enemy—a rapier-thrust in the back which had about it something of the elegantly sinister quality of the swordplay of the Italian Renaissance.

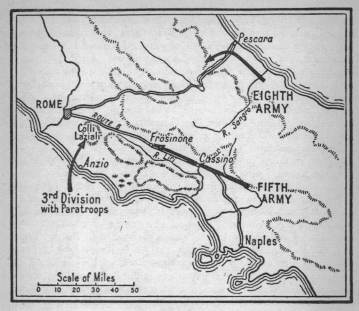

THE FIRST ANZIO PLAN

The place chosen for this rapier-thrust (which received the very un-Renaissance code name of 'Shingle') was the little sea-port of Anzio some thirty miles south of Rome.

Anzio thus seems to enter history apologetically, almost as a footnote in a chapter designed to celebrate greater and better-known names. It was not to be the big show. If all had gone as planned it would have had its small hour of headlines and then have slid back into the peaceful obscurity which had invested it since the fall of the Roman Empire.

But the accidents of war have a habit of suddenly transforming quiet, out-of-the-way places into symbols of courage that men cannot forget as long as they retain their respect for the valour of the ordinary soldier. The name of Anzio, for all who fought there, has become so invested with this exceptional quality that they find it hard to picture the place as it was before the war, living its ordinary, everyday life,

16

no better or worse than a dozen similar small towns scattered along the coast of Italy.

Pre-war Anzio was a pleasant little bathing resort which well-to-do Romans could reach in fast cars within two hours of leaving the capital. The port and town stood on a small promontory which jutted out from the low, sandy coastline. In 1698 Pope Innocent XII had begun the construction of a mole, which was later extended to form a small harbour for fishing boats.

On either side of the harbour white sands, backed by pine woods, swept away into the distance. The town buildings with their gay colours and ironwork balconies were comparatively modern, and there was a sprinkling of holiday villas along the bright strip of beach that lay southwards of the port, christened by the town fathers with pardonable pride the 'Riviera di Levante'.

Immediately behind this beach rose the white dome and terraces of Anzio's greatest hope and bitterest disappointment—the Casino, which was designed to make Monte Carlo look to its laurels but which, alas, never got a licence to function. Further on in the midst of its shady umbrella pines lay the Villa Borghese, a handsome palace built in the days when architects flattered their princely patrons with pillared reception-rooms, ornate staircases and parapets peppered with classical statues.

A mile apart from Anzio was the twin town of Nettuno, again a small place of about 4,500 inhabitants, with a castle and a mediaeval walled town in the centre of a ring of more modern buildings. The ancient streets within the walls were narrow and twisting, and the ground below was honeycombed with catacombs and tunnels constructed over the centuries in the soft volcanic rock. Now they were used as wine-cellars. Great vats of Vini di Castelli, maturing quietly beneath the houses, occasionally sent a rich perfume drifting through the streets in the quiet of the warm summer nights.

The two little towns, linked by the dark green woodlands of the Borghese gardens, looked charming from the sea. Behind them over a level plain rose the graceful Colli Laziali, the Alban Hills. These hills have always fascinated those who have looked towards them from Anzio or from Rome. They sweep up to over 3,000 feet. Their slopes are covered with vineyards and white-walled villages and towns, while in the dark volcanic hollows below the summits lie the mys-

17

terious, deep-sunk lakes of Nemi and Albano. On the far side of the hills to the east lies one of the important roads of Southern Italy, Route Six, curving up through the mountains from the Liri valley, Cassino and Naples on its way to Rome. It is clear at a glance that whoever holds the Colli Laziali holds the keys of the great city itself.

But no one in pre-War Anzio could have thought of the hills and the port as being linked in any way. They were a delightful backdrop to the holiday scene on a clear day, when the sun shone, the band played in the kiosk on the Riviera and children paddled offshore in the placid Mediterranean, riding their gaily painted water-tricycles. Anzio was snug, friendly, a little *bourgeois*—a place to sit and laze in, where the classically-minded could remember that it was once the ancient Antium, the birth-place of Nero and Caligula and the site of the great temple of Fortune celebrated by Horace:

> O Diva, gratum quae regis Antium, . . .
> Te pauper ambit sollicita prece.[1]

They might also have remembered that it was in the theatre of ancient Anzio that Nero is supposed to have fiddled while Rome burned.

But on this first occasion of appearing in the planners' files Anzio was not summoned to drama or greatness. Its gaiety departed with the War, and when the Germans moved in they cleared all the citizens back from the waterfront and prepared the harbour for demolition. Coastal batteries now sprang up along the Riviera and amongst the sand dunes, while the houses were used for battle-training and soon began to look somewhat care-worn and abandoned.

But Anzio was still a place of comparative quiet where battalions which had been through the furnace of the fighting further south were sent to rest and recuperate. Their chief task was coast-watching. The men who manned the Anzio batteries looked out over the calm sea and thanked their good fortune that they were away from the hills around Cassino. If the intelligence reports issued by the German High Command in Italy were true the coast-watchers at Anzio were not likely to be disturbed.

---

[1] 'O Goddess, thou that rulest pleasant Anzio, . . . Thee the poor peasant entreats with anxious prayer.'

STALEMATE IN ITALY, DECEMBER 1943

For the advance so boldly planned by the Allies to begin in November had run into trouble. The weather of sunny Italy had turned traitor, and the whole countryside was being lashed by freezing winds and drenching rainstorms.

19

On the east coast the Eighth Army fought its way forward across the Moro river into the battered town of Ortona, where enemy resistance became so strong that the Canadians had to struggle in the ruins for days, clearing the place cellar by cellar. The rivers flooded and the roads froze into skidding death-traps. The exhausted Eighth Army was forced to a halt, still twenty-five miles south of Pescara.

The Fifth fared no better as it pushed through the mountains towards the Liri valley. The weather was, if anything, worse than on the east coast, and the Germans disputed every rocky knoll and every farm and stone-wall in the mountains. They had been reinforced and were determined to gain time for their engineers, now working furiously around Cassino to complete the Gustav Line. By mid-December the Fifth were only a few more hills forward from the position they had held when the offensive began. It would clearly take weeks to get into the Liri valley. There could be no question of reaching Frosinone and thus no hope of making a landing at Anzio. Many of the landing craft which had been set aside for the operation were now required to sail to England to start their preparations for the Normandy assault. It was not possible to ask for a further delay.

General Clark had a fleeting idea that the Anzio operation might be launched on its own with no relation to events on the main front, but General Truscott of the American 3rd Infantry Division which was scheduled to do the landing, said firmly: 'We are perfectly willing to undertake the operation if we are ordered to do so and we will maintain ourselves to the last round of ammunition. But if we do undertake it, you are going to destroy the best damned division in the United States Army, for there will be no survivors.' [1]

A few days later, on 22 December, the plan was abandoned.

As this drab and wintry December approached its end there were few soldiers fighting in Italy who felt they could wish themselves, with any confidence, a Merry Christmas and a Happy New Year. The position was disheartening. The Fifth and Eighth Armies were slowly coming to a complete standstill, while before them loomed the immensely strong Gustav Line. The plan for an outflanking landing had been abandoned, and the fleet was losing most of its landing craft to the concentration for the Second Front in England. Win-

---

[1] Truscott, *Command Missions*.

ter had firmly set in and conditions were bound to get worse in the mountains for the next two months. There was a final reason for disillusionment with the Italian campaign; most of the stars of the Mediterranean theatre were due to leave it in the New Year. Generals Eisenhower and Montgomery, Admiral Sir Andrew Cunningham, Air Chief Marshal Sir Arthur Tedder, were all assigned to the preparation of 'Overlord'.

More than ever the troops began to feel that they were fighting a side-show. Would it not be better to call it a day and stabilize a front which, in the grim icy weather, seemed already to have put itself into cold storage?

At this critical moment there arrived in the Mediterranean a personage who was determined that 'the show must go on': a dynamic leader who had always been a partisan of the Anzio move and who, moreover, had the power to re-animate a scheme which had been set aside by its original proposers. With his arrival it comes to life again. And in no uncertain fashion!

2

The Code Name is 'Shingle'

On 11 December 1943 Mr. Winston Churchill landed from Cairo at El Alouina Airfield in Tunis. He was on his way home after the strenuous conferences at Teheran and Cairo with Stalin, Roosevelt and Chiang Kai-Shek. He was met by General Eisenhower.

As they drove together to 'Ike's' villa near the ruins of Carthage the Prime Minister, who had recently celebrated his sixty-ninth birthday, reluctantly admitted that he was 'at the end of his tether'. That fabulous physical machinery of his, which for years had run along happily on his astonishing regimen of perpetual oratory, relentless travel, continual dictation of memoranda, cigars, brandy and conferences at two o'clock in the morning, had at last begun to creak a little. That night he became feverish. Next day the doctors diagnosed pneumonia. So, as he explains in his history of the Second World War, there he was at this pregnant moment on the broad of his back amid the ruins of ancient Carthage.

But as soon as Mr. Churchill became convalescent he began eagerly turning over the problems and the possibilities of the war situation and especially the situation in Italy. His body may have temporarily collapsed, but his mind retained its clarity of analysis and its fertility of invention. As he sat up in bed and reviewed the position of Britain he had much to comfort him. Italy alone—the campaign which was nearest to his heart and for which he felt himself personally responsible—showed no dividends. As his fever left him he began calling again for memoranda and figures, turning over in his mind the irritating problem of Italy and the Mediterranean. 'Were we,' he asked himself, 'to leave it a stagnant pool from which we had drawn every fish we wanted?' [1] Something could surely be done to draw out the most tempting fish available—Rome.

He naturally inquired what had happened to the Anzio scheme, or the 'cat claw' stroke, as he called it. For Mr. Churchill always had some difficulty in understanding why the Americans persisted in calling it an 'end run'. Several long and complicated memos passed to and fro before he fully grasped the tactics of American football and realized that, in this strange and violent game, an end run occurs when the forward lines clash together into immobility and the backs race round the supine mass towards the goal. But whatever metaphor was used, a stronger 'cat claw' would undoubtedly lever the Italian front loose and push the whole affair forward.

On 18 December Mr. Churchill was well enough to receive General Brooke, the Chief of the British Imperial General Staff, who was flying back to England after a visit to General Montgomery's headquarters. The date marks the beginning of Mr. Churchill's battle to re-animate Anzio, in which he made such rapid progress that the scheme cancelled officially on 22 December was back again in the centre of the Italian picture by 23 December.

It was the powerful and persistent advocacy of Mr. Churchill that put it back there: this is the unanimous testimony of all the leading figures in the Italian campaign who have so far published their memoirs. Anzio, they say, was Mr. Churchill's pet project, and no one has hurried forward to relieve him of the responsibility for it.

[1] Churchill, *The Second World War*, Vol. V.

The Free World and Britain in particular owes so much to Mr. Churchill, and he himself was right on so many occasions, that a student of the Anzio operation cannot dismiss 'Shingle' out of hand as 'one of Mr. Churchill's Dardanelles schemes'. In late December 1943, confronted with the intractable problem of the Italian campaign, there were others who felt that the 'cat claw' was not such a wild-cat project after all.

General Brooke, one of the key figures in the planning of Britain's war strategy, supported it and Mr. Churchill felt entitled to claim that General Brooke had, by a separate route of thought, come to the same conclusions as he had. Brooke flew back to Britain ready to overcome the difficulties at home that beset the revival of the plan, while Churchill tackled the commanders on the spot.

The attitude of the Americans was quite another matter. They naturally did not have the same feelings about Mr. Churchill as their British colleagues. There were moments when they regarded him as a most dangerous tempter, whose eloquence—unless they took the most stringent precautions—would invariably lead them from the strict path of military virtue as laid down by General Marshall. They exhorted themselves to Stand Firm every time they entered the Great Enchanter's presence. They knew that Washington wanted no further commitments in Italy.

Mr. Churchill therefore first put all his returning energy and his formidable powers of persuasion into the task of winning Washington's consent. He had a bare month in which to mount the operation, for by 1943 the conduct of the war by the Allies had long since lost any element of sudden improvization it may have originally possessed. All was now governed by plans and agreements arrived at months and even years before the event. 'Shingle', in its new form, therefore presented itself to Washington almost as an unexpected baby arriving to upset the carefully planned family budget. Mr. Churchill had to use all his charm and above all his great personal influence with President Roosevelt in order to get it accepted. Many things become possible, it has been pointed out, when a President and a Prime Minister can speak to each other as intimate friends.

Mr. Roosevelt's help was doubly valuable when it came to the vexed question of the availability of the LSTs, the core of the struggle to re-launch Anzio.

A landing in war against a heavily defended shore is a highly technical job, demanding a whole circus of specialized craft. By 1943 the Allies had devoted immense sums of money and intensive effort to building up an invasion fleet of small and big ships, each with its special duty to perform. There were craft designed to land the first wave, craft to give anti-aircraft protection, to fire rockets, to make smoke screens, to blast concrete emplacements at close range. The men who manned them were unorthodox seamen, trained to do as a routine job the one thing that orthodox naval officers regard as the last desperate measure—to run their ship aground!

Of these specialized craft, the ones that were most indispensable and which had some title to be considered amongst the most important of the Allies' war-winning inventions were the LSTs. These were designed to carry the tanks and guns which had to be got quickly on shore, as soon as the first assault went in, to repel the inevitable counter-attack. They were our biggest landing craft and looked like small oiltankers with tubby bows and engines placed astern. When they beached, the great doors in the bows opened and the LSTs fairly vomited their loads onto the sands.

Like so much else of importance they could partly trace their origin to one of those fruitful if irritating 'prayers' of Mr. Churchill. As far back as June 1940 he was demanding in the sentences of an Old Testament prophet, 'Let there be built great ships which can cast up on a beach, in any weather, large numbers of the heaviest tanks.'

When America entered the conflict she took over the major production of LSTs, although a great many were built in Britain. Over a thousand of these wonderful maids-of-all-work were constructed before the end of the War, but, maybe because of the predominance of the United States in their building programme, the majority of them went to the Pacific. Europe, and especially the Mediterranean theatre of war, never seemed to have enough LSTs for its needs.

Without enough LSTs there could be no invasion, no landing in Anzio, but they were in short supply in Europe. This meant that every planner tended to hoard the landing craft assigned to him like precious gold. LSTs were schemed for, fought for, prayed for. Each assault from the sea was preceded by weeks of argument and juggling with figures before the jealously guarded LSTs could be released from the claims of rival planners and sent sailing off to the business in hand.

There was some justification for Mr. Churchill's acid complaint to General Ismay that the whole business of LSTs had become an obsession with some people, who insisted that 'the greatest operations of war turn on three or eight being kept here and sent there'. But it was part of the tragedy of Anzio that the power behind the first punch, which alone could bring success, was entirely controlled by the number of LSTs available. This was one operation of war that did depend upon three or eight LSTs being rushed here or there.

Mr. Churchill had revived the Anzio plan because he was convinced that it was the only way of breaking the deadlock in Italy. But he also saw that the Germans would take notice of this threat to their rear only if it was made in strength or at least gave the impression of being strong.

If four divisions had landed in the assault there could be no question that the Germans would have been very worried men, with their minds firmly fixed on extricating their armies south of Rome before their supply line was cut. Three might not have been so effective, but would have formed a strong threat. The man-power situation in the Mediterranean did not make it too difficult to find the divisions. Mr. Churchill and his planners soon found, however, that it was much more difficult to find the landing craft to put them in: in fact it was clear that they would have to cut their coat according to the cloth available or released to them, on coupons, by the Americans.

In his story of the Second World War the Prime Minister admitted that he was so much occupied in fighting for the principle of the landing that he did not dare to demand the necessary weight and volume for his 'cat-claw'. He wrote ruefully: 'If I had asked for a three-division lift I should not have got anything. How often in life must one be content with what one can get!'

What he got was a two-division lift, and he only got that because his experts performed one of the war's most remarkable juggling tricks, with loading weights, sailing time-tables, repair schedules and the rest of the complicated calculating techniques which were now the commonplace of planning in 1943.

Juggling tricks can be expensive. The hunt to find LSTs

for Anzio set up stresses and strains in the war machine which affected events in the distant Pacific, in the Indian Ocean, in the Eastern Mediterranean and in the date of 'Overlord' itself, so hopelessly interlocked had the various theatres of war become in this fifth year of world conflict.

Memoranda flew in all directions, a sudden hurricane blew through the British Admiralty and the War Office, operations were cancelled or deferred and anxious cables rained on Washington. Mr. Churchill himself had to use his persuasive charm on the President to retain the vital fifty-six LSTs in the Mediterranean which were due to sail to England for 'Overlord'. Well might the Prime Minister note with some satisfaction that when the President's reply came 'it was a marvel.' He hastened to assure his great ally that the word in Italy was now, 'Full speed ahead!'

Not quite. There was a final flurry of anxiety when the generals discovered that, after all the cabling and hurried re-drafting of schedules, the Anzio plan allowed for only seven days' maintenance, after which the LSTs would be with-drawn and sent sailing on their way. There was a further appeal to Washington, after a top-level conference at Marrakesh, whither Mr. Churchill had removed as he slowly recovered from his illness. Again his eloquence obtained a reprieve.

In the early weeks of January 1944 the vital LSTs and the rest of the shipping required assembled in Naples and the neighbouring ports. Mr. Churchill had now succeeded by various means in obtaining, not merely fifty-six but eighty-eight LSTs, enough to launch two divisions and their supporting arms in the first wave of the assault. His 'smash and grab' raid had been a brilliant success, but the Chiefs of Staff devoutly hoped that there would never be need to repeat it.

So the LSTs rode at anchor in the Bay of Naples and the preparations for the landing went on feverishly on shore. But there were one or two strings attached to these invaluable craft which were going to tangle up the Anzio plans in no uncertain way.

Every one of them had a time limit marked clearly on its sailing schedule. The landing had to be hurried forward to take place before the end of January. There could be no delay or pause for reconsideration. It had to be done soon or not at all.

And when all was said and done, there were still only eighty-eight LSTs, still only enough for landing two divisions in the initial assault, although it would be possible to bring up a third division later.

But it is the weight of the first wave that counts in an assault from the sea, and that weight was now strictly limited to two divisions. Mr. Churchill had no doubt that two divisions boldly handled might still do the trick, and he had his supporters, especially on the British side. At Army Group and HQ in Algiers, where General Wilson had now succeeded General Eisenhower, they drew comfort from two factors which were firmly in the Allies' favour—their excellent intelligence and their complete air superiority.

Critics of the Anzio operation have been outspoken about the men who put their trust in these two factors. The intelligence reports have been castigated as 'day-dreaming optimism' while the Air Forces have come in for much ironic comment about 'brash claims of their ability to isolate the battlefield'.

It is easy to be wise after the event and not easy to see the position as the planners saw it in early January 1944. Let us take the Intelligence Department first.

Intelligence at 15th Army Group Headquarters forecast that if the landing was successful the enemy would first attempt to seal it off and would thereby be manoeuvred out of his positions around Cassino. Fifth Army Intelligence also put itself on record with the opinion that there were serious signs of the lowering of enemy morale. Its report went on with easy optimism:

> In view of the weakening of the enemy strength on the front . . . it would appear doubtful if the enemy can hold the organized defensive line through Cassino against a co-ordinated army attack. Since this attack is to be launched before Shingle it is considered likely that this additional threat will cause him to withdraw from his defensive position once he has appreciated the magnitude of that operation.[1]

In the event, these Intelligence appreciations seem staggeringly wide of the mark until we note one important point. In

[1] General Alexander's Despatch, *London Gazette* Supplement 38937 (HMSO).

their estimate of German reactions the Intelligence Department of 15th Army Group, at any rate, had to work on the supposition that the Anzio force was going to move where it was supposed to move—straight onto the Alban Hills. They were not asked to explore German reactions to a landing which, as actually happened, sat down a few miles from the beaches, but rather to a threat seriously delivered to Kesselring's communications.

If the landing force had driven swiftly inland Kesselring might have reacted differently. It is anyone's guess what might have happened: the whole force might have been 'put in the bag'. But it is hardly fair to blame Intelligence for not foreseeing that the Allies would refuse to drive for the hills while they had the chance.

As for the power of the Allied Air Forces to 'keep the ring' around the battlefield, this must also have seemed a reasonable proposition to the Higher Planners as they looked at the Allied air strength in Italy.

At the close of 1943 the British and the Americans had over 2,000 aircraft of various kinds in the peninsula. Against this force the Luftwaffe could muster a bare 350 aircraft of all types when the landing began. If ever the air arm was to justify its claim to be the dominant weapon in modern warfare, the new Queen of the Battlefield, now was its chance.

The ground commanders are unanimous that this chance was missed, yet there is this to be said straight away—without complete air superiority not only the Anzio landing but the whole campaign in Italy and, later, the Normandy assault and the invasion of Germany could never have taken place at all. Our mastery of the skies made possible our advance on the ground.

Nothing was more striking, to anyone who flew on a daylight sortie in Italy, than the complete contrast between the two sides of the front line. As your aircraft flew north to bomb you could look down on a busy countryside. Great columns of lorries moved on the roads, traffic jams formed on the outskirts of the towns and jeeps raced everywhere, even on the narrow tracks in the mountains.

You crossed the line of smoke that always marked the front line and looked down on another world. On the German side the roads were deserted, the railway lines empty. Nothing moved in a dead and lonely landscape. The shadow of air power lay over it all.

The men on the ground might sometimes take this power too much for granted. 'They always will,' said Sir Harry Broadhurst of the Desert Air Force, 'until we get a statue of an Air Marshal on top of a whacking big column in a London square!'

Yet without the fighter and the bomber, glittering in the sky overhead, the man on the ground could never have reached the beaches of Anzio. The Germans were highly critical of the way in which the Allied commanders always moved under the protection of their air umbrella. They felt that the Anglo-American forces could have been flung ashore much further north than Anzio, outside the range of fighter protection, with damaging results to the German defensive position in Italy.

But the Germans had no real experience of big-scale landings from the sea against a modern opponent armed with modern weapons. They had little idea of the vulnerability of an invasion fleet at sea to even a small-scale air attack. The Allies made many mistakes in Italy, but they were not so stupid as to abandon their air umbrella when they took to the sea.

Their reply to German criticism was given by a British Intelligence officer who was listening to a German Staff officer detailing the British mistakes during his interrogation after surrender in Italy. 'You are absolutely right, old chap,' agreed the British officer, 'but you have forgotten our biggest and most dangerous mistake. We won!'

Could we have won more quickly and with fewer casualties if all our high hopes of the air had been fulfilled? Maybe, but in the winter of 1943 these hopes were, perhaps, pitched a little too high. The truth was that at this period the many complex problems that surround the correct deployment of air power in support of the Army had not yet been completely solved. Above all, no one realized how difficult an obstacle the Italian mountains were to the airman as well as to the footslogger.

I admit that I found it hard to understand the problems of the Air Forces when I first came out to Italy as a war correspondent in late 1943. Fresh and appallingly vivid in my mind was an air raid over Berlin, on which I had flown as an observer in a Lancaster bomber. We found the sky over the German capital a nightmare of light—flak poured up in red-hot streams from below, the air was filled with flares that drifted past our wings like flaming chandeliers, while the night-fighters seemed to dive on us straight out of this ambush of glaring night. That night seven hundred aircraft had crashed through the hedge of searchlights that encircled Berlin like the barriers of some fantastic bull-ring of the air. Hapless bombers were impaled on the searchlights like giant moths struggling on a pin. They did not struggle long. I remember looking back at the bomber following us and seeing a glow suddenly flood the cockpit. The wings seemed to float apart and the wreck plunged downwards, flaring like a piece of burning oily rag as it dropped into the fires eating up the ground 20,000 feet below. . . .

That picture haunted my mind when I heard the pilots in Italy talk of their difficulties. Could an attack on the marshalling yards of Pistoia or a bridge in the country beyond Florence compare with the terrors of a raid over one of the big cities of Northern Europe?

In mid-January I had the chance of flying with a wing of the Desert Air Force from Foggia. We took off to destroy a bridge in the wild mountains of the Maella range. The view from 15,000 feet was of a breath-taking beauty, for the whole countryside was buried in snow. Down in the sugar icing of the valleys little red bulbs started to flash, and black cotton wool puffs of flak burst in the clear blue sky around us. The cold air rushed in through the rear hatch and hit us like a blow in the face. But, as we peered down, we got more and more worried. We could not, for the life of us, pick up any feature we could recognise. We dared not drop our bombs in case they hit our own troops. We turned tail and flew disconsolately back over the bomb line. We were the second mission that had gone astray that very afternoon.

So there it was, clearly outlined by personal experience. The problem in Italy was not how to break through to your target but how to find it at all! The Air Forces did their best and the Beachhead could not have been held without them. But the air could not isolate the battlefield completely, because it was fighting not so much the Luftwaffe as the winter weather.

One last unpleasant surprise remained. No one had realized—indeed, how could they until the fact had been demonstrated in actual practice?—that the Germans now possessed an astonishing resilience under air bombardment. Just as the Allies had built up their tactics upon strong support from the air, the Germans were developing an equally impressive technique for doing without it altogether. They moved by night, built up their forward supply dumps in periods of bad weather, and, most important of all, got their soldiers to accept the fact that they would have to fight without the aid of the Luftwaffe.

And all the time the foul, unpredictable winter weather of Italy threw a cloak over them whenever it seemed that the Allied Air Forces had got them to breaking point.

This bitter knowledge was concealed from the supporters of the Anzio Plan in the Higher Command. They felt that Allied air superiority would be the decisive factor in the coming battle. Yet if it had been possible at this point, in mid-January, to draw up a provisional balance-sheet for the expedition, the Board of Directors might have been less optimistic about the prospects of the company.

On the credit side could be set the one overriding fact that Anzio was the only sensible way to break the Italian deadlock. The Allies had air and naval superiority in the Mediterranean, and a landing behind the German lines was the only method of exploiting this superiority. Success would give them the valuable prize of Rome, hustle the Germans back to the Northern Apennines, pin their reserves and open up important contacts with the Balkans. In addition the landing would be a strong reply to the implied criticism of the Russians, who were launching their winter offensive in equally bad weather conditions. The Western Allies could not sit back and wait for 'Overlord' in June. The Kremlin would be entitled to make some pointed comments if they did.

On the debit side one disagreeable item stood out, threatening trouble ahead no matter what the directors decided to do: there were only eighty-eight LSTs and therefore only two divisions could get ashore in the first assault. We have seen exactly why this was so. Mr. Churchill was enthusiastic for action on the Mediterranean front, but, in the matter of LSTs, it was the Americans who held the purse strings. He had used his personal influence to persuade the President and Washington to allow the landing, but even he could not get enough ships to make it a sure-fire success. But it would be idle to pretend that there was much enthusiasm in American circles for the venture. Two divisions to challenge the Germans looked a very slim force in American eyes. They would far rather have been on the side of the big battalions.

Yet war is not entirely a matter of logistics. Two divisions in the hands of a man who believed in the attack and was resourceful and resolute might yet work the trick.

That is just what the Anzio landing failed to get. The character of the general chosen to command the venture had a decisive influence on its fortune. There is still a violent dispute as to which side of the ledger, credit or debit, it should be placed.

3

The Shadow on the Plan

Mr. Churchill might plan, plead and pray for the staging of his great venture of Anzio; he might sweep aside all difficulties of policy and supply to ensure that the assault should start from Naples as soon as possible, but he could not control it once it had started. Its ultimate success now lay in the hands of the soldiers.

At the head of the chain of command stood Sir Harold Alexander. He had been appointed C-in-C, Allied Armies in Italy, in the great December reshaping of the higher command. True, Sir Henry Maitland Wilson had been appointed to an even higher post, that of Supreme Commander, Mediterranean, but in this exalted position General Wilson dwelt in the administrative stratosphere, dealing with the broader question of politics and strategy. The actual battle in Italy was fought under the higher direction of General Alexander, who had both the American Fifth and the British Eighth Army under his control.

There have been no two opinions about General Alexander's quality as a commander; both the British and Americans admired and trusted him. He answered perfectly to the American picture of the best type of British officer: fearless, handsome, immaculate in dress and with great courtesy and charm of manner. His fault, if indeed it can be considered as such, was a reluctance to insist on his own point of view when it came to overruling his American subordinates. But no one knew better than General Alexander that a team of allies must be driven with a light hand, especially when it included General Mark W. Clark of the American Fifth Army.

On the whole General Clark has had a cool Press, which seems rather hard on a man so aware of the value of publicity. He was tall and handsome in what the British might regard as the typical Western film-hero manner. A London critic, reviewing General Clark's book, *Calculated Risk*, declared that General Clark's experiences read as if they had happened to Gary Cooper.

He had great personal charm, and there is no question of his courage or of his abilities as an administrator of armies. He also had the good quality, as General Truscott testifies, of making great efforts to support his subordinates.

The reservations about Clark stem from what seemed to many to be his excessive concern with personal publicity. He travelled with a retinue of photographers and Press men and had the knack of catching the limelight on all occasions. Some of his entourage caught a little of the General's flamboyance. After the final attack had been 'laid on' at Anzio a subordinate explained: 'General Clark has got fifty-seven different plans and he's going to use every one of them!'

But it would be grossly unfair to General Clark to put all this down to personal vanity. A general has got to put his personality over to his troops if he is to get the best out of them, and in the appalling complexity of modern war one way for him to do so is by boldly using his public relations service.

The 1939-45 war was the first to be fought with full-scale Press and PRO coverage. The Americans expected their generals to make full use of their new opportunities, but the British leaders were more reluctant. In their heart of hearts they still felt it was not quite 'good form'. Eyebrows were raised in Whitehall and elsewhere at General Montgomery's frank use of publicity, so that when he wrote that one of his attacks would succeed 'with the help of God', the critics murmured, 'At last, Monty has mentioned the Almighty in despatches!'

The American GIs, who came from a nation devoted to publicity, had no objection at all to their generals being publicity-minded. They admired General Patton for his ability to hit the headlines as hard as he hit the Germans, and fought all the better for him.

General Clark's publicity machine, like that of General Patton, was zealous in his cause, and there would have been less criticism of it if Clark had been blessed, as Patton was, with the chance of winning a series of swift victories. Clark, however, had been assigned one of the most thankless tasks that can be given to a general—'keeping up the pressure' in a campaign which all his men knew was regarded as a 'side-show' by the American High Command. He had to push his men to the attack in a war where the defence was bound to gain all the glory. It is to his credit that he succeeded in keeping his front moving.

Anzio presented him with one opportunity for keeping his front in action, and, officially, he approved. But he has admitted that he felt it was a military scheme which had been shaped to fit a political decision.

In truth, General Clark was in a difficult position, caught between two fires. The Higher Command had given him the job to do and, as a soldier, he had accepted it. But when he turned to the men he had assigned to make the landing he started to meet protests from below. In fact, the nearer we approach the men who were to step ashore on the actual beaches the more we sense their deep distrust of the buoyant plan that had left Mr. Churchill's conference-table at Carthage on Christmas Day—which brings us to the most controversial figure in the complicated history of the Anzio affair, General John P. Lucas, commander of the Sixth Corps of General Mark Clark's Fifth Army.

On his unhappy head fell the wrath of all those who were chagrined and disappointed by the early failure of the landing. His British subordinates distrusted him and assumed, gloomily, that he owed his elevation to the principle known in British administrative circles as 'Buggins's turn'. Buggins is a mythical character, the quiet chap who has stooged along in the office for years until his decent-minded colleagues feel that he should be given a chance to do something before he retires. How otherwise, they asked, was a general appointed to command this dangerous operation who was fifty-four and who clearly did not have his heart in it? General Lucas appeared to them as the final and most serious liability with which the scheme had been burdened on its way down from Mr. Churchill. If Mr. Churchill had been so keen on the show, why had he not made it an all-British venture under a British commander?

This had, indeed, been Mr. Churchill's hope, but Anzio had to be launched from a Fifth Army base and was therefore a Fifth Army responsibility. The Prime Minister rarely interfered in such things as appointments at corps level. Of the two American corps commanders available Clark chose Lucas, who had commanded Sixth Corps in the methodical advance through the mountains north of Naples. He had gained there the reputation of being a reliable organizer of battle.

But General Lucas's character had another side to it which had an important effect on the fortunes of Anzio. He was a cautious commander who tended to lean heavily on the advice of his subordinates. Was he, indeed, too cautious a man to be placed in charge of so bold an enterprise? His Anzio diary does not ring with buoyant self-confidence. He wrote on his fifty-fourth birthday: 'I am afraid I feel every year of it.' Next day's entry read: 'I must keep from thinking of the fact that my order will send these men into a desperate attack.'

At no time, however, did he convey a feeling of dynamic leadership. The historian of the Irish Guards describes the impression the General made on the British troops when he inspected them before the landing:

By a carefully timed coincidence he saw No. 1 Company returning from a route march, very fresh and smart—as well they might be for they had come from just around the corner. They saw a pleasant, mild elderly gentleman being helped out of layers of overcoats. The Corps Commander remarked that they were big men, expressed the opinion that the main guard, under the command of Sergeant Bird, was 'mighty fine', drank a cup of tea and drove away, leaving the Battalion slightly puzzled.[1]

It was even more serious that General Lucas conveyed the same feeling of puzzled indecision to his immediate subordinates. His juniors knew him, somewhat disrespectfully, as 'Foxy Grandpa' and he tended to evolve his operational pro-

[1] Fitzgerald, *History of the Irish Guards in the Second World War*, p. 201.

posals in conferences which often resembled debating societies. Luckily the question of whether or not to abandon the Beachhead was never put to the vote!

General Lucas laboured under another disadvantage as the commander of an Allied force; he never understood or trusted his British colleagues, and they certainly returned this distrust. It is, however, not so easy as it appears for military men of different nations to understand one another, especially when they claim to speak the same language. Each army develops its own way of doing things and a jargon of the trade which is peculiar to that particular army: to an outsider the professional jargon of the British Army can seem very peculiar indeed.

Instinctively the British officer tends to avoid the vivid word, wisely feeling that he can reduce the horror of war to manageable proportions if he can describe it in everyday terms drawn from the world of sport. If he is a senior officer that sport will be fox-hunting. When General Montgomery told a group of Americans that his men had their 'tails well up', a puzzled colonel asked a British officer in the group, 'Excuse me, up what?'

In the Anzio fighting a British officer was putting the Americans 'in the picture' about a tank clash on the Albano road. 'Well, gentlemen,' he proceeded, 'our tins were hacking along the road with their swedes out of the lid when they got a bloody nose. The question is, shall we thicken up the party or do an Oscar? In any case we'll have to tie the whole thing up on the Old Boy net.' Said the Americans hurriedly, 'Are we advancin', or are we retreatin'?'

A general in charge of Allied troops has to penetrate swiftly below such surface difficulties and differences, and this Lucas seemed unable to do. He could quote his favourite, Kipling, by the yard but was never the vibrant man of action so esteemed by the poet.

This may seem an ungenerous description of a man who was called upon to take responsibility for one of the most delicate operations of the war and who was compelled to drink the bitter draught of removal from his post after the German attack had been held. But Anzio was a grim destroyer of reputations. As the Germans swept down the Albano road and whole battalions melted overnight in the furnace of their gunfire, there was no time to consider personal feelings. General Lucas was sacrificed to restore the confidence of the defenders.

In truth, he was a competent professional soldier, well-liked in Army circles but placed in a position where competence is not enough. There was need in Anzio of a man of steely resolution and resilience.

Fortunately for the Allies there was such a man at hand on the Beachhead. General Lucien K. Truscott had landed in command of the American 3rd Infantry Division. He had a fine record of service in Sicily and Italy. He was forty-nine, with greying hair and an air of resolute toughness. He developed laryngitis just before the landing, but this made his growling rasping commands doubly effective. He wore a leather jacket, a lacquered helmet and a silk scarf around his neck, a get-up which gave everyone who met him a feeling that the General was just back from the front. He usually was, for he had strong views about commanders who did not stay as far forward as possible. Where General Lucas asked for advice General Truscott gave an order. His manner left the recipient in no doubt that it had to be obeyed, and in double-quick time!

The generals of the various nations at war sometimes seem to have modelled their manner and their attitude to battle upon the most successful commanders that their country produced in the past. British generals, with their laconic speech and their courteous but occasionally frigid air, have a hint of the great Duke of Wellington in their bearing. Those who met the French General de Lattre de Tassigny and read the communiqués issued by General de Montsabert had no doubt that the source of their inspiration was the Emperor Napoleon himself. In General Truscott his British comrades-in-arms saw hints of the tough, hard-hitting cavalry leaders of the American Civil War plus an attractive dash of Teddy Roosevelt and his Rough Riders. This was how they hoped all American generals would be!

Truscott, with all his forceful character, was a man who had thought long and deeply about the best way of getting the American GI trained for battle and the art of leading him in war. He also had a gift for diplomatic cunning which stood him in good stead in the shifting scene back-stage in Italy and the Mediterranean.

Truscott had another asset which was invaluable at Anzio. He had been posted to London when America entered the War and had an insight into the strength and weaknesses of the British military machine. He was thus able to get on good terms with his British colleagues, particularly with General Penney of the British 1st Division and General Templer of the 56th. The fact that they used to drop into Truscott's command post for a drink at the end of the day was not without its influence on the history of the Beach-head. In the crisis of the battle Truscott poured the two British generals a particularly powerful tot. 'The Doc's given us a special dispensation,' he grinned. 'The gin's run out. This is medical alcohol!' That night the German counter-attack was very roughly handled indeed.

Truscott cared little for histrionics and felt uncomfortable when invited to take part in General Mark Clark's triumphal ride through Rome. But his personality 'got over' to the troops. The Duke of Wellington's men did not give him the enraptured cheers that the French soldiers gave Napoleon; they simply growled with satisfaction when they saw him in battle, 'Here comes the long-nosed beggar who beats the French.' In the same way the men of Anzio felt a new wave of confidence when 'Old Gravel-mouth' took over.

A granite personality, with no frills, General Truscott emerged from the Anzio battle as the Man of the Beachhead.

These were the men who took the decisions which meant life and death to the soldiers who went to the Beachhead. Because Mr. Churchill had insisted that the risks and dangers were to be shared by the Allies each nation chose one of its best available divisions for the first assault.

The British division was the 1st Infantry Division, which had a long and varied history. It had been at Dunkirk under General Alexander and, after a period of training in England, had fought with distinction in Tunisia and ended with the capture of Pantelleria. Since then it had been in reserve in North Africa undergoing training in mountain warfare. In December it was brought over to the mainland of Italy and concentrated near Foggia. The staff expected to be ordered to the east coast to join the Eighth Army.

Divisions, like individuals, acquire a character: they are probably the largest units in an army which can do so. Corps and armies become vast, impersonal things, but a division is still small enough for the executive officers to get to know each other well and for the general to make an impression on his troops.

The 1st Division was proud to regard itself as a completely typical British division. It contained battalions from Irish and Scottish regiments as well as those utterly dependable, solid English county units which are the hard core of the British Army. One brigade was a Guards Brigade, and these remarkable soldiers won new glory at Anzio, although they might sometimes give the impression that they were fighting a different, maybe a more gentlemanly war from the rest of the division. This was the Guards' way. The sight of them meticulously saluting and then pipe-claying their equipment in the chaos of battle along the Albano road was worth many a well-directed salvo of artillery fire to the defenders.

The divisional commander was General W. R. C. Penney. He was a man of fine presence, energetic and with a strong independence of mind. He had studied under General Montgomery at the Staff College and was proud to feel that he was one of 'Monty's boys'. He visited Monty just before he went across to Caserta for the final planning of Anzio. General Montgomery, in a typical gesture, first filled his car with cigarettes for the troops and a few bottles of sherry for the staff, then said firmly, 'Now don't forget that, whatever happens, you are commanding a division. Not a company, not a battalion, but a division. . . . Then all will be well.'

General Penney imported some of the Montgomery quality into the Beachhead. He drove himself hard—perhaps too hard on occasions—and he drove his staff hard as well. The Americans felt that he lived a little too much on his nerves but he was, in fact, a realist who had become impatient with what he felt to be the fumbling direction of Sixth Corps. Like General Montgomery he saw no reason why he should conceal his impatience.

Few generals have been tried so severely in war as General Penney. Upon his division fell the full weight of the German counter-attack. He himself was wounded in the crisis of the battle, yet not before he had succeeded in holding his front against the full fury of the German all-out drive to the sea. His was an achievement which has not yet got the recognition it deserves.

Amongst the many ironies in which Anzio was so rich, General Penney, a front-line general if ever there was one, must have felt that the most ironic of all was the method of his wounding. In the round of farewell visits he paid before leaving for 'Overlord', General Patton, who was much admired by General Penney, called to see the British commanders who were preparing for Anzio. His parting shot to General Penney had all the famous Patton vigour. He lifted his glass and said, 'Here's to the British and the hell and damnation to any God-damn commanding general who is ever found in his own command post!' General Penney was wounded by a shell which destroyed his caravan, just after he had returned from the very centre of the battle.

Following the decision that Anzio was 'on', the 1st Division received orders to move to the west coast and concentrate around Naples.

The divisional planning group reported to Caserta still unaware what was in store for them. As they entered the courtyard of Army HQ a worried staff officer noticed their divisional sign on their jeeps, which had not yet been removed. He raced across to them. 'Ah!' he said, 'the very people I've been looking for. Can you tell me how many additional troops you will require?' The leader of the column replied, 'How much of the Russian army have you got?' On this note the 1st Division got down to the detailed consideration of what it should do to prepare for Anzio.

The American 3rd Infantry Division was the obvious choice for the US contribution to the first assault. We have already met its tough, staunch-hearted commander, General Truscott. His division was a reflection of his own personality and he took great pride in it. Nothing is more heart-warming in Truscott's war memoirs than his constant reference to the skill and courage of his old division long after he had risen to the heights of corps and army command. The 3rd, to him, is always the finest division in the US Army. It was as typically American as the 1st was typically British. It learnt fast from its early mistakes in Tunisia and was at the top of its form at the time of the Anzio landing.

Anzio was not a new name to the staff of the 3rd Division. They had been actively planing for the first scheme and had now simply to continue where they had left off. The 3rd had been brought out of the line in preparation for the original landing and then, after this was cancelled, had been included in the scheme for a renewed drive through the mountains around Cassino. The division began to concentrate around Naples and left to the American 36th Infantry Division the attempt to cross the Rapido river. The 3rd gained nothing in ease but a great deal in glory by the exchange.

Both the British and American sectors needed special troops for special tasks. The 2nd Special Service Brigade, comprising No. 9 and No. 43 Commandos, were assigned to the British, and the Rangers, who had received special training in the technique of street-fighting, strengthened the Americans. In addition there were all the extra units, from tanks and guns to beach-groups, which a corps requires to support its infantry in a landing.

Finally there were the paratroopers. Mr. Churchill made a special effort to obtain the services of the American 504th Parachute Regiment. Paratroops always had a strong appeal for Mr. Churchill, and there were moments when he could hardly picture an operation without them. He felt with justice that there is something profoundly intimidating for an enemy in the thought of an army of desperate paratroopers swooping silently down from the skies and armed to the teeth, ready to capture the nerve-centres of resistance far behind the lines.

He sent one of his eloquent appeals to Washington to obtain their services. General Marshall agreed, and Mr. Churchill got his paratroops. Their presence was not exactly welcome to the Sixth Corps planners. As we shall see, they were visualizing a far different sort of landing from Mr. Churchill.

These were all the troops that could be carried to the first assault. They would be the men who would have to capture and hold the initial beachhead—who might have to defend it against immediate counter-attack or drive inland swiftly to the objective of the Alban Hills. There were two other divisions waiting in Naples for the moment when the armada of LSTs, troop-ships and assault-craft returned from the first landing—the American 1st Armored Division (less one combat team) and the American 45th Infantry Division.

These two divisions would be available to General Lucas as a follow-up force. It would take some days to load and send them to the beachhead. By the time they arrived the pattern of the beachhead battle would have taken firm shape.

The troops had now all been assigned to the task. The commanders had been chosen, and vast stores of war material were beginning to pile up on the docks. The great armada of ships needed to transport the divisions selected for

41

the assault filled the wide circle of the bay of Naples. It remained for General Lucas and Sixth Corps to outline their plan of attack and issue their operational orders.

Mr. Churchill had inspired the move and, with his Chiefs of Staff and the tempered approval of Washington, had obtained the ships that made it possible. But he never interfered in the detailed planning of operations of war. This was the responsibility of General Lucas, supervised by the planners of Fifth Army.

In the early days of January the divisional commanders who had not yet been 'put in the picture', assembled at Caserta, where Sixth Corps had now established their headquarters alongside that of Fifth Army.

The great palace of Caserta lay on the edge of the hills some fifteen miles outside Naples. Built by the Bourbon kings of the old Kingdom of the Two Sicilies, it was an enormous classical structure, a super-Versailles in the Italian sun. General Mark Clark had set up his caravan in the grounds near the rococo marvel of the ornamental waterfall, where nymphs and gods writhed in stone amongst the cascading streams. Before them stretched wide, lily-strewn pools, or, as General Clark describes them, 'a series of ponds at different levels'. He used one of them as a landing ground for his cub plane, fitted with special floats.

At Caserta, in the bare, echoing rooms where Lady Hamilton had once met Nelson—'the only place where I've had my hat blown off indoors', as one irreverent officer remarked —General Lucas met his new subordinates. The ball was now at his feet and his must be the decisions on the immediate tactics of the landing.

The divisional commanders got a surprise. They may have assembled expecting to receive their orders from a general and his staff who had reached clear-cut decisions and who were ready with their plan. Instead they found themselves invited to join a debating society.

That first conference left a strange impression on the minds of the British generals and their staff officers. They sat before the big maps, ready to take precise notes of the proceedings. General Lucas's spokesman produced a suggested scheme for the assault: there were protests from General Truscott, counter-suggestions from Colonel Darby of the Rangers and urgent requests for enlightenment from General Penney. The speaker, with an obliging air of 'Well,

42

if you don't like that plan, what about this' unveiled another scheme prepared for their approval. The British representatives were somewhat bewildered by it all.

As the conferences multiplied one thing became clear to his subordinates: General Lucas was not going to commit himself to a swift advance inland immediately on landing. A glance at the map of the area around Rome will show straight away that it is not enough to land at Anzio and establish a beachhead. If the enemy is going to take serious notice of a threat to his rear the invaders must push inland onto the Alban Hills. From these hills alone can they be in a position to cut the main German supply line of Route Six, which lies beyond these Colli Laziali away from Anzio. But these all-important hills are some fifteen miles inland from the port and the seacoast. And General Lucas had only two divisions with which to capture them!

The more he thought about the task ahead the less he liked it. He determined that he would base his plan on insuring against possible disaster and not on exploiting an extremely problematic success and surprise. 'Army has gone nuts again,' he wrote in his diary. 'The general idea seems to be that the Germans are licked and are fleeing in disorder and nothing remains but to mop up. . . . They will end up by putting me ashore with inadequate forces and get me into a serious jam. Then who will take the blame?'

Sixth Corps had been fighting on that dour southern front themselves for the last few months and they knew the obstacles ahead. They also knew Kesselring and had bitter memories of his swift reaction at Salerno. Everything conspired to make General Lucas cautious.

Kesselring was known to have assembled strong counter-attack forces in the Rome area which might crash on Lucas's two divisions before they had time to consolidate their landing. In the circumstances he felt that he should base all his planning on first securing his beachhead.

General Penney pressed for a definition of the plan of action after landing. He received an operational instruction which stated clearly: 'This directive does not include plans for an advance from the beachhead to or towards the final objective. Such plans are extremely tentative: this advance is not likely to take place unless it is synchronised with operations of the remainder of the Fifth Army in close vicinity of the beachhead.'

One by one the more daring aspects of the landing plan were eliminated. All suggestions for mobile columns striking swiftly for the hills were ruled out, the parachute drop was cancelled and commando raids forbidden. Everything was to be concentrated on the defence of the beachhead against the swift counter-attack on the first day which Lucas, from his Salerno experience, felt sure would come. Two divisions was a small enough force with which to repel it.

'I want every man I can get onto those beaches,' he said, 'even if they have only got a stone in their hands!'

It is impossible not to spare a little sympathy for the unhappy General Lucas as he sat in his office in Caserta planning against time. Suggestions and counter-suggestions rained down on his head from the higher authorities some of which, to say the least, were more than unhelpful.

Take the supply problem. General Lucas had two divisions in his assault, each with different weapons, different spare parts, even with different forms to fill in for rations. A quartermaster's nightmare!

Colonel O'Neil, the Sixth Corps supply expert, came forward with an ingenious plan for the driving of pre-loaded trucks straight out of the LSTs to the dumps and sending back empty trucks in their place. This trick promised a saving of twenty-four hours on the orthodox method of bulk-loading. Higher Authority promptly vetoed it. Sixth Corps mysteriously ignored the veto, and the plan had an important part in saving the Beachhead.

Even more extraordinary was the insistence of the Higher Planners that there was no need to rehearse the landing. Now if there is one operation of war that demands a most careful rehearsal it is a landing from sea at night.

True, soldiers like Colonel Scott of the Irish Guards might claim that people overestimated the difficulties of landing from the sea. 'After all,' he said, 'it is only a kind of approach march. You get into boats instead of buses, the difference being that sailors are more reliable than Army drivers.'[1]

But this comment was simply a witty restatement of the British soldier's traditional confidence in the Navy. It was more serious when Mr. Churchill insisted that a rehearsal

[1] Fitzgerald, *History of the Irish Guards in the Second World War*, p. 201.

was pointless. He wanted the troops flung on shore as soon as possible.

The naval commanders, however, jibbed at this. They knew only too well that the sea has a nasty habit of turning traitor on those who entrust themselves blindly to it. They managed to squeeze a rehearsal in, even though it took place a bare few days before the actual landing. Admiral Lowry, of the US Navy, was in general charge of the naval side of the operation while Admiral Troubridge, of the Royal Navy, supervised the British section of the scheme.

It was just as well that a rehearsal took place. The British try-out on the old beaches of Salerno got ashore with few mishaps, but the American rehearsal went badly astray. By an error in navigation the big transports stopped miles out to sea. The LSTs opened their doors too soon; men were drowned and vital equipment lost. What would have happened if the Germans had counter-attacked at dawn on the 'real thing'?

General Truscott raged; Admiral Lowry promised his captains that if they did not go close inshore off Anzio they would get 'a kick in a soft spot by a cruiser'. General Lucas demanded more time for another rehearsal.

General Clark was adamant. He knew that Anzio was being launched on borrowed time and that there was no room for manoeuvre in the tight schedule laid down: the LSTs had to return without fail to England by the promised date. He had no alternative but to tell Lucas: 'You won't get another rehearsal. The date has been set at the very highest level. There is no possibility of delaying it even for a day. You've got to do it.'

No wonder that General Lucas noted at one stage in his diary that he felt like 'a sacrificial lamb and entitled to at least one bleat'!

Sacrificial lambs do not, as a rule, make ideal and resolute war leaders. Admiral Sir John Cunningham, to whom Lucas confessed his feeling that 'this was going to be worse than Gallipoli', told him bluntly: 'If that's how you feel you had better resign.' A Patton or a Montgomery might have done this or got his way. General Lucas did not think that he had the influence or prestige of these generals; he stayed on.

So as the troops worked against time to complete the waterproofing of their vehicles and the last days ran out, the odds against the success of the expedition had lengthened considerably. 'Between the conception and the creation . . . Falls the Shadow,' wrote Mr. T. S. Eliot. The Shadow had certainly fallen on the conception of Anzio from the moment it left Mr. Churchill to the time it reached General Lucas.

It would have been a certainty if it could have been carried out in strength. From a certainty it had now degenerated into a bold gamble—with two divisions only in the first wave and a time-limit on the vital LSTs. A bold gamble needs a bold gambler if it is to have any chance of success. Instead General Lucas was in control, and no one ever suggested that he had a gambler's streak.

He may have been right to decide on caution—the omens were certainly not favourable—but he himself now added one more uncertainty to the many imponderables which had gathered around Anzio. He may have put his American staff fully 'into the picture', but apart from a few directives of the kind already quoted he gave no indication of his intentions to his British subordinates. General Penney pressed in vain for further instructions. He wanted to know what he and his men had to do after they had made good their landing. He was never told. He remained uncertain after he had been ashore for days, and he sailed for Anzio still thinking that he and his men would be ordered to advance with the greatest possible speed on to the Alban Hills.

Small wonder that Admiral Cunningham turned to Admiral Lowry just before the fleet sailed, and told him: 'The odds are about 51 to 49 in your favour. God be with you.'

So far we have been concerned with the preparations for the actual landing: with the battle for the LSTs, the disputes about the structure of the force and the anxieties over the tactics to be employed. Now, on the eve of the assault when there is no turning back, is the time to remind ourselves of the indissoluble link between Anzio and the Cassino front. These two were conceived as part of the same battle. Anzio was to be the master-stroke, the surprise behind the enemy lines, but the main Fifth Army was also to advance to the attack. It was to assault the Gustav Line with such vigour that the reserves which Kesselring might be keeping around Rome to deal with the dangers of a landing would be sucked south, giving the Anzio force a clear field. The main Fifth Army was to deliver a series of fierce punches to the heart which would set the German reeling; Anzio would be the left hook which would finally knock him out.

General Alexander and General Clark planned to begin these blows on the Gustav Line a week before the Anzio landing. They chose the toughest part of the defences to attack. Before their troops rose the grim bastion of Cassino, daunting in its inaccessibility. The River Rapido, swollen with winter rain, ran like a moat at its foot. From Cassino down to the sea stretched the Gustav Line, one of the strongest defence lines constructed by the Germans in the whole course of the war. The troops which were now to attempt to crack it were no longer fresh. They had been fighting their way for months through the rainy hills towards this grim barrier which the Germans had prepared to receive them. Worse still—they had been given insufficient time to prepare for the date of this Cassino attack had been determined by the time-table for Anzio. General Clark might well have repeated to his corps commanders on the Cassino front the words he had already used to General Lucas: 'There is no possibility of delaying it for a single day. You've got to do it.'

The battle opened with an attack across the lower Garigliano by the British Tenth Corps on the night of 17 January. A little later the Free French Expeditionary Corps advanced through the mountains north of Cassino in the hope of taking it in the flank. In the centre the American Second Corps waited to cross the Rapido river and push into the Liri valley as soon as the British had gained their objectives. This attack was timed for 20 January. Two days later the Sixth Corps were due to land at Anzio.

If all went well, the main Fifth Army would have broken the enemy front at the very moment that the Anzio expedition was rushing ashore, and the prospects would be bright for a swift link-up between the two forces.

Unfortunately things went very far from well. Neither the British nor the French advance went deep enough to cause the Germans concern. In the centre the Americans met with a bloody repulse.

On the night of the 20th, while the Anzio fleet was busy with its last preparations in the curving beauty of the Bay of Naples, the American 36th (Texan) Division advanced towards the dark banks of the flooded Rapido to experience what has been described as 'the biggest disaster to American arms since Pearl Harbour'. This was an exaggeration, but the

47

reality was grim enough.

Fog handicapped the infantry as they moved down onto the river banks. The Germans had every crossing place covered: the assault boats were swept away, covered with dead and dying men. No sooner were bridges built than they were smashed by a hurricane of enemy fire. All through the night and on through the next day, the Texans struggled to cross, but by the afternoon of 21 January—as the convoys were now moving out of the Bay of Naples towards Capri and then north to Anzio—the 36th Division was back where it had started with the loss of 1,681 men. The division had been smashed as a fighting force.

The Texans were bitter and clamoured, after the war, for a Congressional Inquiry into the conduct of General Clark. He was completely vindicated. He had no option but to order the attack if the main front was to fulfil its task of holding the enemy while the Anzio 'end run' was in the making. The ease with which the Beachhead forces landed owed a great deal to the sacrifices of the Texan and other divisions around Cassino.

For the Rapido affair did not end the battle on the main front; General Clark kept up the pressure. The Americans assaulted the mountain bastion north of Cassino town, the French struggled for the heights near the monastery, the British away on the left flank fought their way slowly forward into the foothills of the Aurunci mountains. These hard and sour battles went on well into February, when at last they foundered in snow and rain. But it was the repulse on the Rapido, at the beginning of the attack, that gave warning to the Allies that the Germans were going to hold the Gustav Line as a Verdun, which Kesselring's men had sworn the Allies should not pass.

All this was not very encouraging to General Lucas and his staff as they prepared to sail for Anzio. They could not know the full extent of the Rapido disaster, but they sensed the savage nature of the task confronting the main Fifth Army, and they realized that, almost before they left port, one of the main props of their hope had been swept away. There was now little chance of a quick link-up between the two forces. Lucas would be 'out on a limb' as soon as he hit the beaches.

Yet nothing is certain in war. Bold leaders have mocked at greater odds and snatched victory from more desperate positions. When the expedition approached the shores of Anzio Fate offered it one more chance of success—slender and fleeting, maybe, but still a possibility. We shall see how General Lucas dealt with it. In the meantime his army was embarking on the invasion fleet, fortunately unaware of the anxieties which vexed the mind of its leader. The soldier in the lower ranks has much to put up with, but he is spared one thing—he has no need to worry about the future. That is decided for him in no uncertain measure.

So passed the sunny days of 19 and 20 January. The troops already embarked for the rehearsal remained on board and looked longingly back at Naples as their ships swung at anchor. The empty LSTs lay like stranded whales on the loading beeches that fringed the bay, their steel jaws open to swallow their last quotas of tanks, guns and lorries.

In the ships the men gathered in their cramped quarters to be given a final briefing. The ordinary private is the last man to be told of the plans for an attack in which he must play the leading part. Perhaps this is just as well: if he had realized some of the things that had gone on during the preparation of the Anzio plan he might have promptly tried to wriggle to the rear. Rumours fly around, of course, and the 'gen' passed on by canteen gossip assumes weird and wonderful forms, but it is usually a relief to the Tommy and GI when they are told what they actually have to do. The reaction is 'Well, not as bad as we thought!'

It was certainly so on the landing craft I embarked on for the assault. As we listened to the young signals officer explaining what we had to do we began to feel almost optimistic. The plan looked feasible on paper and on the maps and we knew nothing about the actual strength available to carry it out. The anchorage around us was bulging with vessels, the air forces roared over our heads on their way north, and we were away from the snow and the rain and the mountains. This was all that counted. Our only preoccupation was with the actual moment of stepping ashore. If we managed to make it through the surf unopposed we had no doubts that it was 'Rome in ten days' for us. Especially when our signaller outlined the cover plan.

For, before any venture is launched on the scale of Anzio, an elaborate cover plan is drawn up. In a city like Naples, with a swarming population swollen by refugees from all over southern Italy, it was obvious to even the least observant that a great fleet was going to sail soon. The Allied air supremacy had made German reconnaissance flights a risky undertaking, but information was bound to leak out that an invasion was being prepared. The Allies employed a whole series of stratagems, from bombardments from the sea to the broadcasting of false messages, to convince the Germans that the landing was going to take place further north at somewhere like Civitavecchia.

Yet always the generals were haunted by the fear that their real plans might be discovered. Teams of naval officers, floating in rubber boats in the dead of night, had gone in to examine the beaches around Anzio, and the last of these teams had not returned. Had they been captured by the Germans?

An officer still ashore after the final briefing was on his way to join his unit when he dropped the notebook containing his instructions. It lay in the middle of the road until it was picked up by an Italian peasant. He handed it to a sapper lance-corporal, who gave it to his unit HQ. Had the Italian read the book and could he understand what it was all about? No one could say. It was too late to do anything, but the security officials were worried by the picture of the fate of the landing resting on a small notebook, lying in the mud of a Neapolitan road.

Now all the last-minute changes had been made, from the loading of guns to replace those lost at the rehearsal to the unloading of a harmonium and hundreds of hymn-books, which, by some administrative mistake, had been included in the stores urgently needed by the assault troops as they waded ashore in the face of enemy fire.

Thirty-five thousand men with their tanks, guns and supplies lay packed on board their appointed ships ready for the signal to sail. The majority of them had marched up the gangplanks in that mood of cheerful pessimism which is the hallmark of the good modern soldier. One or two units embarked with more panache. The Irish Guards, for example, swung down the hill to their embarkation point at Castellammare headed by their band playing the regimental march. The Italians lining the pavement cheered themselves hoarse while the Colonel, standing on the pedestal of a convenient statue, took the salute. Says their historian, 'This is the way men should go to war.'

Some Americans had a different version of the Hero's Farewell. As General Truscott stepped on board the headquarters ship, *Biscayne*, the band of the 3rd Division broke into the division's uproarious signature tune, 'The Dog-faced Soldier'. A hundred voices sent the words echoing around the docks at Naples:

I'm just a dog-faced soldier with a rifle on my shoulder,
And I eat a Kraut for breakfast every day.
So feed me ammunition,
Keep me in the 3rd Division,
Your dog-faced soldier-boy's O-Kay!

The commander of the force received a less exhilarating send-off. General Lucas was not in good health, and he had been depressed by the mishaps at the rehearsal. The closer zero hour approached the less confident did he feel about the task ahead.

In his round of farewell visits General Patton also came to Lucas's Headquarters. He had pronounced views about the concept of Shingle and expressed them in those uncensored terms of which he was an acknowledged master. He said to General Lucas, 'John, there is no-one in the army I'd hate to see get killed as much as you, but you can't get out of this alive. Of course, you might be badly wounded. No one ever blames a wounded general!'[1] He urged him to read his Bible and then turned to one of Lucas's aides and added, 'Look here; if things get too bad, shoot the old man in the backside; but don't you dare kill the old fellow!'

General Clark's counsel to his chosen standard-bearer was hardly more encouraging. He advised Lucas, 'Don't stick your neck out as I did in Salerno.'

Back in London Mr. Churchill felt his mind continually turning to what he called 'this considerable stroke', and on the eve of 21 January he cabled to Stalin: 'We have launched the big attack against the German armies defending Rome which I told you about at Teheran. The weather conditions seem favourable. I hope to have good news for you before long.'[2]

As the cable went on its way to Moscow the Anzio ar-

[1] Morison, *A History of United States Naval Operations in World War II*, Vol. IX, p. 328.

[2] Churchill, *The Second World War*, Vol. V.

mada was already putting out to sea. The weather forecast was good and the Met. officers predicted that these conditions would hold for four days. The American ships had been moving out from their shore base since the first light of dawn. There was just enough breeze to ruffle the calm sea. The sky was flecked with feathery clouds and the air ceiling was at 6,000 feet, which gave the air forces ample room in which to operate.

From time to time the sun broke through and glittered on the ungainly barrage balloons that billowed behind the larger vessels. There was a feeling of holiday relief in the air such as always arrives once an expedition starts at last—'This is it! There can be no turning back!'

By the afternoon the British Task Force (code name 'Peter') was also out and assembling in the blue waters off Capri. The ships floated on the very seas through which Nelson's seventy-fours had sailed into Naples after the Battle of the Nile. The gallant Admiral Troubridge, on his deck in the British headquarters ship, *Bulolo*, could reflect that his great-grandfather had been one of Nelson's paladins even though his ship had run aground on the sandbanks at the beginning of the Nile battle. Naval traditions would thus be firmly maintained.

Captain Kershaw, of *Bulolo*, felt therefore in a strong position when he requested a senior officer of 1st Division to go below as he was improperly dressed. The officer was standing on deck absorbed in the view, but was not wearing his hat! The official Russian observer, with his hat firmly on his head, remarked grimly, 'I have been in an operation like this once before in the Crimea. But then we were going the other way.'

So the great fleet moved out of the Bay of Naples, 253 ships in all, of a variety unimagined before this war. To see this armada moving over the blue Mediterranean water was to realize how far the Allies had come since the far-off days of Dunkirk. No recce plane tried a quick dash to capture a tell-tale photograph. No German bombers came in to disturb the white wakes of the ships, turning to take up their assigned positions. The Allied Air Forces were supreme in the Italian sky.

In the background lay the curve of the Bay of Naples with Vesuvius sending up its lazy plume of smoke towards the jagged outline of the Sorrento peninsula. The fleet moved out to sea past Capri and its plunging cliffs, turning first to the southward to deceive any hostile watcher on shore. A destroyer raced through the lines with General Alexander on board, flying the signal, 'Good luck to you all.'

Before dusk fell the main convoy turned north and the smaller craft, which were taking the inshore route, were also on their way.

Night closed in, bringing a touch of crisp cold, and the stars sparkled over the blacked-out ships moving northwards. They passed the dark outline of the island of Ponza. Away to the east the soldiers on deck could see the flashes of gunfire: it was the artillery rumbling among the grim mountains around Cassino. The fleet was slipping in the darkness of the night around the back of Hitler's Italian fortress, and for the moment there was no more to be done.

The Allies had committed their fortune to the waters.

4

The Landing

The chill dawn of 22 January disclosed to the astonished eyes of the Allied commanders one of the most unexpected sights of World War II. Their troops were pouring ashore in the thousands, and the great armada of ships which had brought them safely through the night lay calm and unmolested a few miles from the beaches. Landing craft hurried busily to and fro. Tanks and guns churned up the sand as they pushed out of sight inland. But of the foe there was no sign: the occasional bark of a lonely SP gun somewhere away in the hinterland, the odd pop of a rifle from the quiet woods—that was all!

The unbelievable had happened; the invaders had caught the Germans completely by surprise.

The reports poured in: the British were firm on their objective to the north of the port, the American Rangers had swept into Anzio itself and caught the German engineers who had orders to blow up the harbour. The 3rd Division was driving fast towards the Mussolini Canal, which was to form the flank protection of the Beachhead to the south.

Baker Force, a small group of guns and scout cars, was setting off to reach the banks of the little Moletta stream, the flank guard to the north-west.

There was an air of boundless opportunity over everything in sight!

We were seventy odd miles behind the Gustav Line and we were all possessed with a strange feeling that we were free to drive off anywhere. In the afternoon I got into the port of Anzio from Peter beach, on which I had landed.

DUKWs were already chugging in from the big Liberty ships lying out to sea, and long lines of tramping men were marching through the empty streets. Notices were sprouting in profusion on every telegraph pole as the army lost no time in imposing its own geography on the newly occupied country. Bull-dozers flung aside the rubble near the quays and engineers festooned every wall with endless rolls of signal wire.

But just off the main highways the town was deserted, looted and abandoned. The Germans had cleared out the inhabitants and left nothing but haphazard wreckage in the houses they had once occupied.

As I wandered through the side-streets I felt that not even Pompeii seemed as deserted as newly captured Anzio, away from the dust and engine noise around the harbour. I had a sensation of almost indecent eavesdropping into the pathetic secrets of ordinary family life.

I picked my way over the rubble into what had been a small private school. The schoolbooks had been tumbled into the dust and the carefully filled report forms flung into untidy heaps which would have vexed the heart of the headmistress. But would anyone now care if T. Ghilberti had won Honours in Ancient History?

The nearby church had been split apart, and a British soldier wandered open-mouthed in the ruins. 'This is a beautiful place,' he said to me; 'all the statues are of real plaster.' Two sailors came bicycling down the road on one of the self-propelled trolleys from the railway: they were seized with that air of holiday release which hangs over back-streets of captured towns, where, for a few moments, a man can dodge discipline.

On the door of the house opposite was a large German notice, 'Kommandant'. Someone had scrawled in chalk beneath it, 'Resigned'.

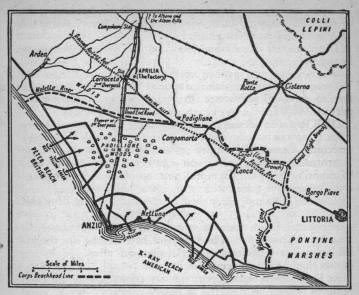

THE LANDING, 22-23 JANUARY 1944

Then came the swift roar of engines overhead, and a plane swept past at roof-top height. German markings! The staccato popping of the light ack-ack echoed through the town followed by deep, bass poundings as the 'Chicago pianos', the multiple pom-poms of the bigger ships, joined in the fury of sound that crackled all around. The Germans had got six raiders through the screen that protected the fleet.

The whole anchorage filled with the reek of high explosive as the sky above it blossomed quickly with the black smoke-bursts of exploding shells. The DUWKs chugged on through the great columns of spray thrown up by the falling bombs.

Suddenly there came a sharp crack, and a huge fountain of dirty water lifted itself high over the Beachhead. Some-one shouted, 'They've hit a LSI, the bastards!' and a black scum of oil waste and wreckage spread slowly over the blue waters. Patrol boats raced into it to fish for survivors.

But what were small air-raids, the odd shell hitting the harbour, the occasional outburst of rifle-fire in the distance, compared with the great over-riding fact that the Allied forces were triumphantly ashore and everywhere advancing almost unopposed onto their first objectives? By midnight on D-day 36,000 men had been landed with 3,000 vehicles and ample supplies, roughly 90 per cent of the first assault convoy. After the mishaps of the rehearsal and despite difficulties with sand-bars the American and British Navies had made a resounding success of the job of putting the soldiers ashore.

And in front of the troops—nothing! At dawn on D-day there were only a few units between them and Rome. The German General Westphal afterwards admitted that the German High Command had only two weak battalions at hand to defend the city and that an audacious flying column could have penetrated to the gates with ease.

General Alexander signalled to the anxious Mr. Churchill; 'We appear to have got almost complete surprise. I have stressed the importance of strong-hitting mobile patrols being boldly pushed out to gain contact with the enemy, but so far have not received reports of their activities.'

Mr. Churchill replied: 'Thank you for all your messages. Am very glad you are pegging out claims rather than digging in beachheads.'

But this was exactly what General Lucas was not doing. No strong, hard-hitting mobile patrols were on their way down the roads towards Albano or Cisterna. Instead the troops were going forward methodically to occupy what had been designated as 'the Corps Beachhead Line'—a perimeter drawn in an eight-mile circle around the port of Anzio, from the Moletta river mouth in the north-west to the Mussolini canal in the south-east.

Behind this line General Lucas had planned to consolidate and repulse the expected German counterattack. He was in no mood to alter his plan in view of the Great Surprise for the very simple reason that, all through D-day, he was more surprised than his enemy.

When his troops poured ashore unopposed on that astonishing winter's morning General Lucas had no hesitation in deciding that the empty countryside before him held dangers which would soon be revealed. He had based his plan on the possibility that he might have to fight for his beachhead: to find himself unattacked by mid-morning of 22 January was a bonus he had no right to expect.

He had been told by his intelligence that Kesselring had two divisions in reserve near Rome, the 29th and the 90th Panzer Grenadier formations, and, although General Alexander felt confident that these units had now been dragged south into the battle around Cassino by the strength of the Fifth Army attack, Lucas was not sure. He determined to keep his troops well in hand.

At any moment on that first day he pictured the German armour arriving on the scene. He held two brigades of the British 1st Division in reserve under Corps command in case they should be needed to restore a Salerno situation.

For most of the morning the 1st Divisional Commander was still unhappily afloat in *Bulolo*, panting for the permission to go ashore and join his men on the Beachhead. General Lucas's craft came alongside in time for him to warn General Penney: 'Alert your boys. They will be attacked at four.'

General Penney, still afloat, was in no position to alert his boys and was left in some doubt about the Corps Commander's intentions. Were General Alexander and General Clark left equally in the dark?

They had both dashed up by a fast speed-boat to the scene of the landing as soon as they heard of its success. General Alexander had gone ashore early in the British sector, and the troops had been cheered to see him driving along the coast road, squeezed in a jeep beside the ever-buoyant but generously proportioned Admiral Troubridge.

He stopped to have a few words with the Guards and told Colonel Andrew Scott: 'I am very satisfied.' The first German shells were beginning to come over, and Admiral Troubridge chuckled: 'This is most unfair, as I am a non-combatant on land.' The General had a good look at the expanding beachhead before he left and saw most of the commanders, including General Lucas. Was he indeed 'very satisfied' with the way things were going and with the decision of Lucas to stick to his policy of slow build-up against counter-attack? Lucas certainly got the impression that Alexander was pleased with him and noted in his diary that the C-in-C felt that he had done 'a splendid piece of work'.

A commander-in-chief bears the ultimate responsibility for the operations in the theatre of war assigned to him, but a British C-in-C who has command of American forces must tread warily. Could it be that General Alexander had memories of previous occasions when he had given orders over the head of the Fifth Army Commander to one of his subordinates?

General Clark himself had some compunction about prodding Lucas into precipitate action on the first days of the landing. He, too, had his memories of Salerno, which had been reflected in the deliberate vagueness of the directive he had issued to Sixth Corps—instructions carefully worded (as Lucas noted at the time) 'so as not to force me to push on at the risk of sacrificing my Corps'.

Whatever their reasons for not applying the spur, General Alexander and General Clark sailed from the Beachhead in the afternoon leaving the impression behind them that they were satisfied with the progress made and that they approved the policy of waiting for the German counter-attack. As the Anzio wits remarked, 'They came, they saw, they concurred.' Their speed-boat shot away to the southward carrying with them the last chance that the Allies might risk anything to take advantage of the Great Surprise.

At that moment elements of the Hermann Goering Division were entering Cisterna and anti-tank guns were being hurriedly wheeled into position at Campoleone. The first frail outline of a German screen was beginning to form around the Beachhead at places which, at dawn, had been completely innocent of the sight of a single German uniform.

The American and British troops were not in the confidence of the High Command and did not worry about the way the operation ought to develop in the future. As far as they could see on D-day it was doing very well at present. The sun was warm, they were moving inland and they revelled in the sensation of having caught the Germans napping. Very few of them doubted that they would soon receive orders to sweep forward to the hills and Rome.

Field-Marshal Albert Kesselring had been in control of the German armies in Italy since November 1943. Those who fought against him recognize his exceptional qualities as a war leader. He shared to the full the strange blindness of the German professional soldier in political matters, but there is no question of his remarkable technical skill.

After the Sicily landing in 1943 his star had been somewhat under a cloud. Hitler was drawn to the more spectacular figure of Rommel and was inclined to take his advice about the Mediterranean. Kesselring was also suspected of being too tender-hearted with the Italians. But after his success in slowing down the Allied advance had restored his prestige, Hitler had appointed him C-in-C Southeast and placed the two armies in Italy under his command. The Fourteenth Army was formed from the units scattered north of Rome, coast-watching or reforming in the valley of the Po; the Tenth Army stood facing the Allies along the whole length of the Gustav Line.

Kesselring had always been aware that the Allies might land behind this line. He had deliberately run the risk of making his stand south of Rome because he felt that, with a properly placed reserve, he could repulse a landing without letting go of his defences in the south.

He had made elaborate preparations to meet the danger which threatened him from the sea. His first care was to see that he had ample reserves in hand that could be rushed to the spot as soon as the alarm-bell rang. His main source of supply was obviously the Fourteenth Army units coast-watching or training in North Italy, but there were units in the south of France and even in the Balkans which could be called upon in time of crisis.

In December, while the fortifications of the Gustav Line were being hurried forward, elaborate plans were being made to deal with any attempt to outflank it.

A complete survey had been made of all the available routes southward from Northern Italy. Five areas had been nominated as the sites for possible landings and arrangements perfected for reinforcing the local defenders by a stream of reserves from Lombardy and further afield.

Routes had been plotted in advance, parties were standing by to de-ice the mountain passes and emergency fuel-pumps had been hidden along selected roads. Engineers were waiting with pontoon bridges which could be floated out over rivers at night after the Allied bombers had gone back to their bases. As soon as the codeword 'Case Richard' was flashed from Headquarters the whole vast machinery of reinforcement would be set in motion.

But reinforcements might take some time to come down from the north. Kesselring felt that he should have a reserve closer at hand behind the Gustav Line. He got his extra reserve by withdrawing two divisions from the Tenth Army and stationing them near Rome.

As he reviewed his position from his headquarters at Monte Soracte north of Rome on the end of the big Allied offensive on the Cassino front, which was to be the prelude of the Anzio landing, he could feel that he had done all that a prudent general could do to prepare for the blow. But the Fifth Army attack in the Garigliano sector of the Cassino Front was more effective than the Allies realized at the time. The commander of the German Tenth Army began to clamour for the immediate return of the two divisions: he feared that his right wing, held by inferior troops, would be driven in.

Kesselring was now faced with one of those harassing dilemmas which are reserved in war for commanders-in-chief. He tells us:

> I could plainly see the enemy's operational possibilities. The alternative possibility of a landing was merely a hunch: there was no indication of when or where. If I let the Tenth Army commander down his right wing might be driven in and no one could tell where it would be able to halt a retreat. At the time I could foresee a development such as actually occurred in the May offensive. If this uncontrolled retirement coincided with a landing the consequences could not be vouched for. How would Rome with its million population react? . . . Against such a threat half-measures are useless—the counter-blow must of necessity be swift and effective. The need was to clear up the mess at one point so as to have the strength available to meet any fresh challenge.[1]

The Commander-in-Chief made his decision: he would risk the landing and restore the position on the Gustav Line. He sent up the two divisions, which were flung into the battle just as the Anzio expedition prepared to sail. The southern front had done its first job and sucked in Kesselring's immediate reserves.

His two carefully hoarded divisions were now committed, but Kesselring had another problem on his mind. As soon as the Cassino attack began he had ordered an emergency warning throughout Italy. Would this attack coincide with a landing? But as the days passed and the anxiously expected fleet did not appear on the coast, his staff began to warn him that he would overtire his troops if he kept them continually standing-to. Against his better judgment he

[1] *The Memoirs of Field-Marshal Kesselring.*

countermanded the stand-to order for the night of 21-22 January, the very night of the Anzio landing!

After the Anzio battle had opened he could also reflect upon another ironic coincidence. Admiral Canaris, the chief of the German counter-espionage system and a man who played a strange part in the later history of the war, visited Kesselring's headquarters. The staff officers naturally wanted to know what the leading German expert in the matter thought of the possibilities of an immediate Allied landing; above all, they wanted to know the whereabouts of aircraft carriers, warships and landing craft.

Admiral Canaris admitted that he was unable to give precise details and figures, but he assured everybody: 'There is not the slightest sign of a fresh landing; shipping in the port of Naples is quite normal.'

Admiral Canaris left Kesselring's headquarters on 21 January!

As dawn strengthened into daylight on the morning after Canaris had left and revealed the Allied forces pouring ashore seventy miles behind the German lines Kesselring might well have cursed his counsellors and his luck.

In spite of all his care and foresight he had been caught off balance. He had given away the swift counter-punch he had so prudently prepared. The two divisions which were designed to crash down on the Americans and British slowly advancing inland were now fighting furiously away to the south. He had ordered 'Case Richard' to be put into operation immediately and reinforcements were beginning to move as planned, but it would take the whole morning to get even the first elements near the Beachhead. Only one depleted battalion from the 29th Panzer Grenadier Regiment had been left in or near the area of danger, and this unit had been too badly mauled to be ordered back into the line.

Well might Kesselring's Chief of Staff lament that there 'now had occurred the very thing that should have been avoided at all costs'. The road to Rome and the Alban Hills was wide open. Which way would the enemy move? The Germans could not conceive that the Allies would not move at all: they waited with deep anxiety for news that powerful, thrusting columns of tanks and guns and lorried infantry had seized Cisterna or Campoleone. Above all they looked

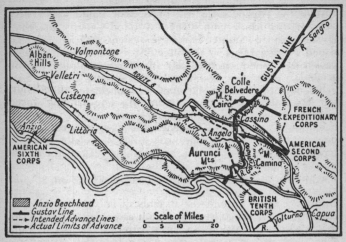

THE GENERAL ASSAULT ON THE GUSTAV LINE AND THE BEACHHEAD, 22-23 JANUARY 1944

uneasily over their shoulder at Rome itself, where Allied aircraft had just showered two million leaflets over the Capital announcing the landing. What would happen when the first reconnaissance units reached the city suburbs?

Those early hours of 22 January have about them a dangerous aura of hope for the Allies. Was Kesselring right when he declared that the Allies had a 'uniquely favourable chance of capturing Rome and opening the door on the Garigliano front'?

The opportunity—'a breath-taking situation', as General Westphal called it—could only be measured in hours, for a commander of Kesselring's calibre does not remain off-balance for long. He had set his reserves moving and he would soon assess the weight behind the Allied punch. Yet for one fleeting moment on the morning of the landing Kesselring might well have felt, like Cardinal Wolsey, that he was indeed 'naked to his enemies'.

His enemies, however, did not move.

The Germans, it has been said, were repeatedly surprised in the last war, but they were rarely panicked. There was a flurry of uncertainty in Rome when the news broke of the landing at Anzio, hurried packings by officials and quick burnings of papers; but the C-in-C knew that his first duty, come what may, was to hold the high ground of the Alban Hills and stop the Allied flood pouring through Velletri onto Route Six and the road to the south. He flung every small packet of soldiers he could lay his hands on onto this vital ground, wondering all the time if it was not too late.

But as the morning developed Kesselring permitted himself a cautious feeling of optimism. The landing forces seemed to be sitting down quietly in the narrow ring they had drawn around their beaches. He drew the correct deduction from their inaction: the Allies were not going to move swiftly inland because they did not yet feel themselves strong enough. Kesselring records: 'That morning I already had the feeling that the worst danger had been staved off.'

But before he could think of a counter-attack he must first throw a cordon around the Beachhead and seal it off from the Hills. He drew this cordon with astonishing speed, using scattered units of the anti-aircraft batteries of the Luftwaffe. The German anti-aircraft gun was a formidable weapon—when it was not pointing to the sky it could point equally well at a tank. By rushing all the available guns to the scene of the landing, Kesselring soon had a complete ring of batteries around it which it would be hard for tanks to penetrate without a stiff fight.

He then put an active subordinate, General Schlemmer, onto the task of pushing forward every soldier he could collect to the support of the anti-aircraft units. Kesselring toured the front in the afternoon, driving on his men with a sense of vital urgency. As he went from point to point he kept looking from the high ground towards the storm centre of Anzio. There lay the armada of ships, with the barrage balloons flying above them like silver specks in the sunshine, but there was still no sign that the Allies were preparing to march away from those comforting ships.

At this moment Kesselring might well have offered a sacrifice to the old Roman Goddess of Fortune at Anzio. From now on it was clear that she had already left the Allied side and come over to the Germans.

The remarkable thing about this cordon around the Beachhead was the skill with which Kesselring and his commanders welded together a mass of miscellaneous units into strong and efficient fighting groups. Kesselring describes the position as a 'higgledy-piggledy jumble—units of numerous divisions fighting confusedly side by side', but it was not long before order was swiftly evolved out of this apparent chaos.

While British and Americans always found it difficult to give of their best when taken out of their familiar framework of battalions and brigades, the German soldier had become used to these sudden improvizations. He did not seem to mind, but attacked and defended with the same efficiency, no matter what officers were suddenly placed over him. As long as those officers knew their business they would be briskly obeyed.

Kesselring now needed a solid administrative frame for his rapidly growing Beachhead force. He ordered the staff of his First Parachute Corps into the area and quickly reinforced it with the staff of the Seventy-sixth Panzer Corps from the Adriatic front. They set to work immediately on their task of co-ordinating the mass of mixed units which were now rushing to the scene of the landing. Within two days Kesselring could feel that he had created the nucleus of an army around the Beachhead.

On 23 January General von Mackensen, the chief of the Fourteenth Army in Northern Italy, reported to Kesselring's headquarters. In giving him the overall command at Anzio Kesselring felt able to tell Von Mackensen with some pride: 'I regard our position of defence as consolidated and we no longer have to fear any major reverse.'

It was a remarkable achievement. Odd elements of eight different divisions had been welded into a coherent defence cordon, while five more divisions were hurrying to the danger point. The Allied Air Forces were out in strength, but they could not stop the long columns moving by night or down quiet roads towards the strong ring which now lay around the quiescent Beachhead.

The formidable Hermann Goering Division held the Cisterna front facing the Americans, the 3rd Panzer Grenadiers were forming in the path of the British near Campoleone and the 65th Infantry Division was busy organizing a defence zone beyond the Moletta stream. As the Allied effort died on the southern front Kesselring even found it possible to withdraw divisions from the very point at which the Allies fought to pin them, and send them back to Anzio. He then looked across to the Adriatic coast and rightly judged that the Eighth Army was incapable of making any further advance. He ordered the 26th Panzers to leave the Adriatic front and join the Beachhead ring.

Some days later, on 28 January, Mr. Churchill cabled General Alexander about the situation at Anzio: 'It would be unpleasant if your troops were sealed off there and the main army could not advance up from the south.'

Two days after the landing Kesselring had already made certain that this was exactly what would take place. He had already laid down the pattern of the Battle for the Beachhead.

As D-day turned into D plus 1, and then into D plus 2, a slight unease began to possess the Allied rank and file. The exhilaration of the Great Surprise had worn off, to be succeeded by the anxiety of marking time. The men could not share the thoughts of the Corps Commander and know nothing of the factors which had influenced him to consolidate on the Beachhead. They only sensed that for the moment there seemed to be no strong enemy before them.

The commander of the British 1st Division, who was as much in the dark about General Lucas's intentions as his men, thought ruefully of the entry he had made in his diary on the eve of embarkation:

> Trying to apply Monty's dictum of seeing, at least in the mind's eye, how the battle should develop . . . the 24th Guards Brigade should be ashore by 1600 and the Division on assault scales by midday D plus 1. By that time I hope that 24th Guards Brigade will be on its way towards Albano with 3rd Brigade, on the night of D plus 1, following them up.

On the evening of D plus 2 the Guards, who had expected to play a dashing role in the race for the hills, were still in reserve in the woodlands of Padiglione. The men were 'brewing up' while their officers, playing bridge to pass the time, were unhappily reminded of the Suvla Bay landing in Gallipoli in 1915, when General Stopford had also consolidated on the beaches instead of driving for the hills. The Irish Guards, in particular, had hoped to race for Rome. One enthusiastic Guardsman had declared on landing: 'We'll give the Holy Father a holiday and make Father Brookes [the Padre] acting unpaid Pope!' This happy inspiration had faded, the sunshine of D-day had melted into rain and there was a general air of damp anticlimax abroad.

The German shelling began to increase in volume—nothing heavy as yet, but with a proof that the enemy were gathering somewhere out in the mysterious country beyond the Corps defence line. Shells fell into the harbour and splashed amongst the LSTs bringing in the follow-up troops and the rear echelons. 'Hey, bud,' said one astonished new arrival from the Pay Corps, 'this isn't on the schedule. You ought to push the war further back!'

As dusk fell on 23 January, the first of the really big air attacks swept in on the anchorage to serve notice that the Luftwaffe was back in business. The Allies had been so used to having things their own way in the air that this sudden reappearance of the Swastika on the fusilage of planes racing overhead was disconcerting.

The Germans attacked the roadstead with aerial torpedoes and their new glider-bombs. These strange missiles had already been used at Salerno with success and the Navy's experts had hurried forward all possible counter-measures to check them.

At first sight the glider-bomb seemed a fantastic, Wellsian nightmare of the same order as the V1 or the Rocket. The bomb, furnished with vanes that allowed it to glide rather than fall, was carried under the belly of the parent aircraft. While the dive-bombers plunged headlong into the attack and the torpedo-bombers skimmed the waves, the glider-bomber stayed well clear of the fountain of flak which rose into the Anzio sky as soon as the first raiders were detected. The pilot encircled the anchorage like a wolf prowling round a sheepfold, ready to launch his bomb as soon as he spotted a gap left by the watchdogs of the Navy. He guided it onto the target by remote control and radio beam, while he himself stayed high up and well clear of the inferno over Anzio. He thus operated on his enemy with clinical detachment. At least he did in theory—in practice the weapon revealed a fatal weakness. The radio beam, on which everything depended, could be detected, jammed and bent.

Quickly the US and Royal Navies equipped three destroyers with special jamming apparatus and with teams that could monitor the wavelengths of the Luftwaffe so completely that they could detect the glider-bombers warming up on the airfields around Rome. As the raiders approached the roadstead a battle of wits began—the glider-bomber pilot struggling to keep his bomb on course, the jamming team huddled over their instruments in the blacked-out control room on board their racing destroyer, striving to get onto the beam and twist the bomb away from its target. The jamming teams quickly became expert and again and again sent the raider's bombs plunging harmlessly into the sea. Yet there were moments when the most skilful operator would miss the beam and the German pilot would score a success.

At the height of the raid on 23 January a glider-bomb got through the defences and hit the British destroyer *Janus*. She sank in twenty minutes with the loss of her commander and over 150 men. The survivors clung to the wreckage, some of them singing 'Roll Out the Barrel' until they were rescued. Later the Germans hit and sank the hospital ship *St. David*, which was lying out to sea, fully illuminated in accordance with the terms of the Geneva Convention. There were more losses to come in the succeeding days.

The sea itself began to show the same hostility as the Germans. The calm of the first days of the landing gave way to a swell which rolled in from the westward and ended all unloading on the British beaches. The wind rose, and by the 25th it was blowing at fifty miles an hour, driving steep, breaking waves onto the American beaches as well. Pontoons broke loose, landing craft were driven ashore and the Allies got a sharp reminder that a beachhead which did not expand rapidly would be a costly affair to maintain from the sea.

The High Command now started to put as strong a pressure on General Lucas as the sea and the Germans. Mr. Churchill waiting in London for news of the fast columns seizing the Alban Hills, hastened to inquire from General Alexander when these desirable prizes were likely to be in our hands, for, as he pointed out, 'In all his talks with me Alexander envisaged that the essence of the battle was the seizure of the Alban Hills with the utmost speed. . . .'

General Lucas still felt no desire to push far inland, but was beginning to see that his present beachhead was a little too constricted. He looked out from his defence perimeter towards the small towns of Cisterna and the railway station of Campoleone.

These two names now assumed an importance in the battle for Anzio which they never lost in the long weeks of anguish which lay ahead. They had, of course, featured in the preliminary plans for the landing; they would have to be occupied during the course of the breakout as useful road centres, through which our troops would drive on their way to the Hills. Now they became important objectives in themselves. Unless Lucas got them he would have no breathing-space in his beachhead even if he had no intention of going any further.

Cisterna was a small country town on the edge of the Pontine marshes, where the road to Velletri wound down to more level ground. Through it passed the main railway line from Rome to Naples and the coast road to the south, known as Route Seven.

The little settlement came to life on market days, when the farmer from the hills came in to the main square to sell his produce before the strange ornamental fountain, a rococo rockery peppered with small statues. The importance of Cisterna to the invaders lay in its position. It blocked the way into the Velletri Gap, so that whoever held it could disrupt communications in this important area.

A road led from Cisterna to Anzio, one of the two main roads out of the Beachhead. Along this road the Americans were to fight their bitterest battles, and Cisterna, battered until only the strange fountain remained recognizable from the days of peace, became their main objective, the centre of their thoughts.

Campoleone was a much smaller affair, a mere railway station on the main line. It lay at the point where the comparatively level ground round Anzio started to rise in a series of gently swelling slopes to the town of Albano perched high on the Alban Hills. Here again was a communications centre which could be important both for attack and defence.

General Lucas had known from the beginning that he needed both Campoleone and Cisterna as strong-points for his expanding beachhead, and he could have taken both with ease on the morning of the landing—if he had dared. They were his for the asking even if he had decided to go no further toward the Hills. But on D-day his thoughts had been concentrated on immediate counter-attacks, and Cisterna and Campoleone looked too far away from the beaches. Now they seemed eminently desirable properties which he would have to possess to make certain of his defensive line.[1]

He was encouraged to go for them by the arrival on 24 January of the first of the follow-up forces, the 179th Regimental Combat Team of the American 45th Infantry Division, with the rest of the division due to land in a matter of days. An American RCT is the equivalent of a British brigade, and General Lucas now felt free to release the bulk of the British 1st Division from Corps reserve. He gave General Penney permission to probe towards Campoleone while General Truscott was to test the going towards Cisterna.

On the morning of the 24th the first British patrol went forward from the flyover bridge on the Anzio-Albano road into the silent, waiting countryside beyond.

At the same time General Lucas received two startling bits of news from Allied Intelligence: the Germans had already moved forty thousand men into the Anzio area and Hitler had issued a special Order of the Day to the Southern Front, in which he said: 'The Gustav Line must be held at all costs for the sake of the political consequences which would follow the successful defence of it. The Führer expects the most bitter struggle for every yard.'

The Germans now meant to fight to the death; long before the patrol had started to move up the deserted Albano road the last frail chance of making the Anzio landing a success had gone.

5

Advance at Last

In the British sector the first patrol was sent out by the Grenadier Guards. A handful of Bren-gun carriers and anti-tank guns assembled at dawn around the flyover bridge, about eight miles out of Anzio along the Albano road. For

[1] But his diary still reflects caution. On 25 January, four days after the landing, he noted that the situation would not be resolved 'until I can get my feet under me and make some further progress. I am doing my best but it seems terribly slow. . . . I must keep my feet on the ground and my forces in hand and do nothing foolish.'

days this bridge, which carried a sideroad across the main road, buttressed by short embankments on either side, had been the limit of our exploration. The little force passed under it and moved slowly off down the deserted roadway.

The little party of Grenadiers were unaware of the speed with which Kesselring was throwing his cordon around the Beachhead like a Roman *retiarius* in the Colosseum catching the heavily armoured *secutor* in his net. They were in a mood of exploration and felt that they might easily reach the gates of Rome.

Their road first led them straight for three miles towards the cluster of houses marked on their map as Carroceto. The electric-railway track from Anzio to Rome ran close alongside, and the roadway itself was lined with trees now bare after the winter. In the growing light they could see that the farmhouses on either side of the road were still heavily shuttered, but here and there the peasants were stirring, pausing as they went out to attend to their cattle to look at the strange procession rumbling down the road.

Now immediately ahead a second bridge crossed the road. It seemed to serve no useful purpose but simply carried over the main road what looked like a disused or never completed railway. The surface was strewn with cinders, and Lieutenant Hargreaves, in charge of the patrol, noted it as 'The Embankment'. The Bren-carriers now pushed cautiously through the bridge. There was no sign of the enemy, but every house in sight still had its shutters closed.

The leading carrier moved in among the houses until it came to the point where the road turned a little and continued on its way north. The men looked along it to the Alban Hills, which now seemed very near. They could see the small towns among the vineyards, the hollows holding the lakes of Nemi and Albano and—seemingly very close to them in the crisp, morning air—the next railway station up the road, Campoleone. The little task force set off gaily to reach it.

As the first carrier moved out of the shelter of the last house in the village there was a sudden crack of gunfire and a small shell spattered against the white wall of the house. The carriers swung hurriedly back into shelter again.

The opposing forces had made contact, and the first shots on the ground between British and German had been fired at last.

The shots came from a large fortress-like building a few hundred yards to the north-east of the village of Carroceto; it was promptly christened 'the Factory' by the newcomers as they took hurried looks at it from the shelter of the houses in Carroceto. They were unacquainted with the niceties of Fascist architecture and the way its practitioners harked back to the severe brickwork of Ancient Rome.

The Factory was, in fact, Aprilia, one of the big agricultural settlements built by Mussolini as centres for the peasants he had placed in the new farms on or near the reclaimed Pontine Marshes. Behind the stern, red-brick outer walls lay a village square, a church, a town hall and Fascist headquarters together with rows of shops, a health clinic and the municipal wine store. Such was Aprilia, a natural stronghold for whoever possessed it, dominating the surrounding countryside and therefore destined to become a key-point in the subsequent fighting. In the centre of the square stood a bronze statue of St. Michael with a drawn sword. By some strange freak of war, after all the shells and high explosive had been emptied over the Factory in four months of fighting, this statue alone remained intact upon its pedestal.

Two self-propelled guns now waddled slowly out of the Factory while, to their left, the patrol saw a group of Germans hastening down towards the embankment. It was time to withdraw, amid a hail of bullets.

But the patrol had done its job and pinpointed the first centre of German resistance. It was much further forward than the Allies expected. The 29th Panzer Grenadiers from the 3rd Panzer Division had moved into Aprilia, and Sixth Corps had been forestalled.

But the enemy might still be in small numbers, a screen that could be swiftly brushed aside providing the British advanced in strength at once. General Penney pressed Corps to let him issue the order; they hesitated, agreed, hesitated again and finally, in the afternoon, released the Guards Brigade from reserve and gave General Penney permission to advance. The attack was laid on for 0730 hours next day. The Guards were to clear the Factory area in preparation for a further advance towards Campoleone, while the 2nd Brigade would push forward into the Moletta area to the east to guard the left flank.

In the cold light of early dawn of 25 January, four days after the first landing, the Guards marched to the attack,

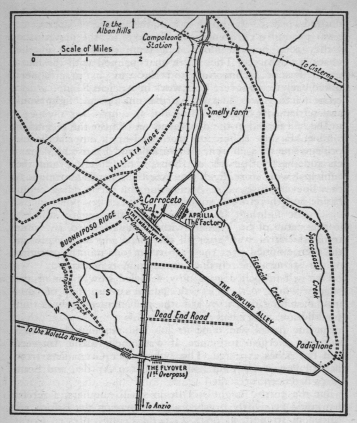

THE LANDMARKS ALONG THE ALBANO ROAD

since Corps, in making its landing plan, had not provided for early embarkation of infantry transport. They had concentrated on the repelling of the counter-attack which never arrived.

The fight for the Factory was the first warning to the front-line soldier that the Anzio adventure had lost its early bloom, its promise of boundless opportunity. The Guards had to clear the place by house-to-house fighting, one of the most unpleasant operations that an infantryman is forced to do. It is a deadly game of hide-and-seek, of sudden encounters at close quarters and of unexpected stumblings upon well-armed enemies. Shutters and doors had to be smashed in and grenades flung quickly into rooms where the Germans might be hiding, the Guardsmen ducking hurriedly to avoid the flying fragments. In some houses terrified civilians crouched in the shallow cellars praying that the fight would sweep past them.

The Germans counter-attacked and blasted the Factory with gunfire of an intensity that came as an unwelcome surprise to the Guards. It took twenty-four hours and a lot of casualties before the Factory was ours and the Germans fell back to their next line of resistance before Campoleone. As the Guardsmen grumbled: 'How much easier it all would have been only two days before.'

The net result of the first day's push by the 1st Division up the Albano Road was the possession of the Factory and the houses of Carroceto and a new realization of the strength of the German cordon forming round the Beachhead. It was by no means the flimsy affair that many had imagined it to be; in the days that the enemy had been given after the landing he had clearly built up a strong defensive network. The 1st Division would have to deploy more of its strength to penetrate the German web.

Away on the right, General Truscott and the American 3rd Division had come to the same conclusion. They, too, had advanced out of the Beachhead ring on 25 January and pushed towards Cisterna at the same time that the British had set off hopefully for Campoleone. They had met the same stubborn resistance from the enemy. Every farmhouse bristled with SP guns.

Both the British and Americans had been disappointed, but neither divisional commander was depressed. They had not yet used their full strength. They were all for trying again quickly, and Truscott added that 'done quickly it could be done well.'

Back at Corps Headquarters there was more caution in the air. The spokesman who briefed the correspondents looked thoughtfully at the map on which the chalk marks of enemy units were beginning to make a black hedge around the red outline of our forward positions: 'Today, gentlemen, things don't look so bright for Sixth Corps. Almost anything that is anything seems to be arriving on our front. So far we calculate that in a week's time we'll be facing the best part of seven divisions. If the purpose of this operation was to draw off troops from the Fifth Army front, it's certainly done it!'

General Lucas was beginning to find himself in an unenviable position. His enemies were gathering swiftly round him, and he still did not have enough room on his Beachhead. Forty-thousand Germans were already opposed to him, and more were arriving every day. Almost as hostile as the Germans were the criticisms which were beginning to reach Lucas from Caserta and farther afield. Mr. Churchill was putting pressure on General Alexander, who, in turn, passed on his impatience to General Clark.

On 28 January Clark himself, after being nearly killed on the deck of his PT boat, arrived at Anzio and admitted that he felt 'Beachhead progress was lagging unnecessarily'. Lucas was in the mood for action at last, for the follow-up divisions had sailed from Naples to add strength to his Beachhead.

The American 45th Infantry Division, under General Eagles, took over some of the ground held by the British 1st, who concentrated for a renewed advance on Campoleone. The bulk of the American 1st Armored Division was also ashore and gave Lucas a striking-force. Its tough, stocky commander, General Ernie Harmon, was a Vermonter who believed in speaking his mind plainly and had a touch of Patton about him. He reported himself to Lucas immediately he landed at Anzio. Says Harmon: 'Lucas rose from his desk in his map-hung office, laid down his inevitable corn-cob pipe and shook hands. "Glad to see you," he said briefly, "You're needed here."'

Harmon and his tanks were urgently needed, for Lucas was about to attempt a break-out against an enemy who was preparing to break-in on him.

28 January was the date originally set at Kesselring's headquarters for the beginning of the German counter-offensive which was to drive the Allies back into the sea. The Anglo-American Air Forces had, by their vigorous bombing of his communications, delayed Kesselring's troop concentrations, but his men were forming up on the ground, his tanks were getting ready and his artillery registering their targets.

The advance about to be undertaken by General Lucas assumed that the main German line of resistance lay further back from Cisterna and Campoleone along the lower slopes of the Alban Hills. Instead the enemy was already well established in Cisterna and Campoleone, busy organizing his own offensive. He had no time to construct the type of defences which barred the Allies at Cassino, but he had laid minefields at danger-points, driven tanks and self-propelled guns into every farm building and sited machine-guns wherever they had a clear field of fire.

The solidly constructed farmhouses were always an asset to the defending Germans and a liability to the advancing Allies. Each farmhouse required a separate small-scale operation, supported by tanks and tank-destroyers, before it could be cleared of the enemy.

This was the hornets' nest into which the British 1st and the American 3rd Divisions were now to be thrust. Little wonder that the spokesman at Corps, as he explained the way it was hoped the battle would develop, said to his audience: 'Well, gentlemen, tomorrow has all the makings of a bloody day.'

The plan decided upon for the attempt to break-out from the Beachhead ring called for a two-pronged advance. On the eastern flank the American 3rd Division was to push to Cisterna, cut Highway Seven and get ready to move on to Velletri. To help them the 504th Parachute Regiment and Colonel Darby's Ranger Battalions were assigned to this front. The main effort was to be made on the western side in the British sector. Here the British 1st Division was to advance towards Albano. They would first seize the road and rail junction of Campoleone by advancing from the Factory. Meanwhile General Harmon's tanks would be out on their left, making a wide swing round Campoleone to come in on the Alban Hills from the west.

Military plans inevitably look tidier and more plausible when described on paper after the event than they looked in the field at the time. I write about Corps calling for a two-pronged advance or of General Harmon preparing to swing his armour round Campoleone, but this is only a convenient shorthand to bring some sort of simplicity into a most complicated series of movements.

I remember the general air of hurry and uncertainty that

surrounded all plan-making at Anzio in the days following the landing. I think of the last-minute conferences before the maps at Corps HQ in the bleak, bare house in Nettuno—meetings which, in General Truscott's opinion, too often turned into debates; of the arguments between divisional generals about ground and the hurried radio messages summoning worried colonels to report to brigades for briefings; above all, of how totally pointless accidents can cause tragic and unexpected delays—no one is to blame for them, yet they have an utterly unfair influence on the result of an attack. One such accident, in the British sector, made certain that the break-out from the Beachhead would get off to a bad start.

To launch his attack in good order from the positions he held around the Factory General Penney wanted first to capture a lateral road which crossed the main road and the railway out of Anzio at a point about a mile and a half short of the station of Campoleone. He required this feature as a 'start line' for his main attack.

The concept of a start line—an essential part of infantry tactics—is simply a matter of applied common sense, as indeed are most of the accepted doctrines of war. Just as in a race in athletics all competitors must line up at a starting-point or else the race ends in chaos, so, in the infinitely more exacting race of an infantry attack, the unit—be it battalion, brigade or division—needs some feature on the ground along which the troops can be lined for the take off. This feature can be a hedgerow, a road or the edge of a small creek; no matter what it is, it will serve as a start line as long as it is clearly marked on the ground and can therefore be equally clearly recognized on a map.

The artillery, firing its heavy concentrations of high explosive and smoke shells to help the infantry forward, can use the start line as a reference in plotting where to drop its barrage. Reserves can be grouped behind it. A good start line will ensure that the attackers will sweep forward in a powerful wave rather than in ragged, unco-ordinated bunches. General Penney had assigned the 24th Guards Brigade to the task of capturing his start line. Then 3rd Brigade would jump off from this lateral road and capture Campoleone.

On paper all looked well, but within two minutes a burst of fire from a German automatic and some hand grenades threw the whole scheme out of joint.

The Grenadier Guards, who were to get the start line, sent their company commanders across to the Scots Guards for a final briefing. Their jeep took the wrong turning and ran straight into the German outposts. There was a swift storm of bullets and the jeep was left burning in the road beside the bodies of three officers and the maps and orders for the attack.

There was nothing for it but to delay the attack. A battalion which goes into action immediately after losing three of its company commanders is fighting blind. The Irish Guards took the place of the Grenadiers, and the Corps Commander granted a twenty-four hours' delay. In his turn, he was compelled to delay General Truscott's attack for twenty-four hours, to ensure that there would still be a co-ordinated double punch out of the Beachhead. This delay had a most unfortunate effect on Truscott's advance.

His plan of attack was based upon a daring use of Colonel Darby's crack American Rangers. This fine body of fighting men had been specially trained on the lines of the British Commandos, and Truscott himself had been responsible for their original formation in Northern Ireland in 1942. He had foreseen the need for such Special Service troops in the American Army and had chosen the title of Rangers for them, an honourable and glamorous name in American history associated with bold adventure and the upkeep of law on the wild frontier. The men were volunteers, personally selected after an interview with their leader, Colonel Darby. They had already made a name for themselves in Sicily and on the mainland of Italy.

Truscott and Darby proposed that, before the main attack went in, the Rangers should infiltrate deep into the German lines and capture Cisterna. Here they would turn houses into strong-points and dislocate the enemy's defences. As the bulk of 3rd Division fought its way towards the Rangers the Germans would be caught between two fires. Two flank attacks would be linked with the main effort, the 7th Infantry Regiment pushing north-west of Cisterna and the 504th Parachute Regiment advancing into the marshy country out on the left flank.

The road that runs from Nettuno to Cisterna, the axis of the American advance, is not as straight and flat as the Anzio-Albano road along which the British were going to make their effort. Just before it reaches a cluster of farms with the musical name of Isola Bella it runs over the crest of a low hill which gives a superb view out over the country ahead.

In one sweep the observer can see the white houses of Cisterna, a mile or so beyond Isola Bella. The Alban Hills, the Velletri Gap and the high, rugged mountains of the Lepini range form the background. To the right lies the wide level of the Pontine Marshes, dotted with the white-walled, newly built farmhouses. A narrow artificial ditch runs across this reclaimed land to a point near Cisterna. It is marked on the map as the Fossa di Pantano and is deep enough to give cover to soldiers working their way forward silently in the night. Truscott and Darby planned to send over seven hundred Rangers along this damp watercourse so that, by dawn, they would have slipped clean through the thinly spaced defenders. It was the sort of plan that wins battles—if all goes well! The Rangers were ready for their attack on the night of 28/29 January.

But now came the fatal twenty-four hours' delay. That very night units of the 26th Panzer Grenadiers, brought across from the Adriatic front, were coming in to reinforce the elements of the Hermann Goering Division, which had been clinging to Cisterna. Unknown to the men of the 3rd Division and the Rangers their enemy was no longer thin on the ground. He had increased his strong points and rushed in more tanks and SP guns. The gaps through which the Rangers were hoping to creep had been closed.

In the thick darkness that held the whole Beachhead on the night of 30 January the 1st and 3rd Rangers got ready for their daring adventure.

Each man carried two bandoliers of ammunition slung over his shoulders and had his pockets stuffed with hand-grenades. Some were equipped with bazookas, a few had portable wireless sets on their backs. They were thus lightly armed raiders, depending on their individual skill and daring to surprise the enemy.

They moved off after midnight under a cloudy, moonless sky, creeping carefully along the ditch and freezing motionless against the banks when German sentries walked by almost overhead. As dawn broke the head of the long, snake-like column came out onto the Cisterna road half a mile from the town. Success was within their grasp. They quickened their pace in a rush for the first houses of the outskirts.

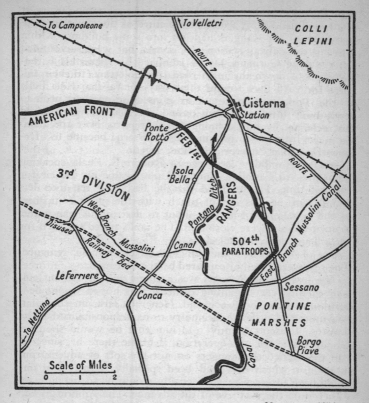

THE ATTEMPT TO BREAK OUT IN THE AMERICAN SECTOR, 30 JANUARY 1944

They ran straight into a tornado of bullets. The Germans had detected their approach, allowed them to advance and were waiting for them in deadly ambush. SP guns opened up at point-blank range, snipers picked off the Rangers as they struggled out of the head of the ditch, and soon tanks appeared across the flat fields, firing as they came. The lightly armed Rangers, unequipped with anti-tank guns, took refuge in houses and in drainage canals, but could not hold off tanks with bazookas and sticky grenades.

At 0730 the 3rd Battalion HQ radio broke silence and gave

the anxious Truscott and Colonel Darby, listening back at their command post, a dramatic picture of the situation. The remnants of the Rangers had got into some buildings within sight of the railway station of Cisterna, but were surrounded by attacking Germans. Darby launched his remaining battalion straight down the main road from Nettuno to their aid. Yard by yard they fought their way forward to Isola Bella and beyond, with tanks and SP guns close on their heels to blast every farmhouse they passed. But their advance could not possibly be quick enough. The reports over the radio from the little group hanging on in Cisterna became less frequent, but their calls for help more urgent.

Just after midday 1st Sergeant Robert E. Ehalt, speaking from the 3rd Battalion command post, came on the air for the last time. He reported that he had only ten men left round him, he was out of touch with the other companies of the battalion and he was about to destroy his transmitter as enemy tanks were closing in. The tanks rolled forward for the kill and the radio fell silent.

Out of 767 men in the Rangers' attack only six returned. The rest were killed or captured by the Germans.

The loss of the Rangers was a tragic and depressing episode at the very beginning of what was hoped would be a break-out from the Beachhead. General Clark, in particular, was upset and ordered an inquiry to fix responsibility for the disaster. Truscott bluntly told him that he would shoulder all the blame for the operation, if blame there be, since he had despatched the Rangers on just the sort of adventurous attack for which they had been specially trained. No one could have foreseen that the enemy would be so strongly reinforced on the very eve of the advance. The Americans had expected to creep through a widely spaced defence and not into a close-knit web of strong-points.

The 3rd Division gritted its teeth, regrouped and continued to fight its way forward. All through 31 January and into the next day the battle raged towards Cisterna. At one point the Americans reached the Cisterna-Campoleone railway line, at another they got within a thousand yards of the town.

This was still not far enough. The 3rd Division had now suffered three thousand casualties since the landing and was not strong enough to continue. The unexpected tenacity of the enemy reinforced the warnings already given by the loss of the Rangers: the Germans had built an iron ring around the Beachhead and General Lucas had lost the race to Cisterna. The 3rd Division ceased to attack, hurriedly adjusted its line and prepared to go on the defensive.

The right-hand punch of the Sixth Corps attack had thus jarred to a stop. Was there any better hope from the left?

It was here after all that General Lucas was putting his greatest weight behind the punch, with two divisions, the British 1st and the American 1st Armored, pushing towards Albano through and around Campoleone. The Corps commander was now more anxious than ever to secure some elbow-room for his beachhead and to get his armour moving. At his meeting with General Penney and General Harmon before the attack he declared, 'It's time to go places. Ernie, give them the works.'

The problem that confronted the two divisions, however, was that there were not many places to which they could go. The battlefield which looked so wide on the map was curiously confined on the actual ground.

The main road from Anzio to Albano was the only surfaced road in the area, the only one along which tanks could easily deploy. But it was already the British axis of advance and the Germans had covered it with formidable road-blocks. Clearing it to Campoleone was an infantry task.

The tanks were therefore given the country to the left flank over which to make their sweep towards the Alban Hills. The air photos showed it as treeless, rolling and open, good country for armour. But the air photos deceived. These bare rolling downs concealed a bitter disappointment for the American tankers. The British were also to meet their full share of bitterness.

At the same time as the Rangers, far out to their right, were getting ready for their adventure against Cisterna, the Irish and Scots Guards moved forward from the Factory area to make their bid for the start line. Behind them the 3rd Brigade of the British 1st Division, consisting of the 1st Duke of Wellington's Regiment, the 2nd Sherwood Foresters and the 1st King's Shropshire Light Infantry, formed up in the darkness. They would go through as soon as the Guards had reached their objective and drive for Campoleone. Tanks and SP guns moved out from the protective walls of the Factory; they would be needed to support the Guards as dawn brought the inevitable German counter-attack.

No one knew what lay out ahead amongst the vineyards which lined the low ridges on either side of the road. Corps had given 1st Division the information that the main lines of German defence now lay behind Campoleone. The Guards set off into the darkness.

The moon had not yet risen, and the only light came from the occasional flash of a distant gun. The mail had come up during the night, but many of the men were in no mood to read even the long-awaited letters from home; they stuffed them into their pockets and carried them into the attack. The Scots advanced up the main road and the right-hand ridge while the Irish tackled the line of the railway and the left-hand ridge, known as the Vallelata ridge.

As the Irish column moved out from Carroceto village they stumbled against the broken overhead cables, dangling from the shattered standards along the railway line. To the anxious men, advancing in the stillness of the night, the twanging of the wires made the sound of a series of gigantic harps which might give away their approach to the enemy. The gunfire then crashed down ahead of them and the soldiers quickened their pace behind its protective screen.

A Very light soared up. The Guards were outlined starkly as targets for the waiting Germans. The enemy was in far greater strength before Campoleone than anyone expected. The Guards had not been ambushed like the Rangers, but they were advancing head on into a most carefully prepared network of machine-gun nests reinforced by hidden tanks. Their losses were heavy and crippling. But, depleted and exhausted as they were, they yet got onto the much desired start line.

But could they stay there? Dawn was coming up fast, and with the dawn would come the German tanks; our own tanks must be up with our infantry before the enemy arrived. From both Scots and Irish Guards came fervent wireless appeals to Brigade Headquarters for immediate tank support, or as the Guards put it—'Send up our heavy friends.'

Brigadier Murray, commanding the Guards Brigade, had to make his decision. He had very few 'heavy friends' in hand; to whom should they go? He felt that his right flank was his danger point, for beyond the Scots Guards there was only the ever-vigilant Recce Regiment of 1st Division patrolling the wide stretch of country towards the American sector. He gave the order, and five tanks went forward to support the Scots who were fighting desperately to hold the German counter-attack. The Irish Guards would have to withdraw.

But now came a nightmare difficulty. The Irish Guards had one set left to maintain their wireless communication with Brigade; at this critical moment it was out of commission. The orders to withdraw were being broadcast urgently, but there was no set to receive them. The Irish would stay until they were cut to pieces, huddled in the shallow pits along the track to which they had so grimly fought their way.

Since midnight Lance-Corporal Holwell, the signaller of No. 2 Company, had crouched apart from his comrades in a small pit in the front line. He was carefully taking his wireless set to pieces by the light of a shaded torch at a time when the slightest gleam of light produced a storm of machine-gun fire and mortar shells. He accepted all risks to get the vital set working again, but, as the hours passed, the radio remained stubborn and silent. The orders to retire were being broadcast in vain and the companies isolated on the roadway waited for the German tanks to roll forward.

Suddenly, at a quarter-past six, the signallers at Brigade HQ reported to their officer, 'No. 2 Company is back on the air. It's Corporal Holwell talking.' The vital orders were given—'Come back as fast as you can.' Again the set went off the air and Corporal Holwell fell dead a few minutes later; but he had saved his comrades.

The survivors of the two hard-tried companies of the Irish Guards came back down the railway line, through the driving smoke laid down by the Divisional artillery, the rear-guard halting from time to time to turn savagely on their enemies. At the same time, miles away to the eastward, the American Rangers were caught in their ditch before Cisterna and the German tanks were moving in for the kill.

As the sun came up warm and strong on the morning of 30 January the Brigadier of the 24th Guards Brigade could share the American Colonel Darby's feelings when he heard of the plight of his Rangers. For the Guards also, 'things didn't look too good.'

The Scots Guards were firm on the right, but the Irish were back to where they had started. General Penney's start line had to be attacked all over again.

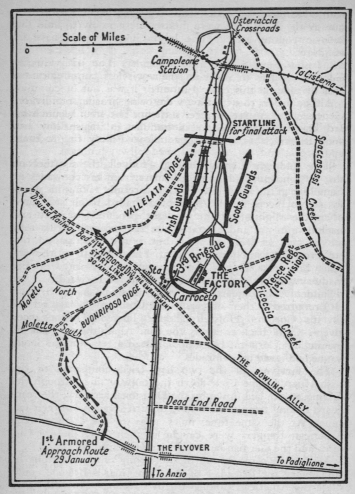

THE ADVANCE TO CAMPOLEONE, 29–30 JANUARY 1944

The divisional artillery flung a fierce and concentrated barrage over the whole area, and with the help of a company from the KSLIs, the 3rd Company of the Irish Guards with tanks of the 46th Royal Tank Regiment and the American 894th Tank-Destroyer Battalion, attacked again. The tank-destroyers advanced line ahead like battleships of old and blazed at every farm building. Soon it became clear that the Irish Guards' night attack had not been in vain; the Germans had been badly shaken and were prepared to fall back on their main defence position.

Although the short winter's day was wearing rapidly on, General Penney now had his start line and could launch his 3rd Brigade towards Campoleone. But all this delay had been dangerous. Every hour had allowed Kesselring to bring up more defenders to the threatened railway junction.

It was not until just after three o'clock in the afternoon that two battalions of 3rd Brigade made their advance on Campoleone station. The KSLI on the right went fairly easily forward and soon, with a hundred prisoners to their credit, were on a good ridge just short of the railway embankment before Campoleone. The Dukes had a harder time and seemed to be running into strong opposition as they strove to push beyond Vallelata Ridge to get up to the embankment in their sector. To complete the picture the Recce Regiment, out to the east, reported that the Germans were digging in strongly in their area too.

As night fell on 30 January, General Penney might well feel uncomfortable for his division. It had now advanced twelve miles from the sea up the Anzio-Albano road, and the ground it held got increasingly narrower the farther it advanced. Now it had reached the first slopes of the Alban Hills. On the map the divisional position looked like a thin pencil thrust deep into the German defences. Well might a company commander of the KSLI, who were now at the extreme tip of the division's advance, declare: 'We feel like the lead in the pencil!'

General Penney looked anxiously to his left. Here, on ground which had appeared open and rolling in the air photographs, the American 1st Armored were making that wide sweep which was designed to carry them round Campoleone and on to the Alban Hills. A successful advance by the Americans would greatly ease the British position and help them into Campoleone itself.

Unhappily 30 January was as disappointing a day for General Ernie Harmon as it was for General Penney.

The Italian campaign, so prodigal of unpleasant surprises in so many directions, seems to have reserved particular frustrations for the commanders of armoured divisions.

Italian geography is unfriendly to the tank, and there were moments when tankers must have felt that the whole country was one enormous, endless anti-tank ditch. The spectacular triumphs of armour had been won on the great open plains of the world. Guderian's Panzers broke the armies of France on the bare chalklands of the Somme and ran riot over the Russian steppes; Rommel and Montgomery used their tanks like rival fleets of battleships on the sand sea of the desert; while Patton had the level plains of Northern Europe as the scene of his triumphs.

In Southern Italy there were no wide, open spaces where the armour could be 'shaken loose' for one of those historic scythe-like sweeps into the rear areas of the enemy. Instead the tanks had to crawl through mountain passes on narrow roads that made them sitting ducks for well sited anti-tank guns or else fight their way through villages where every house could be converted into a tank trap.

The armoured divisions were not idle in the Italian campaign. They never sat behind the line waiting for a breakthrough by the infantry, like Haig's cavalry on the Somme, consuming its own weight daily in fodder brought up by transport which could have 'passed the ammunition' to the hard-pressed foot-slogger.

In the Second World War the tank had become an essential part of infantry tactics, the armour-protected gun which could lie close to the battle and help the infantry forward. In anything like open country infantry formations were bound to feel naked and defenceless, unable to stand up against their enemy without a strong skeleton of tanks and SP guns. Each division that landed at Anzio had this armoured skeleton attached: the 46th Royal Tanks, mainly Welshmen from Liverpool, did yeoman work with the British 1st Division, and the American 3rd Division looked with respect on its 751st Tank Battalion.

But close infantry support was hard, nervous work for the men in the tanks. They had to learn how to play a deadly game of hide-and-seek around houses which might conceal anti-tank guns; how to avoid the innocent-looking field which had been sown with mines all set to blow off the tanks' tracks; how to skulk, hull down, in every fold of the ground out of sight of the German artillery-spotters.

Gone were their memories of North Africa and the Desert, of swift pursuits of a retreating and beaten enemy across open country. They now had to move at the pace of the man on foot! One look at Cassino eliminated all hope of an Italian *Blitzkrieg*.

All this was galling to the men of the armoured divisions and disappointing to their public—in this case, the rest of the army. Armour has an aura of speed; its *mystique* demands the 'breakthrough'. There was something particularly out of place in the sight of this mass of mobile gun-power—the Allies had nearly two thousand tanks with their front-line units in Italy by early 1944—being continually held up by broken bridges, holes blown in roads, houses tumbled across narrow streets and the rest of the endless tricks in the German demolition repertoire. Critics began to ask why we did not take bigger risks with our overwhelming reserve of tanks. We could surely afford to lose hundreds if their loss would achieve decisive results. The American 'tankers' were aware of the criticism and simply asked for a small patch of open country where armour could at last show what it could do in Italy. The rolling downs that lay west of the Anzio-Albano road seemed on first sight to offer the armour its long-awaited chance.

On 29 January General Harmon sent out a strong reconnaissance force to find a good approach to his start-line. He had marked this on his map as the bed of the disused railway line running north-west from Carroceto—the same track first reconnoitred by the Grenadier Guards' patrol five eventful days ago and christened 'the Embankment'. This cinder-strewn track, rough and narrow as it was, cut across the rolling ridges and shallow valleys of the Upper Moletta stream and seemed to offer the armour a good chance of advancing north along the parallel ridge which sloped upwards from it towards the Alban Hills. It looked as good a start-line as any other in this deceitful countryside.

But Harmon had first to find an easy line of approach to the Embankment, independent of the obvious one straight up the Anzio-Albano road to Carroceto. A modern division, especially an armoured one, needs a mass of transport to keep it supplied, and as it moves creates a traffic problem which it takes experts to solve. In the ideal attack each division is assigned an independent axis of advance, a separate road down which it can send its long transport columns without cluttering up the movement of its neighbours. The Italian road system, however, seemed to be cunningly designed to spoil all textbook battles.

The only feasible line of approach to the left of the Anzio-Albano road was a country track which started a mile west of the Flyover (First Overpass) and then meandered northward over the shallow valleys of the Upper Moletta stream. On the afternoon of 29 January, while the Guards were sorting themselves out in preparation for their night attack up the main road, the 1st Armored reconnaissance force, with its light and heavy tanks, its assault guns, jeeps and half-tracks carrying infantry set off from the Flyover and started to make its way out along the track which led, first down into a shallow hollow and then up onto the ridge marked on the map as Buonriposo Ridge. They went a mile through a deceptively quiet countryside and then started to push off their road across the open country. Immediately the tanks and half-tracks bogged down. The division had met its first disappointment—this open country, sodden with winter rain, was soft and treacherous and would not permit that swift movement away from the constricting frame of roadways for which the tankers longed. It concealed another and more deadly surprise.

The small streams that ran at the bottom of the shallow valleys were not the innocent watercourses that they had appeared to be from the air. They had cut their beds deep into the soft earth; their banks, in some cases, were crumbling, bramble-covered dykes twenty or thirty feet high, forming a series of perfect anti-tank ditches. They were deeper, more winding and altogether more sinister than the Pantano ditch, far away on the right flank of the Beachhead, along which the gallant Rangers were preparing to crawl that very night. The 1st Armored had, in fact, uncovered the natural booby trap which was to plague every unit which had to fight in this sector during the history of the Anzio adventure. The British troops, with their memories of the Desert, christened these winding cracks in the ground 'the Wadis'—after the Arab name for the dry watercourses of North Africa. These wadis were far from dry in the winter of 1943-4. In addition they supplied perfect cover for the Germans.

It was difficult for anyone who had not penetrated this

warren of watercourses to appreciate exactly what the nature of the ground—and thus of the fighting—was bound to be in the wadi country.

The staff officers from Corps never visited it during the critical days of the Beachhead battle, and it was not until General Truscott took over that a really high-level Corps 'brass hat' made a tour of the wadis. General Truscott was taken round by General Penney. After the visit Truscott's Chief of Staff rang up Penney to say: 'We know now what you've been talking about. You need never mention those God-damn wadis again.'

But on that January afternoon no one knew what the 1st Armored were running into. The infantry waited to hear that, at last, the armour was 'going through'. The only thing it went through was the sticky, muddy earth. The reconnaissance tanks sank into the ground after they had 'lagered' for the night, and their crews had to spend six hours winching them out. At dawn the rest of the tanks assigned to the wide armoured sweep came up to the old railway bed of the Embankment at Carroceto. They did not get much farther. The Germans were strongly posted on the ridges to the west and north-west, and the wadis acted as moats which the tanks could not cross.

General Harmon tried to get his 6th Armored Infantry into action. An armoured division in this fourth year of the war had become a most complex formation, including artillery and infantry as well as tanks. The infantry, trained to work closely with the armour, could be used to clear up such obstacles as well-defended road blocks, which a tank could not tackle.

All through the afternoon the infantry strove to advance. The Germans had observation, and the attack foundered five hundred yards north of the start line.

Nothing could be more infuriating and frustrating to the Allied command than the sight of their armoured division, with all its potential punching power and speed, stuck in the mud and pent up between twisting cracks in the deceitful, waterlogged ground. They now felt that they were fighting with one hand, the most useful and dangerous of all, tied behind their back.

The wide swing to the west had clearly to be abandoned, yet there was desperate need to get the tanks loose, out of the bottleneck that was now building up along the Anzio-

Albano road. There was only one thing to do. The armour must return to the main road even if this involved a dangerous traffic jam. The British infantry would make a final, all-out effort to capture Campoleone station and reach the cross-roads, marked Osteriaccia, just beyond it. Then, at last, the armour would 'go through' and fan out onto the lower slopes of the Alban Hills.

In the darkness of the night of 30 January there was an intense scurry of activity behind the Allied lines. The tanks of Taskforce Hightower, named after Colonel Louis V. Hightower of the American 1st Armored, were moving into the Factory area ready to drive forward as soon as news came of the capture of Campoleone. Two battalions of 3rd Brigade lay on the ridges in front of the railway line before Campoleone station, within sight of the railway bridge and embankment that crossed the main road. (This road was over-prolific in defensible bridges and embankments! This was the third one to bar the Allies' advance and would prove the most formidable of the lot. It carried the railway line from Cisterna, which ran from the south-east to link with the Anzio line at Campoleone.)

The Scots and Irish Guards were further back, holding the ground they had won the night before. Out on the right flank, which was beginning to seem very exposed indeed, the resourceful Reconnaissance Regiment tried hard to give an impression of strength. There was a drone of aircraft overhead as the enemy's nightly air-raid went over to bomb Anzio harbour.

The men who were to make the attack were the Sherwood Foresters. They had not yet been committed in the Anzio battle but waited amongst the vines, well back from the two forward battalions of 3rd Brigade. Solid, steadfast soldiers from the Midlands of England most of them: they had received their orders and would carry them out without emotion and without question. They had the inner bravery of men with long tradition behind them.

The farther away you are from the actual scene of a battle the more anxious you become. 31 January was going to be a critical day for the Beachhead, and, in company with everyone at Anzio, my thoughts were centred on Campoleone and its station and embankment. I found it hard to remain waiting and inactive and felt compelled to see what was happening.

I drove first to the mobile battle room of 1st Division, located in a trailer placed on the edge of the woods not far from the very spot on which I had landed ten eventful days ago. I ducked under the camouflage nets and found that the officers plotting the position on the maps were reasonably optimistic. The reports, coming in fast over the network of radio which now covered the Beachhead in a complex web, were quickly translated out of the jargon of the radio operators into pencil marks on the map. The trailer was filled with voices:

'Hullo, Love. Ref. our last natter with Mike Zebra Mike, your proposition is agreed to.'

'Hullo Love. Sunray Minor dealt with the proposition. Love Roger Wait Out.'

I asked when the Foresters' attack was due. There was a series of hurried inquiries.

'Andy, have Johnny's boys gone up over the railway yet? . . . I see . . . Johnny's party is definitely on. I'll put them near the railway. 10.30, this morning, looks like the show.'

The chalk pencil made a neat mark on the map, but, as the major in charge said ruefully, 'Pencil marks do not put battalions on objectives. Go up and see what's happening.'

For eight miles out of Anzio I drove through a long series of traffic jams, wriggling our jeep onto the verges and over ditches. It was easy to see the problems that arise when both an armoured and an infantry division try to use the same axis of supply. The columns of guns, lorries and tanks were bumper to bumper and moved forward in jerks as the Military Police waved them on. I felt grateful that we were still in the shelter of the Padiglione woodlands: no one would dare risk this congestion in open country.

Beyond the Flyover the traffic thinned out. 'Nothing like an odd shell to keep traffic moving, it's the best traffic controller we've got,' said the MP at the edge of the woods.

Near Carroceto we pulled off the road to have a word with HQ of the Guards Brigade; it was always common sense to get as much information as possible when you were driving towards a front which, in military parlance, 'was still fluid'. The Guards worked in a farmhouse while, in the huge barn near by, twenty Italian families cluttered all the available space. The children laughed and romped round us, women cooked on little open fires burning against the wall and everyone seemed strangely unaware of the war only three miles down the road. The Brigade Major brought out his map onto the steps of a truck.

'Here we are; form at a glance. We reckon we're too strung out here. The Hun is thickening up on our left and the Brigadier wants to thicken up a bit, too—with something in hand in case the Hun gets nasty.'

'And the 3rd Brigade attack?'

'Well, what do you think? We're not too happy about it. You know, I can't help regretting that we didn't go for the Big Thing straight away after we landed.'

Air bursts were pock-marking the sky over the Factory and we scurried hurriedly towards 3rd Brigade HQ. The further forward we went the more we felt like cringing against the ground. A troop of our guns, brought forward since yesterday well in front of Carroceto, were dug in behind us and their shells went screaming overhead as I talked to the young Intelligence Officer. We lay in a ditch for safety, for the Germans were trying counter-battery work.

Five shells suddenly whistled round us and sank into the earth with a damp series of 'phuts'—it was hard to believe, but every one of them was a dud!

'How often does that happen?' I asked thankfully.

'Not often enough,' replied the IO with fervour.

Then I noticed an odd thing; the shells had been fired from almost right behind us.

'These were shorts,' I gasped, 'from our own guns!'

'No, they were from the Boche all right. We are so far up the road and so thinly spaced that he can catch us right in the flank. The sooner the Foresters get across that railway line the better!'

'Have they started?'

'Five minutes ago. The proof of the pudding is now in the eating.'

The taste of that pudding was bitter and set our teeth on edge. From a slit trench north of 'Smelly Farm' I watched the attack go in. It is difficult to make sense out of a modern battlefield as you look at it from the touchline.

All we could see were the quick fountains of black smoke thrown up along the railway line, a tank belching fumes from behind the walls of a broken farm and a cloud of white dust hanging over the spot where we imagined the station to be. The Alban Hills seemed startlingly near. The noise ebbed and flowed over the leafless vines, now rising to a general thunder as the guns cracked out on both sides, now dropping to a treacherous lull. Small figures now appeared, popping up from holes in the ground and half crouching as they ran. There seemed so few of them. And yet everything depended on what they were going to do in the next few minutes. Behind them were the hundreds of guns, the masses of tanks, the huge dumps of ammunition, the great fleet at anchor in the roadstead at Anzio. This huge war machine came to an abrupt end on the shell-torn ridge the Foresters were now crossing. It could advance only if they advanced. We saw them drop out of sight and heard the swift outburst of the machine-gun fire that welcomed them. Were they over the railway line? Was Campoleone ours?

Back at Brigade Headquarters they 'put us in to the dismal picture'.

Punctually the two companies of Foresters had gone forward along the ridge to the right of the main road. They passed the slit-trenches of the KSLI and struggled through the low and tangled vines. SP guns, out on the right, hosed them with fire, but they pushed on resolutely until they reached the Cisterna-Campoleone railway. And there they stuck, bloodily and brutally, against the strongest defence line yet encountered.

This railway line was the perfect tank and infantry trap, almost designed for stopping our advance dead in its tracks. It was part of the main line from Rome to Naples, built right across the foothills of the Colli Laziali in a series of embankments and cuttings. When the infantry tried to cross the embankments they made perfect targets against the skyline; when they dropped into the cuttings they were trapped between the walls of rock.

In every house and railway building on the far side of the line the Germans had placed a tank, which fired through the windows protected by the thick walls of the building. Machine-guns swept every inch of the main road, and minefields were laid under the bridge. Again and again the Sherwood Foresters tried to rush across the line, with its mocking double track of shining rails. The bullets ricochetted off the metals and beat the Foresters back. One small group did get over, but, like a spent swimmer exhausted by the effort, had to drop back into the cuttings to their death. The two companies were losing strength fast.

The spearhead of the American armoured force came forward, turned off the main road and strove to get onto a ridge to the left where the tanks might trade fire with the German tanks and help the infantry forward. They could not hope to cross. Nothing is more vulnerable than a tank slowly crawling over a steep embankment—with its gun lifted in the air and its belly exposed to the anti-tank gunner.

A last desperate expedient was tried. The forward troops were ordered to move well back from the railway, and the full weight of the formidable artillery which we now possessed in this western half of the Beachhead was brought down on the German defences. Then the two reserve companies of the Foresters, passing through the depleted and exhausted ranks of their comrades, rushed to the embankment. Again they could not win over to the other side. No one could doubt the courage and devotion of the Foresters on this bitter day. As the afternoon ended, General Harmon, anxious to see for himself what was holding up the advance of his armour, went up to the embankment. He says:

I came up in a tank—a jeep wouldn't have lived long there—to watch my tanks, spread wide on the level ground to the right and left, trade fire with the Germans. I decided I would plough up the steep slope where the Foresters were entrenched. My tank climbed the hill, and then I called a halt and got out to walk. There were dead bodies everywhere. I have never seen so many dead men in one place. They lay so close that I had to step with care. I shouted for the commanding officer.

From a fox-hole there arose a mud-covered corporal with a handle-bar mustache. He was the highest-ranking officer still alive. He stood stiffly to attention.

'How is it going?' I asked. The answer was all around me.

'Well sir,' the corporal said, 'there were a hundred and sixteen of us when we first came up, and there are sixteen of us left. We're ordered to hold out until sundown, and I think, with a little good fortune, we can manage to do so.'

The losses of the Sherwood Foresters were amongst the heaviest suffered by any battalion in the Anzio battle. The Commanding Officer, the Adjutant and all company commanders were casualties; 'A' Company was commanded by an NCO since all the officers had been killed or wounded; no company totalled more than forty all ranks, and one company was down to twenty. The total strength of the battalion, as it mustered at the end of that desperate day's fighting, was 8 officers and some 250 men. No one could say that the Foresters had not tried to break the barrier that now hemmed in the Beachhead.

General Clark, General Lucas and General Harmon took stock of the position and realized that all hopes of an armoured 'breakout' must now be abandoned. The orders were given: the American 1st Armored was to withdraw to the area of the Padiglione woodlands, there to act as a mobile reserve and a counter-attack force. In the dusk and through the early hours of the night the long columns of tanks moved back along the Anzio-Albano road through the positions of the British 1st. Division. The infantry watching them go back to the rear, looked at the signs painted on the Honeys and Shermans—'Berlin or Bust', 'Do or Die', 'Death takes a Ride'—and murmured, 'Well, the Armour's done a Duke of York, so what?' Not a man who watched that return of the tanks failed to realize the full significance of the sight: we had lost the race to Campoleone as finally as the 3rd Division had lost the race to Cisterna. The next round was in the hands of the Germans. For the moment we had shot our bolt.

There was no denying it—tension and even distrust had grown steadily between Sixth Corps and the British 1st Division during the last few doubtful days. A cloud also hung over the relations between General Lucas and Generals Clark and Alexander. The 'bold stroke' of Anzio had turned sour on all those directing it.

After all those long days of planning, after the heavy risks accepted in landing, the desperate attacks against the stern fortifications of the Gustav Line, the devoted efforts of troops like the Rangers, the Guards, the Foresters and the Paratroops, after all this blood, sweat and tears the invaders were now penned into a giant corral built by German guns and defences.

If the Allies travelled ten miles along the sea coast in any direction from Anzio and Nettuno they came up against a well-placed enemy. The Beachhead stretched inland for a mere fifteen miles, and this at two places only—one before Cisterna and the other along the Anzio-Albano road. The whole area was dangerously shallow for the needs of modern war, and the German long-range guns reminded us of this disagreeable fact every day.

Well might Mr. Churchill lament: '. . . I had hoped that we were hurling a wild cat on to the shore, but all we had got was a stranded whale.'

General Clark passed on some of the discontent of the Higher Command to General Lucas, who made a note in his diary.

> His gloomy attitude is certainly bad for me. He thinks I should have been more aggressive on D-day. I think he realizes the serious nature of the whole operation. His forces are divided in the face of the enemy who is operating on interior lines, and now neither of the parts is capable of inflicting a real defeat on the hostile troops facing it.[1]

General Alexander was polite but hardly more encouraging. Lucas felt that he was not really pleased with the way things had gone. The unhappy Corps Commander made another entry in his diary: 'My head will probably fall in the basket, but I have done my best.'

General Penney also kept his notes of those critical last days of January. Of all the commanders engaged in the break-out attempt he had the most reason to feel bewildered and frustrated. He knew only too well that his division was dangerously strung out on a narrow front with the enemy in force all around him. His pencil-point salient was a most unpleasant feature on every map in Corps, Army, and Army Group headquarters.

The most ill-informed observer could see at a glance that this pencil, if it had ceased to move forward hurriedly, ought to move back at equally high speed. General Lucas, however, gave Penney no positive instructions beyond uttering vague warnings about over-extending the division. But Penney had not deliberately thrust himself into the middle of the German defences. It had been the failure of the armour on his western flank that had led to his present exposed position.

[1] Morison, *History of United States Naval Operations in World War II*, Vol. IX, p. 358.

General Clark and General Alexander both vetoed any suggestion that he ought to draw back any of his forces. 'You stay where you are,' they told him; 'don't give up an inch.' General Alexander still cherished faint hopes of renewing the attack, at least to capture Cisterna and Campoleone.

Penney noted with some exasperation: 'This is *not* a Corps battle in the close-co-ordinated sense. Plans are made by Divisions for everything.'

One ray of comfort reached him on the night of 31 January. Certain adjustments of the Beachhead perimeter allowed him to bring up his 2nd Brigade and strengthen the base of his salient. He placed the 2nd North Staffordshire Regiment of 2nd Brigade out to his left on a ridge near Carroceto known as Buonriposo. The 1st Loyal (North Lancashire) Regiment were ordered into position on the right, where all through the hectic days of the advance the Reconnaissance Regiment had been acting as a thin screen. The 6th Gordons came up north of the Factory and settled on the ground won by the Scots Guards in their night battle for the 'start line'.

The Guards were now all grouped west of the Albano road, holding the ridges south of Campoleone station to the edge of Carroceto. As for the 3rd Brigade, it had to remain where it was for the present—the 'lead in the pencil', cramped in amongst the olive groves and vineyards just short of the fatal railway line which had foiled the Allies hopes. The whole front of the Brigade did not extend more than two thousand yards.

The battalions settled into their new positions, and an ominous quiet now held the Beachhead. The forward troops heard tanks moving at night; from time to time the guns on either side of the line barked for a bit and then subsided into silence. The first few days of February were clear, and in the crisp winter sunshine the summits of the Alban Hills sparkled under a light dusting of snow. The question 'What next?' seemed to hang over the waiting landscape.

The correspondents sought enlightenment from General Lucas. He received them in his small villa at Nettuno. He sat in his chair before the fire, and the light shone on his polished cavalry boots. He had the round face and the greying moustache of a kindly country solicitor. His voice was low and hardly reached the outer circle of the waiting Pressmen.

They fired their questions at him, above all Question No. 1, 'What *was* our plan on landing and what had happened to it now?'

The General looked thoughtful. 'Well, gentlemen, there was some suggestion that we should aim at getting to those hills'—he turned to his G-2—'What's the name of them, Joe?'

'But the enemy was now strong, far stronger than we had thought.' There was a long pause, and the firelight played on the waiting audience and flickered up to the dark ceiling. Then the General added quietly, 'I'll tell you what, gentlemen. That German is a mighty tough fighter. Yes, a mighty tough fighter.'

With that official statement we had, for the moment, to be content.

But outside there were signs of the coming storm. The shelling grew vicious at night and, what was worse, the weather changed. On 3 February rain was sweeping the Beachhead, and sweeping away our effective air cover. Everyone knew how the Germans prayed for rain and prepared their most unpleasant surprises under its protection. That evening I drove back from 3rd Division to attend the nightly briefing of correspondents at Sixth Corps headquarters.

Ahead of us two lorry-loads of prisoners chugged along in the rain and then swung off into the cage—a large barn in the centre of a muddy field surrounded with a high barrier of barbed wire. The Military Police, armed with tommyguns, ordered the captured men to jump down and line up in two companies. They obeyed with Germanic smartness. The guards ran in and out of the ranks like fussy sheep-dogs as the prisoners stepped forward for interrogation. They ran their hands over each soldier in the manner of a film 'cop' searching a gangster for weapons. Then every man was tagged like a prize ox and led off to lie in the straw in a leaking barn. Maybe they were lucky. Whatever lay ahead for the Beachhead battle, they were well out of it.

Among the prisoners was an official war photographer who spoke some English. His job was the taking of propaganda photographs, but he had not received much co-operation from the military authorities. He protested to us sadly, as if professional colleagues were allies across the barriers of war.

'You understand, they just couldn't see the importance of

it—they wouldn't let me take my photos.'

'Move on, superman,' ordered the guards.

We looked at the German correspondent marching away along the barbed-wire fence.

'The shape of things to come?' murmured one of my companions.

At Corps we assembled to hear the worst; we sat once again on our hard-backed chairs, like a class at school, and gazed with the eyes of last-minute hope on the map pinned to the wall of this cellar-like room. No hope there! Then the brisk and wiry G-2 of Sixth Corps entered—Colonel Langevin, an attractive man although the American tin-hat he always wore, even indoors, in obedience to Corps regulations bore to British eyes a disconcerting resemblance to an inverted chamber-pot.

He gave us the bad news straight away. 'The major development today is that Sixth Corps is now going on the defensive.'

There was an uneasy stir among his audience. Only three days ago we were still talking about the 'infantry breaking the path for the tanks' and about 'shaking the armour loose'; now we were going to 'hang on with all we've got'. 'We've got enough mines,' the colonel continued, 'but we are not too plentifully supplied with wire at the moment.' I thought ruefully of the last despatch I had sent with its note of optimism and its talk of our 'drive for the hills'.

The Colonel calmly continued his briefing. Army Group intelligence reports had left no doubt about it: the Germans were about to begin a major counter-attack on the Anzio position. General Alexander gave instructions for Lucas to go on the defensive. This order was dated 2 February, and by the morning of the 3rd the divisional commanders were busy making hurried adjustments to their front line.

General Truscott had the watery maze of the Pontine Marshes guarding his right flank and was thus able to draw back into a reasonable defensive position in a curve a mile south of Cisterna. General Penney, with his division wedged deep into the forward German defences, did not have so much room to manœuvre. The narrow salient where he now stood would be, perforce, the ground on which he would receive the German attack.

'There it is, gentlemen,' said Colonel Langevin, 'we shall see what tomorrow will bring.'

Outside the rain increased in intensity. The Beachhead, as we talked and looked at the map, began to seem one vast puddle in which all our high hopes had been washed away.

6

Lancing the Abscess

From his headquarters in Germany, far removed from the the actual battlefields of Italy, Hitler had followed the fortunes of his armies at Anzio with mounting interest and excitement. In this fifth year of war he still nursed an invincible optimism that his stars would not betray him and that soon Germany would once again pass over to a victorious offensive. His technical experts, brooding over the grim news from Russia and counting the ever-growing strength of the Allies, had grave doubts about this long-promised, glorious recovery, but they never dared to express them in The Presence. Hitler would have dealt swiftly with anyone who had ventured to suggest that there was any depression in his House. The Nazi creed had firmly laid it down that victory was bound to come if everyone did his duty under the inspired leadership of the Führer, and in this matter Hitler was the first and greatest victim of his own propaganda.

Thus the Anzio landing appeared to him as a threat to his European Fortress, but also as a great opportunity. Here, at last, was a chance to break that depressing chain of continual defeat in which the German armies had been bound since the end of 1942. More important still, a great German success at Anzio would be proof that it was possible to smash the threatening invasion of Northern France, which hung like a cloud over all German war-planning at this critical time. After that, the new weapons—V1s, V2s, and new long-range U-boats and the rest of them—would enable the Führer to make a swift and devastating 'comeback'.

Six months later, as the German armies reeled back in Normandy, Rundstedt gave his famous reply to Keitel's desperate appeal for advice—'What shall we do? Make peace, you fools. What else can you do?'—but now, at the beginning of this fateful year for Germany's fortunes, no general dared to think in such terms. There was still a chance that the Führer might be right. The OKW approved of the message that Hitler sent at the end of January to his commanders in Italy:

> Within the next few days the 'Battle for Rome' will commence . . . this battle has a special significance because the landing at Nettuno marks the beginning of the invasion of Europe planned for 1944. Strong German forces are to be tied down in areas as far as possible from the bases in Britain where the majority of the invasion troops are still stationed. The object of the Allies is to gain experience for future operations.
>
> Every soldier must therefore be aware of the importance of the battle which the Fourteenth Army has to fight.
>
> It must be fought with bitter hatred against an enemy who wages a ruthless war of annihilation against the German people and who, without any higher ethical aims, strives for the destruction of Germany and European culture.
>
> As in the battle of Sicily, on the Rapido River, and at Ortona, it must be driven home to the enemy that the fighting power of Germany is unbroken and that the invasion of the year 1944 is an undertaking that will be crushed in the blood of British soldiers.

With this call to action from the Führer to inspire them, Kesselring, Von Mackensen and the generals of the Fourteenth Army set to work with a will to lance what Hitler had christened 'the abscess south of Rome'.

It was quite obvious that their attack would have to be made down the Anzio-Albano road. This was the quickest route to the sea, and an advance down this road would split the Allies in two. The maps also showed the British 1st Division strung out along it in a most tempting position for a counter-attack—no general could resist having a 'go' at cutting off such an exposed group of his enemies.

But General Mackensen and his Fourteenth Army did not yet feel themselves ready to strike the major blow which was to lance the abscess. They had acquired a healthy respect for the Allies in the fighting of the last few weeks, and while they were justifiably proud of the way in which they had checked the Anglo-American advance they were still persuaded that the Allies might renew their attempts to advance and might even try a landing north of Anzio. In this they overestimated the strength of Sixth Corps and the determination of its commander. Fourteenth Army, however, were all ready to try a limited attack on the exposed brigade of 1st Division. More troops, guns and tanks were being hurried into Italy in preparation for the real 'knock-out' blow.

The great battle down the Anzio-Albano road, the centre of the Beachhead drama, resolves itself into three acts. First, a preliminary attempt by the Germans to cut off the 3rd Brigade of the British 1st Division. Then, with stronger forces available, the Germans press on to seize the Factory area and Campoleone. From this start-line they finally drive forward with every ounce of power they can muster in a stupendous all-out effort to smash through to the sea. Each act of the drama has its own crisis, surprises, unexpected failures and equally unexpected successes. The Germans prepared for the lifting of the curtain by a careful regrouping of their forces around the Beachhead, bringing order into the somewhat jumbled groups which had been hurried to the scene during the first hectic days of the landing.

First Parachute Corps, which had until now handled the whole battle of the Beachhead under Fourteenth Army, was assigned the western sector from near Albano to the mouth of the Moletta River. It had two divisions under command, the 4th Parachute on the west and the 65th Infantry. The central and eastern sectors were placed under the staff of the Seventy-sixth Panzer Corps, which had been specially brought across from the Adriatic, where it had been conducting the defence of the Ortona area and the Moro River line against the British Eighth Army. Kesselring had rightly decided that there would be no serious attack made against him on this front for a long time to come.

Seventy-sixth Panzer Corps had five divisions under command. The 3rd Panzer Grenadier Division held the important position across the Albano road. Then came the 715th Infantry (Motorized), while to the eastward the front was manned by the 71st Infantry and the Hermann Goering Panzer Division. The bulk of the 26th Panzer Division formed the Corps reserve.

German military practice did not insist, however, upon the sanctity of divisional boundaries. When an important task was planned, units from various divisions, together with supporting arms, were formed into special combat groups. Thus the 3rd Panzer Grenadier Division, attacking the Albano road from the west, and the 715th Infantry on the eastern side were reinforced, indeed intermingled with other troops, and all lumped together under the title of Combat Group Gräser. It was this Combat Group that began the great German counter-attack and fought through the first act of the drama.

Zero Hour was fixed for 11 p.m. on 3 February.

To the waiting British, 3 February seemed a cold, uneasy day, made gloomy by lowering clouds. The troops felt that something sinister was in the air as they worked to deepen their shallow slit-trenches in the damp ground. Divisional HQ had issued the warning 'Strong counter-attacks to be expected' and no one was surprised. The last twenty-four hours had produced plenty of evidence that the Germans would soon move in on the 1st Division.

The ever-watchful Reconnaissance Regiment, who had dominated the wide area north-west of the Factory so successfully that they could make the proud claim that they were 'masters of the night', reported tanks moving into the woodlands lying beyond their outposts. The Gordons heard sounds of intensive firing from the ruined farms before them. The battalions of 3rd Brigade had to beat off probing attacks of company strength. The Irish Guards, digging in on the left of the Albano road, noted in their War History that the stillness of the afternoon of 3 February had been broken by the bleating of a thousand sheep. 'Like a dirty, ragged wave a huge flock surged over the crest of the Vallelata ridges and scampered crazily through No. 3 Company. Those wise after the event later said that it was a typical German trick to use poor dumb animals as mine-detectors, but at the time no one felt anything but gratitude.'

General Penney and his Brigade Commanders, if the incident had been reported to them at the time, would have felt anything but gratitude. It might have symbolized to them their 'thin-ness on the ground'—for they were now very much aware that they were strung out along the Albano road in a way that was certainly never recommended by any of the orthodox textbooks on Infantry Training.

On the small-scale maps our forward positions are inevitably represented by a continuous line—in fact, a 'front' in the old First World War style. It would be better to show it as a series of disconnected dots, some huddled close together, others separated by wide, blank areas.

In an ideal defensive 'lay-out' each dot represents a company of the battalion holding the front, a close-knit little unit with every man dug in as best he can in his slit-trench, all within sight and sound of each other. The company commander will be dug-in close behind his men, with his signaller at his portable set keeping him in touch with Battalion HQ a hundred yards or so in the rear. On his right and left, marked by similar dots on the map, are the other companies of the battalion, so placed that all the unoccupied ground between the dots can be swept by fire from the company positions. Minefields can also be used to deny this blank area to the enemy.

Farther back, but in a position to cover the forward men, are the machine-guns and mortars; farther back still the tanks attached to the battalion for quick action against any infantry overrunning our men. Behind the whole area is the divisional artillery, ready to pour down fire at prearranged signals. The man in the lonely, forward slit-trenches is in theory not so lonely as he seems.

So we can picture the ideal lay-out of a British division on the defensive—a spider's web of mutually supporting units in which the slightest touch on the perimeter of the web produces a swift reaction in all the component parts.

The lay-out of the British 1st Division fell short of the ideal picture we have been painting in one vital particular—the dots were too far apart. There were holes in the defensive web. The battalions holding the front had perforce, in constructing their company areas, to leave wide stretches of ground unswept by direct fire from their slit-trenches. By day the machine-gunners and mortar crews could take care of these gaps, but night brought danger. The companies might do their best to send out fighting patrols to keep control of this treacherous ground, but a patrol cannot stop large numbers of the enemy infiltrating behind company positions if the night is dark enough and the enemy strong and determined. Worse still, the Germans had cover under which they could form up by day ready to attack by night. On the left flank of the 1st Division's 'pencil' (or 'the Thumb', as the Americans called it) were the deep wadis at the head of the Moletta stream; on the right the tangled woodland, watched with such anxiety by the Recce Regiment. Both areas were ideal "jumping-off' areas for groups of Germans setting out to infiltrate into the gaps between the dots.

Infiltration! The word was to become a nightmare to the men of the 1st Division during the coming battle. The unnerving thought that, at night, whole companies of Germans might steal quietly through the gaps in the line haunted them continually, and they soon discovered that the Germans were masters of the tactics of infiltration. In the temporary chaos created by infiltration the gunners protecting the front under attack found it difficult to bring down their devastating 'stonks'—as the troops nicknamed all types of artillery concentrations. They could never be certain that they were blasting the foe and not their friends. The mortar and machine-gun positions could be overrun without the men in the forward slit-trenches realizing that they had lost their support and that their enemy was now behind them. Barbed wire and mines, so comforting to the defending troops, were in short supply. The divisional tanks, waiting for the enemy armour, had perforce to concentrate in front of the Factory in the narrow end of the 'pencil' for there was no other space for them to 'lager'.

General Harmon and his tanks of American 1st Armored were far away down the Albano road towards Anzio, held in the Corps Commander's jealously guarded reserve. General Penney might gaze wistfully towards the woodlands of Padiglione, five miles to his rear, where over two hundred and fifty Shermans lay waiting out of sight in the thick undergrowth. They were not for him!

So the night of 3 February closed in wet and dark, with the British 1st Division awaiting the inevitable German attack in a position which the Divisional Commander ruefully admitted 'was very airy indeed'. His thoughts turned to the men in the forward positions, shivering in their damp holes in the ground, peering into the uneasy darkness ahead of them for the first signs of the enemy's advance. He would have to rely implicitly on their steadfastness and courage, for all the signs pointed to one thing—the battle ahead was going to be very much a 'soldier's battle'. Faced with the test, the soldiers did not let their Commander down.

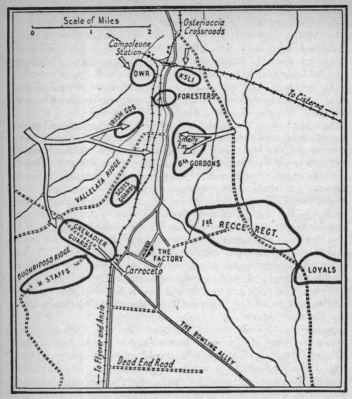

FIRST GERMAN COUNTER-ATTACK ON BRITISH 1ST DIVISION, 3-4 FEBRUARY 1944

In the rainy darkness, stabbed by flashes of bursting shells and the restless stars of the tracer bullets, the three battalions of 3rd Brigade waited for the attack with some confidence. They were reasonably close together, dug in amongst the vines in a compact knot just short of the fateful railway embankment. The gaps in the company areas between each battalion were not too wide for comfort.

The danger-point lay behind them down the road towards Anzio.

The Irish Guards and the Gordons were in position on

either side of the main road, keeping open this vital supply route to the troops of 3rd Brigade now perched uncomfortably at the tip of their thin salient. The Gordons and the Irish Guards were strung out along low ridges and were only too aware of the airy nature of their position. 'But what could we do?' the Irish Guards noted afterwards. 'To scatter sections along the line of the salient would be to invite piecemeal destruction by night. . . . Our present positions were to be held and we had to accept it.'

Punctually at eleven o'clock on the night of 3 February the Germans began their attempt to pinch off the salient. A violent storm of shells crashed down on the Irish Guards, and immediately they were caught in the swirling chaos of a violent night-attack. The Germans had already slipped through the wide gaps in the Guards' position.

There is nothing so disconcerting to the infantryman as to be suddenly trapped by fire from the very point where you had supposed your own friends to be firmly dug-in. The Guardsmen felt that the whole landscape had erupted with attacking Germans. A battalion was now racing forwards to overwhelm a company; there seemed no end to the number of men who were following the first wave.

A mortar bomb set fire to the hay-ricks around a ruined farm and the Germans came rushing out of the darkness into the flickering floodlight of the burning ricks. The machine-guns scythed down the attackers, but the German commanders shovelled in their reserves with deadly efficiency. Their men charged on, shouting the war-cries which German infantry had inherited from the mass-attacks of the First World War, *Sieg Heil! Gott mit Uns!* The machine-gunners poured out their ammunition, eight thousand rounds of it, straight into the shouting, crowded masses. Then the company wireless went off the air. . . .

As dawn broke through the icy rain which now poured down on the Beachhead the enemy next swept in over the Gordons. There was a misunderstanding, a company retired without orders and in a matter of minutes the Germans had torn a huge gap in the British position. By 10 o'clock on 4 February, their tanks were sweeping the main road with fire and the 3rd Brigade was cut off from the rest of the division and in deadly peril.

The Irish Guards fought magnificently, but they and the Gordons had been given too wide an area to hold. The Germans had penetrated into the gaps and were cutting in behind 3rd Brigade. Smoke drifted across the front. The rain sluiced down with a cruel fury, and only radio reports now reached Brigade HQ from its lost units. Somewhere across the wide gap held by the Germans they were holding out, beating off all attempts to overrun their trenches. But they could not hold out for ever. The Germans were closing in for the kill.

The drama now shifts from the men in the midst of the battle to the commanders behind them—from the slit-trench to the command post.

To the soldiers in the centre of an attack such as the one we have been describing, events seem to happen with a terrifying inconsequence, as if in a wildly experimental film directed by a madman. Shells suddenly burst around him; Germans appear out of the dust and smoke; his Bren-gun jams for no reason at all; tracers whip overhead, and incomprehensible orders are shouted across to him from the neighbouring hole in the ground; dark, threatening shapes loom up through the rain. Tanks! Ours or theirs? Who can tell?

And through it all, he fights a battle inside himself to conquer his fear, to stop his flesh quivering against the imagined brutal impact of every piece of jagged metal flying in the air.

There can be no question: in war the man in the front line is the man who counts. But, in the stress of fighting, he cannot see much order or reason in the shambles going on around him.

The generals have a different role in the battle. At all costs they must not get involved too deeply in its emotional stresses and strains. They must impose some sort of order on chaos: their plans must be quickly made and firmly insisted upon. When all is committed to the trial they can still exercise a moral influence on the battle by encouraging their subordinates and coming up to the actual fighting line as often and as close as they can.

As soon as the reports flowed back to him of the danger threatening 3rd Brigade, General Penney sought for reinforcements. General Lucas had already told him, 'You'd better get your boys out of it,' but the problem was—with what? The Corps Commander was determined to keep his 1st Armored Division intact, for he felt that this first German attack was only the preliminary—worse was certainly on the way. There was, of course, the 3rd Battalion of the American 504th Airborne, whom Penney had already accepted with gratitude and placed as a 'back-stop' across the main road before Carroceto village. The British and the Para-troopers got on like a house on fire. The Americans were placed near the 24th Guards Brigade and at first sight nothing could seem more unlikely than a friendship between two such contrasting units as His Majesty's Guards and the tough American paratroops. But the strange alchemy of Anzio was already at work. The fighting soldiers, American and British, never had the slightest difficulty in understanding one another even when their higher commanders were at logger-heads.

The Irish Guards described the vivid impression made on them by Colonel Freeman, of the Parachutists, when they met him a few days later in the midst of the fighting.

His first words endeared him to the Battalion. 'Those Krauts, I sure hate their guts.' From him, and his troops the Battalion leant the word 'Kraut', and never afterwards called the Germans anything else. Colonel Free-man was a tall, melancholy gentleman from Virginia, with a slow drawl and a captivating manner. Every morning, during these days he strolled into Battalion HQ to discuss the previous night and the forthcoming day. Every morning Colonel Scott greeted him, 'Hiya, Colonel, what d'ya know?' and invariably Colonel Freeman replied, 'Morning, Colonel. Not a goddam thing.'[1]

The Parachute Corps were most welcome, but they were not enough to form a counter-attack force. What Penney re-quired was a battalion which could be flung immediately into the attack, before the Germans had firmly settled in on the ground they had won. The longer they were left undisturbed the more dangerous they became. The driving rain had blinded our Air Force and allowed the enemy to bring up his reserves with impunity. Only the accurate shooting of the Beachhead artillery had prevented them from being imme-diately poured into the gap to reinforce the units already there. When night fell, however, our artillery could no longer dominate the battlefield, and General Gräser and his Com-bat Group would be free to build up the sort of divisional defensive web which we have already described.

[1] Fitzgerald, *History of the Irish Guards in the Second World War*, p. 201.

His artillery could arrange their defensive tasks, his tanks and SP guns could take up their positions to give their best support to his infantry, his signal units could perfect their communications. By dawn next day he would be impossible to dislodge and would have shut the last escape door for the 3rd Brigade.

It was vital that he should be hit in daylight before his men could settle in on the ground. The road had to be re-opened, if only for a few hours, before the encircled British could try to get out of the bag.

At this moment a British infantry brigade, the 168th under Brigadier Kenneth Davidson, was completing its disembarkation on the ruined quayside of Anzio. General Penney had no hesitation in describing their arrival as 'providential' and he may well have felt a sense of reprieve in his hour of trial as he hastened to press General Lucas to put them under his command. The brigade were not exactly the fresh troops he needed, for they came direct from the 56th Division, which had already been fighting hard in the mountains round Cassino. It was symbolic of the crisis in British man-power that this much-tried unit was the only reinforcement that could be sent to the British front at Anzio.

General Lucas had wanted it for the general reserve he was striving to build up against the evil days he saw ahead, but Penney was pressing. He got the brigade and immediately ordered its three battalions forward. He chose the 1st London Scottish as the unit for the counter-attack, feeling that the hard-pressed Gordons, across whose ridge the attack would go in, might feel encouraged by the help of their fellow-Scots. Small, emotional things of this sort can count in the stress of battle.

There was no time for long preparation. The London Scottish, who had been barely twenty-four hours ashore on the Beachhead, formed up in the rain-sodden fields behind the Gordons. The tanks of the 46th Royal Tank Regiment moved out on to the road north of the Factory. The attack was timed for four o'clock in the afternoon.

General Penney had now done all he could do at the moment. He went forward and joined the commander of 3rd Brigade, Brigadier James, in his HQ in the inevitable broken farmhouse north of the Factory. The Germans' advance had placed the Brigadier in the unenviable position of being cut off from his own command, but James was one of those steady men who can see a battle as a whole and estimate coolly the exact extent of the threatening danger. He sat in his jeep, while Penney waited in the command truck parked against the farmhouse wall. 'You'll have to get them out by daylight,' he told James. 'Warn them to move.'

James sent his orders by radio across the gap where the Germans waited to trap his men. All battalions were to get ready to break off contact with the enemy. The signal word for the move would be 'Tally Ho'. The DWR and the Foresters would move first, and the KSLI, at grips with the enemy on the right flank of the salient, would have the difficult task of forming the rearguard.

No one need envy a general at such a moment! Penney stood to lose a third of his division within the next few hours, and once he had issued orders for the counter-attack there was nothing more he could do about it. He simply had to wait—wait for news. He sat eating a somewhat tasteless dish of army stew, reading the reports as they came in and listening to the whine of the shells overhead. He could, at least, be a calm, reassuring presence, ready at hand in case things did go wrong.

Four o'clock! The attack had begun. Soon there came good news: the London Scottish were advancing with great determination, backed by the tanks, and had found the Germans not yet consolidated on the ground. They overran the enemy in the same way as the Germans had caught the Gordons that very morning. Prisoners started to crowd back. It was clear some sort of corridor had been opened, for how long no one could say. The London Scottish now ran into heavy fire and slowed down short of their objective, but the time had come to give the signal for the 3rd Brigade to move, even if there were still Germans between them and the farthest advance outposts of the Scottish.

There was danger in delay. The short winter day was drawing to a close, the rain sluiced down with renewed vigour and the German artillery was doing its best to batter the ridge that their infantry had just lost. In the dismal winter dusk the head of the British columns pushed off down the road towards safety.

The British can claim to be specialists in triumphant retreats. This one was on a small scale, but it had all the classic features we expect from such an operation. The weary men stumbled through the rain, the wounded supported by their

111

comrades or flung over the Bren-carriers and the anti-tank guns. The one road was choked with marching columns mixed up with lorries and jeeps. Small groups of Germans still lay huddled amongst the broken buildings of the farms and opened up with machine-guns on their retreating foes. Our own artillery put down tremendous concentrations of fire in a screen around the salient, until the air was filled with the hiss of the shells hurtling overhead.

And always the rain—persistent, dreary, soaking the tired soldier and making the ground a sodden morass, turning into sleet as the darkness deepened. The retreat went on into the night. The darkness was lit by the glare of the burning hay-ricks, and the German shells started to fall with dismal accuracy on to the crowded roadway. To those who watched it, it seemed a chaotic drift towards dubious safety, a mob of defeated men driven before the Germans.

Appearances were deceptive. There were dead everywhere, with tanks on fire and smoke rolling over the shell-torn fields. Very lights soared and tracers flashed in all directions. Yet when the last units got in after midnight and the roll-calls were taken, with the men standing drugged with fatigue half-asleep in their muddy ranks, 3rd Brigade had cause to be proud of itself. The battalions had to leave sorely needed equipment behind; tanks and anti-tank guns were abandoned and lorries left to burn, but the brigade was still intact as a fighting organization (the KSLI had even knocked out two Tiger tanks). This was the reward that had been torn from the jaws of almost certain defeat.

In the wet morning of the next day I recorded an interview with a young soldier of one of the beleaguered battalions.

That salient—I'll tell you what it was like. We were in our slit-trenches—a whole day of it without being able to lift our heads. All I did was to eat my compo rations and dream about what I was going to do after the war. I had to do everything, filth and all, where I was. I've never seen such machine-gun fire. It was taking the heads off the daisies, it was so low, honestly it really was. What the hell could we do? We were perfectly happy!

We got orders to send a platoon out towards the rail-way. Well, I did—by radio. It was just murder. The sergeant set off to lead them, he stepped out from behind a house and his guts were shot out of him over the men following. I don't think they went any further.

In the night we couldn't see a darn thing in the rain. All I did was to pop my head up from time to time to see if a Jerry wasn't going to stick a bayonet into me.

Then came yesterday morning. Nothing but shells and the smoke drifted across to us, from the KSLI I think it came. You couldn't tell where the stuff was coming from. Then, after we'd been firing at everything that moved, I was going to open up on a new mob coming out of the smoke, when someone shouted, 'Christ, those are our boys!' They were prisoners, shouting in English not German, 'It's hopeless. You'd better join us.' Some of our lads got frightened and started to climb out of their slit-trenches to throw down their guns, but the CO shouted, 'Get back into your trenches,' and he would have shot the first one that moved.

We shouted to the prisoners, 'Run and we'll fire on your guards.' Some did, others lay down, so we fired. We killed a good many Germans, maybe some of our boys too. I tell you, that shook me more than anything.

Then, at last, we got the order, 'Get out quick!' But we couldn't, we had to stick there until dark as the Boche had us covered. Then we moved—damn fast, I can tell you. We came running down that main road and all the shells in hell came down on us. Lots of bodies there, too! I fell over one that groaned, but what could I do, I couldn't stay? And then we passed a whole row of burning tanks, all oily waste smoke. It filled the whole place. Nothing but black smoke and what smelt like the stink of frying bodies.

Glad to be out of it, you bet! But we brought a lot of our equipment back. The boys didn't fancy leaving it behind, and now we're perfectly happy, as you might say. You don't know of a job going as Sanitary Man at Corps, do you?

The Germans had failed in their attempt to encircle 3rd Brigade, and the first act in the drama of the counter-attack ended with the British line intact but withdrawn some two and a half miles back down the road towards Anzio. It now lay in a curve around the Embankment and village of Carroceto and the solid, square block of the Factory.

But the fighting of 3-4 February gave a warning to Sixth Corps that soon they would be fighting for their lives. The intelligence reports arrived with the monotonous persistence of the messengers in Greek tragedy, bringing no comfort but only further confirmation of a steady German build-

113

up. More and more units, coming from Northern Italy, the South of France and the Balkans, had reached Fourteenth Army in time to take part in the battle, and the devoted efforts of our Air Forces seemed unable to stop them. Clearly, it would only be a matter of days before the next attack would begin, and equally clearly the enemy would try to continue his advance down the Albano road. On 5 February he had put in a sharp attack on the 3rd Division, but this was obviously not the area in which vital decisions could be reached.

Von Mackensen had his eyes now firmly fixed on the Factory and Carroceto. If he could capture these important features quickly he would have his start line for the all-out drive to the sea.

He knew, from the experience of his troops in the attack on the salient, that our men were thin on the ground. Under the constant harassing of the German artillery the 1st Division could not hope to fortify their new positions in any way —they could not lay minefields and set up wire. Those dangerous gaps between the companies of the battalions would still be there. Infiltration tactics would, once again, pay handsome dividends.

The Allies were only too conscious of the weakness of their front line. Sixth Corps issued hurried orders and began to construct a Final Beachhead Defence Line, from the Moletta across the Flyover on to the 3rd Division front and the Mussolini Canal. There the engineers put down all the mines and wire they could: this was to be the last ditch beyond which, come what may, the Germans were not to pass.

In the days that followed this defence line was continually strengthened, but for the moment the thoughts of British 1st Division were not turned towards the rear. They were occupied entirely by what was happening on their front, where once again all the sinister signs of a new enemy attack were accumulating—in the first clear day for a week our air reconnaissance secured photographs showing a big increase in the number of German gun emplacements around the Albano road sector; intelligence reports from reliable sources in Rome fixed the night of the 7th as the probable date of attack, and deserters began to drift over to our lines in the darkness in order to avoid taking part in the approaching blood-bath.

Our troops knew by instinct what they were in for. Ten

to one the weather would turn foul again, cramping our air support. Then in the darkness the usual sudden hurricane of shells would burst over some exposed point in our forward positions and, before anyone had a chance to take counter-measures, the German advance-parties would have filtered through the gaps, set up their machine-gun posts behind our company areas, and deluged our men with bullets from the rear. After that, the onrushing hordes of yelling infantry, and the wild hand-to-hand struggles around the slit-trenches. As the dawn broke, Tiger tanks which had been lurking off-stage just out of range of our anti-tank guns would roll for-wards into position behind the ruined farmhouses, ready to wipe out any attempt at rescue.

This had now become the standard pattern of the German infiltration tactics—one very difficult to counter without having more men on the ground to cover the gaps. In the last few days the British 1st Division had lost 1,600 men: bat-talions like the 6th Gordons, 1st Irish Guards and 2nd Sher-wood Foresters had been decimated, all this on top of the casualties already suffered in the attempt to capture Cam-poleone. New drafts were hurried through the port of Anzio to bring them up to something like strength, but the new-comers were comparatively inexperienced in battle and never in sufficient numbers.

General Penney had a week hand for the coming game, but it was the only one he had. He grimly re-shuffled his cards and prepared for the next round.

He placed the 168th Brigade, of 56th Division, whose ar-rival had been so 'providential', in defence of the vital Fac-tory area. The London Irish Rifles held the building itself, the 10th Royal Berkshires were out in the fields to the east of it and the London Scottish in reserve behind.

The Guards Brigade held Carroceto village and the dis-used railway track christened 'the Embankment', with the Scots Guards flung out a little ahead of the houses beside the railway and road towards Campoleone and the Grenadiers stretched along the Embankment. The Irish Guards were in reserve behind Carroceto with their invaluable American allies, the 3rd Battalion, 504th Airborne Regiment. Farther to the west lay a battalion of the North Staffs, guarding the important Buonriposo ridge. The rest of 2nd Brigade—the Gordons and the Loyals—were away on the east flank of the divisional front, helping elements of the Recce Regiment to hold the wide open area north of Padiglione; 3rd Brigade, after its ordeal in the salient, was placed in reserve.

Each battle has its own geography: features which, until the fighting starts lie unregarded by the combatants, suddenly assume major importance. Place-names which seemed the centre of the world two or three days before in the previous struggle, now drop out of mind as if they had never existed. On 3 February the thoughts of everyone had been fiercely concentrated on the railway embankment at Campoleone, on Smelly Farm and the Gordons Ridge. By the evening of the 7th these features, for which men had died in hundreds, could have been located on the moon for all the troops cared. Other, even more important points on the map were now dominating their minds.

Over everything loomed the gaunt, square-cut bulk of the Factory. It had been shelled and bombed, but at this stage of the fighting still retained its solid, impregnable, fortress-like air. It stood like a rock over the surrounding countryside. We felt safe as long as it was in our hands, since it controlled a small network of tracks and roads. In this soggy landscape any firm track was invaluable, and the Factory was the key to the network. For this reason the Germans coveted it as strongly as we valued it. The Factory would obviously be the big prize in the coming struggle.

Tied with the Factory in strategical importance was the village of Carroceto a few hundred yards to the south-west, together with the disused railway-bed that crossed the main road by a bridge and embankment in the village. The British knew this track as 'the Embankment' while the Americans called it 'the Bowling Alley'. It gave firm ground for tank movements and that was enough to make it a worthwhile prize.

The whole area would have been a tough nut for the Germans to crack if only we had been strong on the ground. But 1st Division were only too conscious that its lack of men exposed the Factory and Carroceto to danger from two points —out on the right and left flanks there was ground that could be treacherous for the defenders.

When the 10th Royal Berks, still fresh to the Beachhead, moved up to take position they were unpleasantly surprised to find that the front they were to defend had up till then been held only by standing patrols, and no defences had been

116

dug—not a slit-trench, a mine or a coil of wire existed. The ground was absolutely flat, and there was no cover except a ditch and a few scattered buildings. Only 300 yards away to the front was a wood, where the Germans were busy massing troops for further attack. This was the position on the right flank of the Factory and Carroceto.

The left flank was equally unsatisfactory from the defensive point of view. The main road running south from Carroceto to Anzio was paralleled on the west by a low, swelling ridge marked on the map as Buonriposo—'the place of gentle rest': one of those names of unconscious irony which seemed all too prolific on the Beachhead. The Americans had already suffered at Isola Bella, 'the beautiful island', and Campomorte, 'the field of death', while the murderous plain before the Flyover, destined to become the biggest slaughter-pen of the battle, had the sinister title of Campo di Carne, 'the field of flesh'.

General Harmon's tanks, following the track along the ridge in the hopeful days of our early advance, had already uncovered the traps on this flank. Beyond the ridge lay the wadis of the Upper Moletta stream, a tangled maze of narrow watercourses sunk fifty feet below the general level of the ground. One of the wadis, the Fossa di Carroceto, actually cut in behind Buonriposo and the mainroad. This tiny stream, rising near the embankment at Carroceto, had carved a ditch which was surprisingly deep for so small a volume of water.

These details were completely invisible from the main road. A soldier used to the sharp and savage outlines of the mountains on the Cassino front would have regarded the whole area as a dead-level plain. But in war all height is relative and the contours of a landscape change dramatically as soon as a man gets down on his belly to avoid being killed. The infantry who had to attack and defend the Buonriposo ridge felt its slopes as steep as those of Monastery Hill itself. If the Germans succeeded in capturing it they would dominate the main road, and the position of the battalions of the 1st Division holding Carroceto Embankment and village and the fortress of the Factory, would become very uncomfortable indeed.

Buonriposo was held by the 2nd North Staffs. They could not feel firm upon it. To the north they stretched out a hand to the Grenadier Guards holding the Embankment, but the

Guards found the hand difficult to grasp. There was too much space to be covered, and, as usual, the company areas were too far apart. Dead, dangerous ground lay in between both companies and battalions.

And always, over the ridge, the Commanding Officer of the North Staffs was conscious of the hidden wadi system, through which whole battalions of Germans could creep up on him undetected. He was uneasy about the security of his sector, but he was not the only one who felt worried: a general air of anxiety now invested the Beachhead and spread still farther afield.

The shells thumped down in the waters of the harbour. The air raids increased in intensity, and the rear areas began to seem as unsafe as the front. General Penney, after his experience in the salient, looked towards Corps with a troubled eye: they seemed to stay in their cellars at Nettuno and not appreciate the difficulties which were growing around 1st Division. General Lucas, from his point of view, seemed to have lost confidence in the British ability to hold their sector finally and nursed his reserves carefully; there was tension between the Allied command on the Beachhead.

At Caserta, General Alexander and General Clark had earnest debates over the reinforcements to be sent to Anzio. Alexander hoped for some relief for the more hard-pressed British Brigades, Clark—anxious to have every man possible on the threatened beachhead—objected.

> I told him that if any of the British 1st Division was to come out of the beachhead now it was over my strongest objection and that he would have to give me an order in writing. He said the British 1st Division was tired. I told him so was the 3rd but that if the situation got more critical all would have to fight whether they were tired or not.[1]

In distant London Mr. Churchill, as the prime mover of the expedition, felt impelled to initiate a series of cables, more in sorrow than in anger, to his commanders in the field. He had already confessed to Field-Marshal Dill in Washington that 'all this has been a great disappointment to me. . . . We should also learn a great many lessons about how not to do it

[1] Clark, *Calculated Risk*.

which will be invaluable in "Overlord" '.

On 8 February he cabled to the C-in-C Mediterranean:

> Let me know the number of vehicles landed at Anzio
> by the seventh and fourteenth days respectively. I should
> be glad, if it were possible without too much trouble or
> delay, to distinguish trucks, cannon, and tanks.[1]

Mr. Churchill felt that the reply to his query was startling. By the seventh day 12,350 vehicles had been landed, including 356 tanks: by the fourteenth day 21,940 vehicles, including 380 tanks. Thus he calculated that, apart from the 4,000 trucks that went to and fro in the ships according to Col. O'Neil's supply plan, 18,000 vehicles were landed on the Beachhead by the fourteenth day in order to supply a force of 70,000 men.

On 10 February he relieved his feelings with a characteristic Churchillian crack:

> Thank you for your information. How many of our
> men are driving or looking after 18,000 vehicles in this
> narrow space? We must have a great superiority of
> chauffeurs. . . .

This business of the over-mechanization of the army always irritated Mr. Churchill. 'The army is like a peacock—all tail,' he said to General Brooke. 'The peacock would be a very ill-balanced bird without its tail,' replied Brooke, but Mr. Churchill remained unconvinced.

Calculations, exchanges of memos and special arguments were beside the point on 8 February 1944. It was too late to worry about the number of vehicles shipped to the Beachhead. The usual unpleasant signs were multiplying that the Germans were getting ready to renew their onslaught.

Our intelligence got wind through its sources in Rome that the night of the 7th was zero hour, and there was a hurried stand-to along the Allied line. Then deserters drifted across to our forward positions with the news that the attack scheduled for the 6-7th had been put off for twenty-four hours. The Scots Guards captured a German officer who had driven into their lines while looking for sites for the unpleasant *Nebelwerfers*, or six-barrel mortars. This was the first sign of these much-hated weapons on the Beachhead.

[1] Churchill, *Second World War*, Vol. V.

The German took pleasure in telling his captors that he had found excellent sites for his batteries and advised them to 'do a Dunkirk' while there was yet time.

All day on the 7th the rain poured down with that inhuman persistence that the Anzio veterans now felt as a personal attack, as hard to bear as the German shelling. Everyone looked up at the dripping sky and realized that, once again, there could be no question of air support. It was the perfect weather for the enemy, forming up in the wadis and in the ditches and woods of the right flank.

Towards dusk the rain eased off and the night sky cleared a little. There was a strange quiet for a moment along the main road from Carroceto, and then the North Staffs radio came up with the message: '2100 hours. Enemy seems to be infiltrating between A, B and C Company forward positions on Buonriposo ridge. Maybe patrol activity.'

The Germans had crept forward from their hiding-places in the wadis and, dispensing with elaborate artillery preparation, had sent their advance-parties forward to find the gaps between the North Staffs company areas. The tactics were similar to those employed in eliminating the salient. What the North Staffs took to be merely strong patrols were, in reality, highly trained groups of German infantry, armed with light machine-guns, whose job it was to cut communications and organize small strong-points far behind the British forward positions.

When the appointed moment arrived, the Very lights would soar up, down would come the barrage, the infiltrators would add to the confusion by pouring in machine-gun fire from the rear, and then, in overwhelming force, the German main attack would rush, yelling, firing, flinging grenades on to the dazed and bewildered defenders.

At eleven o'clock that night reports began to come in from all along the line—increased shelling on the Loyals, the Recce Regiment under fire, a company-strength attack on the Americans of the 45th Division holding the western section of the Moletta river! Then the North Staffs reported again, shortly after eleven: the whole of Buonriposo ridge had become alive with the enemy; they were rushing towards the forward positions in two-battalion strength, 'A' company cut off, 'B' and 'C' fighting fiercely, enemy penetrating towards the main Carroceto-Anzio road. The battle that was to lead to crisis on the Beachhead had begun.

Von Mackensen had decided to make the same sort of pincer attack that proved so successful on the night of 3-4 February. The 65th Infantry Division was to drive from the west to capture Buonriposo ridge, while Combat Group Gräser would assault across the flat unprotected country to the east of the Factory to reach a lateral track that ran from the Factory towards Padiglione. Once these features were in German hands—and Von Mackensen hoped to have them safe by the early hours of 8 February—further reserves would be poured in to cut the main Anzio road and, on the eastern flank, to penetrate to the Bowling Alley. At dawn the British troops in the Factory-Carroceto area would find themselves in a perilous position, in the same sort of difficulty they had faced in the battle for the salient. The enemy would be across their communications and the Factory would fall.

Von Mackensen hoped that, if all went well, he would be able to report to Kesselring that he held the Factory on the morning of 9 February. The plans of the First Parachute Corps, who were co-ordinating the attack under Fourteenth Army, subsequently fell into our hands and indicated that the Germans had even envisaged the capture of Buonriposo, Carroceto and the Factory in a single night! This would give them the firm base they needed for their final attack, which was already being planned in detail. The quicker they got their start line the more powerful that attack would be.

Such an outline was the German plan. Thus expressed it looks simple and straightforward, but even as he writes the words describing it the historian is uneasily aware that something is escaping him. He can never convey the one thing that worries everybody who has to endure the ordeal of battle—the hopeless uncertainty of it all! No one, from general down to private, can be absolutely sure about what is happening around him. There is no safe rock on which to build.

Uncertainty can explain nearly everything, the wrong decision of a commander and the sudden panic of the men, the unexpected retreats and the equally unexpected successes. It also adds a rare value to the general who can make some sort of coherent picture of events and to the soldier who does not allow himself to be intimidated by the dismaying news, 'They're in behind us! We're cut off!'

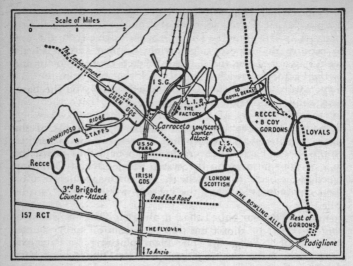

SECOND GERMAN COUNTER-ATTACK ON BRITISH 1ST DIVISION, 7-9 FEBRUARY 1944

This battle for the Factory was mainly a night battle and one which it was particularly hard for tired troops to fight. The only sensible advice a commander could give his men was: 'Stay put. Don't worry if you're cut off in the darkness. Fight it out where you are during the night and at dawn we'll counter-attack to rescue you.' Some did just that— they were supported by a framework of strong discipline and by good leaders. Others could not hold—they were inexperienced or, worst fate of all, their officers got killed early in the fight. This all added to the mind-numbing, overriding uncertainty that covered the whole battlefield.

An orderly narrative cannot convey this utter disorderliness of war, and perhaps the best way to recapture the real feel of it is by reading the regimental or battalion histories.

Anzio, in these histories, does not appear as a long-drawn-out campaign. It takes the form of one or two violent encounters as the battalion, jerked from place to place by order from on high, unfathomable by the private soldier and his young officers, suddenly finds itself in the front of the battle. The battalion historian's Anzio, the Beachhead that the regiment remembers with pride, is always some small feature—the Caves, Smelly Farm, the Gullies—where for one terrible night or through a day of near despair the Loyals, the Dukes or the 'Micks' learnt the full bitterness of war and yet did not break.

For the 2nd North Staffs, Anzio will always be the bare, swelling grasslands of the Buonriposo ridge.

The Irish Guards, after their ordeal in the battle of the salient, had been withdrawn into a reserve position centred on a gully behind Buonriposo ridge about a mile down the main road from Carroceto towards Anzio. No. 4 Company had been sent up to reinforce the Scots Guards before Carroceto itself and the 'Micks' realized that they would also be called on to send support to the North Staffs in front of them, if the enemy struck hard at Buonriposo. The Irish CO confessed that he didn't quite like his role of 'being a little Dutch boy, running up and down plugging holes in the dykes.' but there was no alternative. 1st Division had very little in reserve.

Towards nine o'clock, as the rain cleared and a wan moon shone out for a few hours, the North Staffs radio gave warning of the first German infiltrations. Then at 11 p.m. the messages picked up by the Irish Guards became more urgent. 'They say that all their companies but one are off the air and Battalion HQ is surrounded. The corporal on their set sounds worried!'

He had every cause to be. The Germans had completed their infiltration behind the forward companies of the North Staffs and were now swarming over the ridge in a yelling horde to overwhelm the British by sheer weight of numbers. Men struggled hand to hand, all cohesion between the companies was lost and inevitably the wireless sets were silent.

The British 18 portable radio was never the pride and joy of the infantryman. Its wagging aerial drew down fire on the unfortunate signaller who carried it, and some were tempted to get rid of this dangerous encumbrance in the heat of action. Again and again, in the regimental histories, we come across the same old story—'the set had conked out, Company B were out of radio touch,' and as a result, Battalion HQ goes blind, together with the long chain of communications stretching towards the rear from which alone help can come.

The Staffs, with most of their radios gone, their officers killed or wounded, struggled desperately to hold out, but by midnight one thing became clear in the confusion. They had been pushed off the summit of the ridge. As the remnants of the Staffs strove to rally round Battalion HQ and a company of the Irish Guards set out in an attempt to fight their way towards them to bring them some present help in their troubles, the Germans now had a chance to drive straight through to cut the main Anzio road behind Carroceto.

They lost no time in reforming after reaching the summit of the ridge. They swung left to take the Grenadier Guards in the flank. Once they had pushed the Guards aside they would be out at last on to the main road.

The 5th Battalion of the Grenadiers had been placed along the Carroceto Embankment and some of their companies lay on the north end of Buonriposo ridge and a little forward of it. The gap torn in the line when the enemy overwhelmed the North Staffs put the two forward companies in a hopeless position. In a matter of minutes, as one officer recalled, 'a lot of Germans seemed to have suddenly materialized, as it seemed, out of the air'. The forward units had been under pressure for some time and were holding on until the last round, but the strength of the German attack overwhelmed them.

By midnight the ridge, the gullies and the damp fields just south of the Embankment at Carroceto were the scene of a confused struggle. The full moon now shone down on a battleground that had lost all sense of order. Small groups of Grenadiers still held out here and there on the ridge; a column was trying to retire along the Embankment itself, led by a jeep towing an anti-tank gun, in order to rally round a farm nearer to Carroceto station; the Germans were pouring intense tracer fire across the Embankment and moving to cut the column off, while close to the main road the American parachutists were hurrying up to try to block the gap just north of the Grenadiers' Battalion HQ.

It was just at this critical moment in the battle that the drama of the fighting seemed, for a few brief minutes, to concentrate in a way rare in modern war onto one place and one man.

The Grenadiers had set up their Battalion HQ in the Fossa di Carroceto, the deep wadi which started near the embankment and flowed between Buonriposo ridge and the main road. Today a track still leads down it from the main road which has now been built on the old Embankment site. If you walk down this track in the spring weather, when the broom is in flower and the air is filled with rich scents from the growing herbs, you feel yourself in a secluded and extremely beautiful valley, cut off from the traffic that hurries so noisily a few yards away along the new highway to Naples. By the time you have gone a few hundred yards into this valley you are out of sight of everything except the swelling skyline of Buonriposo to your left, for the right-hand side of the gully is formed of steep tufa rocks which are honeycombed with shallow caves. The Anzio shepherds walk here with their flocks on hot days in search of shade, with their sheepdogs of the white, husky-type breed peculiar to the Campania padding, tongues out, behind them.

On the bitter night of 7-8 February 1944 the valley was bleak and damp. The Grenadiers had driven a truck down the track and set up their HQ at a point where a side gully comes in from the right. Two tents were pitched alongside the truck, one used as the telephone exchange and orderly room, the other for the Commanding Officer and Adjutant. It was a cramped, uncomfortable billet.

The floor of the wadi was covered with thickets of brambles which concealed a booby-trap, a deep ditch cut in the soft earth with crumbling sides that made it difficult to cross. The Italian peasants had made one crossing place, however, almost opposite to the point where the HQ truck was parked.

The Guardsmen of HQ Support Company, under Major W. P. Sidney, covered this crossing-place with rifle-fire, while the American Parachutists guarded the gully farther up towards the Embankment. Support Company and parachutists were not the firm, final defence line which the position demanded. A swift rush by a strong, determined enemy would break the frail screen along the wadi which was now the last defence between Buonriposo and the road.

All too soon this swift rush was upon them. The men in the tiny tents had realized that the human dykes, which up until now had protected them from the enemy, were crumbling fast. As the radio sets went off the air one by one, they sensed the danger racing towards the gully. Rifles and Bren-guns in hand, the last-ditch defenders were now lying amongst the rocks or on the ledges just above the valley floor waiting for their enemy's onslaught. In some of the caves a few terrified Italian civilians still cowered, with their hands, as one of them afterwards told me, either over their ears or held together in prayer.

The rattle of machine-gun fire echoed in the narrow gully. The Germans had swiftly set up their guns on a spur overlooking the whole place. The British and Americans replied as best they could and struggled to get a mortar into action. Then the attack came in.

Hundreds of Germans came running down the slope of the ridge towards the Grenadiers' Headquarters. The moon was cruelly bright and glittered on their rifles and automatics, magnifying their numbers. They shouted hysterically as they ran. Who would blame them? This is the worst moment in war for the infantryman, as he throws himself forward, cringing flesh against flying metal. The first wave reached the bottom of the wadi, a mere twenty yards from the truck. For a moment the Germans paused, they were held up by the brambles and by the ditch concealed in the bramble thickets. The Grenadiers and the parachutists poured fire on them, but wave after wave of the enemy came down the ridge. Soon they found the weak point in the defence line— they had come across the track hewn through the brambles. In a moment they would be over the ditch. Once across nothing could have stopped them reaching the main road. Already the German tanks could be heard forming up on the ridge, ready to cross the obstacle of the ditch once the infantry had seized it.

If ever there was a moment in the battle of the Beachhead when one man held in his hand—like Horatius of old—the fate of an army, this was it.

Major Sidney leapt to his feet and ran forward to the edge of the ditch beside the crossing place. Bullets were whipping in all directions, but he stood upright. He fired his tommygun and cut down the first Germans rushing across the ditch. His gun jammed. He came back from the edge of the ditch and started to fling grenades on any of the enemy who tried to dash over. A few succeeded, but Major Sidney kept flinging grenades at them. Two Guardsmen crawled forward to help him and primed the grenades as he threw them at the Germans. In the excitement of the moment one grenade was detonated prematurely and killed one of his helpers. The fragments flew in all directions and wounded Major Sidney in the legs. He still remained at his post, keeping the dangerous patch blocked to the Germans. Then a stick-grenade hit him in the face, but by this time his own men were alongside him.

All attacks have a critical moment beyond which they cannot be pressed. A check on the crest of the wave, and, somehow, the impetus dies, the attackers falter even though they might outnumber the defenders. The blood runs cool and the men who have advanced with fury and determination suddenly feel exposed and naked; they drop down for shelter and crawl to cover. So the German attack faltered and fell back from the lip of the ditch as Major Sidney himself fell wounded.

Major Sidney was awarded the Victoria Cross. Today he is Lord De L'Isle and Dudley and lives in Penshurst Place, the beautiful house in Kent which was once owned by his ancestor, the great Elizabethan Sir Philip Sidney. The portrait of the Hero of Zutphen must look down with approval on his modern descendant, but Lord De L'Isle and Dudley probably gets more satisfaction out of the typical comment made by a wounded Guardsman when he heard of the award, 'Well, if he was as tough on the Germans as he was on us, he deserves the VC.'

The Germans did not give up after the failure of their first attempt. At 3.30 a.m., with the moon high in the sky, they sent in a new wave of men. Again the wave was held on the edge of the ditch. The thin line between Buonriposo and the main road remained unbroken when, at last, the dawn came up and the German attacks died away.

The western pincer of the double German attack had thus not made quite the progress for which the German command had hoped. But the enemy held Buonriposo ridge and that, in itself, spelt grave danger for the future.

The total strength of the Grenadier and Parachute force still opposing them along this last-ditch wadi was 29 Grenadiers and 45 American soldiers!

We look now across the eastern sector of 1st Division's front. Here the first storm of the German attack had fallen on the 10th Royal Berks. As the North Staffs look on Buonriposo as their greatest ordeal of the Anzio campaign, so for the Royal Berks the Beachhead means the flat fields just to the east of the Factory. They were about to begin their two days' purgatory in this undistinguished patch of damp ground.

The usual infiltration tactics were employed by the enemy, and they knew now that there were gaps in the British line. As the night wore on they succeeded in pushing in between the Berks and the Recce Regiment on one side and overrunning a platoon of the London Irish near the Factory on the other. A major attack broke over the forward companies of the Berkshires at 11:30 p.m. Their Battalion History describes the feelings of the watchers at Battalion HQ as the Germans surged around 'B' Company.

> The steady deliberate, thump-thump-thump of Bren-guns, always so easily distinguished from the ripping sound of the German spandaus, bore testimony that stout hearts were keeping up the struggle in the forward positions. For three hours they fought and held off all attacks. Ammunition was rushed up by cooks, drivers, and anyone else who was available. Sergeant Griffin, the cook-sergeant, stayed with his old company until 2.30 a.m. killing Germans and providing great inspiration to the company. . . . Artillery defensive fire, tanks, rifle and Bren-gun fire, the explosion of grenades, all combined to create a terrific and noisy scene. Gradually, as dawn broke, the fighting died down with both sides exhausted.

As the dawn light strengthened, the danger of the right flank of 1st Division's sector could be seen more clearly. The line had not been broken, but the Germans had pushed back the Recce Regiment on the right of the Royal Berkshires and had overrun a platoon of the Gordons. They had reached one of the tracks that ran from the Factory to Padiglione, but were being kept from further advance by heavy fire from the rest of the Recce squadrons. They had, however, got some sort of a jumping-off ground from which they could launch stronger attacks. The Factory itself was still firmly in the hands of the British.

Once again the harassed General Penney found himself called upon to solve the now familiar problem. His division had been caught by a pincer-attack, and it was imperative that he should himself counter-attack to blunt the pincers. But which pincer should he counter-attack first and with what? He had very little left 'in the kitty', only the two weakened battalions of 3rd Brigade, the 2nd Foresters and the KSLI. Corps were unable to spare him any extra help at the moment, yet he dared not leave the Germans to consolidate their gains. Penney looked at Buonriposo and knew that here was the point on which he must focus every atom of strength that he still possessed.

The thin screen of Grenadiers and American Paratroops along the wadi must try to hold out for the coming day, the Scots Guards north of Carroceto and in the railway station must put up with the continual menace of German tank attacks, and the London Irish must hang on to the Factory with no other encouragement than the sound of our artillery, firing their heaviest concentrations yet into the dangerous ground ahead of them. The Commanding Officer of the Royal Berkshires noted grimly in his diary:

> Men dog tired, I can't write consecutively as so many things happen at once. Brig. says can't send any more help, so I took a risk and ordered the battalion to sleep with minimum sentries for two hours. This, on such a wide front, with depleted companies, was a big risk, but men must sleep.

Buonriposo came first, for it dominated the main road. If the Germans remained firm on it they would eventually push us out of Carroceto and the Factory. The centre of the fighting on 8 February was the all-out attempt of 1st Division, weakened as it was by twelve days' continuous fighting, to get back Buonriposo.

Two infantry battalions, the 2nd Sherwood Foresters and the 1st King's Shropshire Light Infantry, were alerted for the attack, and 'A' Squadron of the Recce Regiment. A squadron of 46th Royal Tank Regiment was also assigned in support, but by now the troops were only too familiar with the country over which they had to fight. They knew that, however hard the tanks might try, they would not get across the muddy, bramble-covered ditch which filled the bottom of the wadis. The infantry would have to go on alone up over the sodden ground that rose steadily to the summit of the ridge. At the top of the ridge their enemy now waited for them, only twenty feet above the level of the infantry start line in the wadis, but those twenty odd feet made all the difference.

The counter-attack failed. The KSLI had been rushed to the scene with no chance of reconnoitring the ground; the Foresters were heavily shelled as they waited for a zero hour which had to be repeatedly postponed. The tanks could not get far on the muddy ground.

All through the afternoon and into the early evening the attackers struggled to beat the machine-guns across the last twenty yards to the ridge.

By six o'clock the light was starting to fade. All officers in 'B' and 'C' Companies of the KSLI were casualties. Then the commanding officers of the other companies fell; the company sergeant-majors took over and were wounded in their turn. There was nothing more to be done but let the men come back, as best they might, to the line of scrub and brambles at the bottom of the Fossa di Carroceto. The senior NCOs—'magnificent' the KSLI war-diary calls them, the solid dependable backbone of the British Army—led the survivors back. The Germans remained on Buonriposo.

The survivors remember vividly the scene at the ruined farm just behind the wadi. The rain had now started to drench down again, and the general misery seemed to clot around the broken farmbuildings. The Recce Regiment cars were trying to tuck themselves behind the walls as shelter for the night, a Quad, towing an anti-tank gun, was vainly trying to do the same thing. The gunner's OP vehicle was stuck in the mud near the door while jeeps and lorries of the admin. train of the Foresters and the KSLI were jammed on the slithery track behind. The wounded men lay in the barns, the icy rain poured in everywhere, and officers crouched in consultation over hooded torches, trying to sort out some order in the chaos. The German shells whistled through the darkness. Where did the troops go from here?

There could be but one answer. The loss of Buonriposo could only mean that the troops would have to go back, back from the vital Factory area—unless something drastic was done about it.

1st Division had shot its bolt as far as any power to make a major counter-attack was concerned. The troops for this could only come from Corps reserve, and General Lucas was still unwilling to release them. The tension increased between Corps and the British 1st Division.

In his caravan on the night of 8 February, with the icy rain pouring down outside, General Penney set down the state of his division after an unsatisfactory interview late that evening with General Lucas. The returns showed him how weak he was getting. He wrote: 'Corps Commander reiterated order to hold where we were and said that he could provide nothing from Corps reserve to help.'

Penney felt curiously isolated. No staff officer from Corps came up to look at his difficulties on the ground, and far too many of the conferences between Division and Corps seemed to take place back in the catacombs of Nettuno and not forward near the scene of the fighting.

Penney clamoured for a firm policy, some clear-cut indication that Lucas was going to prepare a really strong counter-attack. He asked for an appreciation of the intentions of the enemy since those of his own general were veiled from his gaze. It was disconcerting to be told by a senior officer at Corps: 'Your guess is as good as mine.'

By the evening of 9 February Von Mackensen held the Factory. The main bastion of the British front was gone, and a deep anxiety flooded the whole Beachhead. To the defenders there seemed to be a sickening inevitability about its loss.

Their counter-attack had failed on Buonriposo, no fresh troops had come to relieve them, no new, powerful punch was being prepared to shake the Germans on the ground they had gained. The men were tired, their slit-trenches were filled with icy water, they had little wire and fewer mines. Out in the darkness and the rain they could hear their enemy forming up in the wadis and woodlands. It would only be a matter of a few hours before the storm would break over them again. They counted their numbers and saw the big gaps in their ranks. The shivering private in the British front line could only try to grit his teeth and pray desperately that the storm would not break over his tiny part of the front. Where would it break?

All the signs pointed to the damp fields east of the Factory. Von Mackensen had already closed his western pincer and taken Buonriposo: now was the time to put full weight on the eastern pincer. Once his assault force had cut the tracks leading towards Padiglione from the Factory he would be ready to drive straight at the Factory itself. General Gräser was conducting the operation on the spot and he had proved himself bold and ruthless. He had the 725th and

735th Grenadier Regiments of the 715th Division ready by dusk. The German artillery began its preparation. Directly in the track of the advance of Combat Group Gräser lay the weakened Royal Berkshires. The London Irish still held the Factory and the London Scottish lay behind the two advanced battalions of the 168th Brigade.

Brigadier Davidson, in his HQ within sight and sound of the front line, could see the flashes of the tracer bullets in the rain over the flat land where his units lay. The Factory stood gaunt, battered and dark against the gathering dusk. He had no reinforcements in hand to buttress up his line, but he felt he had to send some words of encouragement to his battalion commanders. Words are cheap and the troops would have preferred tanks and shells, but they were all the Brigadier had left. They might help. He dictated a message that evening to go up with the rations. The sentences may not have the incisive ring that a Napoleon could have given them: the Brigadier did not claim to be a literary artist. He was just a good soldier, desperately anxious to hearten his troops. The sentences bring back the tension of that evening when the British 1st Division waited for its worst ordeal yet.

. . . I would like you to tell your soldiers how much their gallantry and steadfast courage is appreciated and I hope you will understand just what I, at this time, am feeling about you. I hope that in the near future you will be relieved, but first we must all produce that extra effort however tired we may be. Good Luck. May God's blessing be on you all. . . .

Soon after midnight the inevitable heavy concentration of German gunfire fell on the forward positions of the Royal Berks. The Germans rushed forward, certain that they would find the usual wide gaps between companies and battalions.

The Berks were overwhelmed where they stood. The final, laconic entry in their war diary shows how they fought: 'Battalion now consists of battalion HQ, two sections of C Company, a few carrier and mortar personnel, totalling 40 men in all.'

No battalion on the Beachhead fought a more self-sacrificing battle, but by dawn the Germans had eliminated them and were on the road between Padiglione and the Factory. Swiftly General Gräser turned to tear the Factory itself out of the hands of the British. He knew that he had the whip-hand for the moment. In overwhelming strength his troops slowly drove the London Irish out of the ruins. The shells burst in the confined space of the Factory and made the men feel that they were fighting in a steel boiler with the riveters working relentlessly outside.

It was all over by the late afternoon. The Factory was German and the Allies had lost a key-point in their defence system. The Scots Guards alone remained in the village of Carroceto. They held it for a day and a night against everything that the Germans brought to attack them. Again this was a great feat of arms, but again it was a case of fresh troops being hurled against tired men, who had no reinforcements in sight. The result was inevitable; by dawn on 10 February the Scots Guards had lost the village, although they still clung stubbornly to the Embankment. And from that battered earthwork nothing could dislodge them.

From the Irish Guards' History we take this vivid picture of the Embankment at Carroceto. It puts the magnifying-glass on one small corner of the Beachhead battlefield and lifts it off the official military map into a grim life of its own.

The embankment was a scene of peculiar desolation. The rain beat down on a litter of smashed equipment and burnt vehicles, shattered ammunition and derelict tanks. Lying on his back was a Gunner officer, shot through the head and then run over by a tank. It was not a pretty sight. Up on the embankment the sodden exhausted remains of two battalions crouched in their slit-trenches. Battalion HQ was in the culvert under the embankment, where the Battalion RAP had been, knee-deep in water and crowded to capacity. Looking tired, but unmoved in the babel, was Colonel Wedderburn of the Scots Guards, surrounded by Americans, Sappers, Gunners—all that could be scraped together to reinforce the Scots Guards and the Grenadiers. Outside, snuggled close up to the embankment, were four American tank-destroyers, the only comforting sight to be seen.

That seems to bring back the smell, dampness, disorder and dogged courage of it all.

There had been confusion of mind and disagreement behind the lines as well as in front. All through the 9th and 10th of February, while the men of the 1st Division were being slowly driven back, their commander, General Penney, was hammering away at his Corps Commander as hard as Von Mackensen was hammering at his harassed troops.

Penney's messages to Lucas became increasingly urgent and insistent: 'The 1st Division must get help. Either relief from the line or a really big counter-attack.'

Every report the 1st Division's commander received from his front told him of more companies overrun, more tanks smashed, more anti-tank guns lost. His command was being eaten away piecemeal, and still Corps did not seem to realize it. Let them send someone up to see for themselves, for it was no good arguing this out in the cellars of Nettuno. Penney did succeed in getting Lucas to release some tanks and the 180th Regimental Combat Team of the American 45th Infantry Division took over the sector of the 2nd Brigade, but Lucas himself admitted that these measures were small and did not solve Penney's real problem—how to stop the Germans in the Factory and Carroceto area.

It would be idle to pretend that at this stage of the battle Penney had confidence in the vigour of Corps leadership or that Lucas felt sure of the British capacity to hold. So the arguments raged behind the lines as the guns thundered around the Flyover, the American tanks slithered once again in the mud south of Buonriposo ridge, the British fell back out of the Factory and the Scots Guards faced their crisis in Carroceto.

By dawn on the 10th Penney felt that a crisis faced the whole Beachhead unless he could force Lucas to do something positive about it. From 5.30 in the morning, all through the early part of the day, he stuck firmly to the task of putting all the power he had behind his attempt to persuade Corps that they must counter-attack or expect the worst. It was a morning of damp misery, disappointment and mounting irritation. The wind rose, lashing the rain in the faces of the troops. The big air programme laid on to blast the Germans in the Factory fizzled out as the rain increased, and at last General Lucas decided on a counter-attack. At 6 a.m. his Chief of Staff telephoned Penney and told him of the decision that the American 45th Infantry Division were to retake the Factory. 'They must do it today,' emphasized Penney, and the Chief of Staff agreed.

At mid-morning, 1115 hours, Lucas came for the first time since the fighting began to the headquarters of the Guards Brigade. General Harmon, General Penney, the Brigade

Commanders of the Guards and 168th Brigades attended the conference. It was a meeting that left the subordinate generals puzzled and their junior officers bewildered. Maybe it was once again a question of the clash of two different methods of approach to a problem, but the British were undoubtedly dismayed to find that after Penney had given his exposition of the situation Lucas sat quiet and then said to General Eagles, 'OK, Bill, you give 'em the works.'

Penney noted, 'No operational appreciation, no orders, no objective, no nothing.' Lucas left and the generals tried to sort out their plans, while the Brigadier of 168th Brigade murmured to his Intelligence officer that he may have seen many American movies but he'd never seen one like that conference. The Americans may have made comments on their own side.

One thing was clear—with this element of misunderstanding abroad there could be no question of the counter-attack smashing in quickly on the 10th; zero hour would now be dawn on the 11th and the Germans would have the whole night to prepare to receive the American attack. The British could not help feeling uncertain about its success. They knew the Factory of old and had attacked it first with the Grenadier Guards: even then they had felt they had not concentrated enough strength on the job to do it quickly. The plan for the counter-attack called for the commitment of the 1st Battalion of the 179th Infantry Regiment and two companies of the attached 191st Tank Battalion. This was certainly not the powerful punch with all the weight of the Allied reserves behind it, for which Penney had hoped.

Nor did the methods of co-ordinating the artillery support between the Allies promise success on the morrow: again there was a difference in method. A British CRA is given more power than his opposite number in an American division. Penney had told Eagles after the conference: 'I've got eight regiments of artillery in action whose guns can all fire on the front of your attack. What do you want?' Eagles sent his artillery commander over to 1st Division after dark to work out details with Brigadier Pasley. The technical experts got on like a house on fire—there was never any difficulty about co-operation at the level of the fighting men —but again it was the differences in the system of command that complicated the issue. The American, with that completely open and unprejudiced approach which is the

135

strength of the US Army at its best, said, 'General, you know more about this part of the country and what to shoot at!' but when Pasley asked him for details of the plan of attack, the position of his infantry and the movements of the tanks, he replied: 'General, I'm only the artillery commander. I know nothing about the infantry!' It was too late to get the information required, and the British artillery, mainly 25-pounders, had to be put on targets other than close support —the very job that they were perfectly adapted to do. It was the British guns which were in the best position to support the American attack, advancing over ground that the British gunners had been fighting over for the last three days and nights.

Thus, in the heat and hurry of battle, do plans made between allies come adrift. There was one more danger. The tanks which were to support the counter-attack would be using the main road, and needed the Carroceto embankment for their jumping-off ground. They would have to pass under the Carroceto bridge to get at grips with the Germans in the Factory. At all costs the 1st Division must go on holding the Embankment. General Penney now put in the last battalion he had left, the DWRs—his final reserve, the last carefully guarded particle of strength. He sent them up in the rain before darkness fell on the night of the 10th to buttress the decimated Guards clinging to their final foothold on the Embankment. At least he had made certain that the tanks would have a start line for the morrow.

Now the 1st Division was really stretched to the limit. Every one of its units was in close contact with the enemy; there was not a battalion which had not been put through the mincing-machine of battle. That evening General Penney wryly recalled his inconclusive discussions with Corps Headquarters. Thinking ahead, and determined to force others to do so, he sat down to write a letter to the Corps Commander to make crystal-clear his views on the present position and the need for vigorous planning for the future. He detailed the state of the British 1st Division.

> . . . The strength of the division is being gradually sapped through the course of the present operations. Desperate defence without stabilisation, and with little in the way of availability or opportunity to make adequate use of defence stores—continued regrouping

whilst in immediate contact: these are outstanding features.

A period for rest, refitting and reorganisation is essential. The process of relief has started, but effective stabilisation can, in my opinion, only be achieved by a strong counter-offensive. The initiative has temporarily been lost, and although it would appear that the enemy, in his present condition, would be susceptible to a hard knock, resources on our side are inadequate. . . .

The division is prepared to go on fighting hard but is being worn down. . . .[1]

Penney was not 'belly-aching' without cause. His mind turned to the complete infantry division and the tanks of the American 1st Armored, which General Lucas still had power to commit to battle. After urging that Corps should issue a positive directive of the action proposed in the event of the failure of the counter-attack 'since there is no effective immediate defence line' between Carroceto and the final Beachhead line, he ended with a firm statement:

Nothing in the above is to be interpreted as critical or defeatist, but troops react to confidences, even if they involve calling on them for super-efforts, providing at the same time it is made clear to those troops that those efforts, and the sacrifices involved, are achieving results.

At 6.30 a.m. next morning, the 11th, the counter-attack began. Neither the efforts made nor the heavy sacrifices involved achieved the results hoped for.

This counter-attack went the way of all the others that the Allies had launched: once again it was too weak and too late. General Lucas was still unwilling to commit his reserves, for he knew that the storm now breaking over his lines had not yet reached its full fury. His theme was: 'There's worse to come.' He was determined to hoard his reserves to the last.

So the Americans tried desperately to force their way back into the Factory, but always in insufficient strength. By dawn of 12 February the counter-attack was back where it had started.

That night the 'Dukes' were recalled from the Embankment, which had been defended with such valour. With the

[1] General Penney's Diary (unpublished).

Germans in the Factory and on Buonriposo the position had become hopelessly exposed. The soldiers scrabbled new slit-trenches in the muddy fields south of the Embankment, and the German attacks died down. Dawn on the 13th was very quiet. For the moment Von Mackensen had got all he wanted.

The stark, unescapable fact was that the Allies had lost their outer rampart and the enemy was now in a position to work furiously, preparing the final knock-out blow. There was no good natural defensive line between the Factory and the last-ditch of the Flyover. The level fields that lay south of Carroceto, the tangled wadi country and the ditches that led towards Padiglione were all points which the Germans could now use in their advance for the final storm of the Beachhead. And 1st Division had been so mauled that it would have to come out of the line.

Its sacrifice had not been in vain. Few Divisions in the British Army had been driven through such a long-drawn-out ordeal, and the 1st had borne the brunt of the German onslaught. Their losses had been grievous, but the stubborn defence of Carroceto had thrown the German time-table out by many valuable days: and they were still to play a noble part in the final Beachhead battle. Yet the brutal fact could not be ignored—the 1st was no longer a powerful fighting force in defence of the Beachhead.

Indeed, was the Beachhead now capable of defending itself? There were quite a few people who began to ask themselves secretly this disquieting, insistent question. Not the fighting men, for it was a curious fact that the nearer one went to the actual fighting the more steadfast were the hearts one found there. It was the men in the back areas, who did not quite know what was going on, who felt the unease of Anzio in those dismal days of early February. And farther back still, at Caserta and farther afield, doubts began to creep in, and the criticisms of General Lucas grew. Was he the stout-hearted leader that the Beachhead clamoured for as its hour of trial approached?

Anzio was now a sinister name to the troops who fought in Italy. 'Beachhead—Deathshead' shouted the German propagandist over Rome Radio. We must look for a brief moment away from the front-line, where the Germans are quiet as they prepare for their supreme effort—back to the rear, to

the rest of this strange beleaguered island in the midst of a
sea of hostile enemies. What does it feel to be in Anzio on the
eve of the attack which is going to 'fling the Anglo-Americans back into the sea'?

7

'Beachhead—Deathshead'

To the anxious watchers in the rear areas, the front line
seemed one enormous boiling mass. They could see the white
fountains of the phosphorus shells vomiting around the Factory as the wounded streamed back down the Albano Road.
Every morning the maps at Divisional and Corps Headquarters showed the enemy positions creeping nearer and nearer
the Corps Beachhead Line—nearer the last-ditch defence of
the 120,000 men who were now penned in the steadily con-
tracting perimeter. The correspondents grew to dread their
visits to the briefing officers at Corps and Division. A glance
at the map showed that, round the red circles that marked
our troops, more and more black circles of the enemy were
gathering, like microbes round the red corpuscles in the
blood. There was no need to ask what the situation was.
'Worse than yesterday' was the inevitable answer.

Every day the guns seemed to be farther back; the range
on which they fired shortened. Now they were dug in almost axle to axle in the soggy ground of the dripping Padiglione woodlands. Day and night they sent their shells hurtling towards the fateful mile beyond the Flyover in which
the life or death of the Beachhead was being decided. The
dead leaves showered down on the gunners with each ear-
splitting crash of gunfire.

Overhead the German shells raced the other way towards
the now hopelessly crowded areas of the harbour and the
ammunition dumps. The 'Anzio Express', the great railway-
gun hidden somewhere up in the Alban Hills, had a sinister
note of personal menace in the explosion of its shells. At
night it seemed to be aimed at each individual who listened
for it to begin.

First you heard a distant, almost discreet cough, away behind the enemy lines, then a slight pause, during which you knew the shell was on its way. Fear wound up your guts as if they were on a fisherman's reel. Then came the sickening crump of the explosion and the sound echoed away like a tube pulling out of the station and racing down a long, black tunnel.

Maybe the shells of 'Anzio Annie' or the 'Anzio Express' did not do such great material damage, but there was no question that they damaged nerves and morale.

The air raids became more frequent, pressed home with more daring. Every evening, as dusk deepened towards darkness, the ack-ack guns around the port began their quick, nervous crackle. The sky over the anchorage filled with red tracers and the sparks dropped off the bullets as they flew, covering the whole sky with glittering bloodshot stars. Through them would shoot a faster, more steadfast star. Streams of fire poured out behind it like a meteor. The Germans had aimed another wireless-controlled bomb at the fleet—a 'chase-me-Charlie' the British seamen called it.

It moved remorselessly through the tracers towards the black hull of a helpless Liberty ship silhouetted against the flaring horizon. The guns of the fleet and the ack-ack ashore fought off the raiders with furious determination, but occasionally a glider bomb or a dive-bomber would get through the screen of fire which poured up into the Anzio sky.

Then the whole beachhead would suddenly become naked in the unreal light of a flare dropped by the incoming German. An angry drumming sound would fill the air, turning into a high-pitched whine. 'Diving!' The savage crump of the bombs would shake the earth like a terrier shaking a rat. Away to the right a huge furnace glow would spring up in the sky. 'They've hit an ammo dump.' The exploding shell and small arms made a monstrous popping and fragments sang overhead.

This was the dusk nightmare that everyone on the Beachhead came to dread.

Anzio had become a sinister name to the troops landing as reinforcements during the height of the battle. As they stood on the decks of their LSTs they could see from miles out to sea the grey cloud of gunfire and the puffs of bursting shells that marked the Beachhead. The long-range shells sent up a fountain of sand and water as their ship entered the harbour. They were hurried through the battered streets to the reception centre just outside the town, which was placed between the cemetery and the field hospital. There was nowhere else to place it!

For this was the macabre quality of Anzio at the crisis of the German attack: the whole area seemed to be shrinking under the very eyes of the troops. As the Germans advanced the front was slowly driven towards the rear. The rear echelons could not move farther back, since they had the sea as a barrier behind them. Formations which in the Desert or on the mainland of Italy would have been miles apart were compelled to stay close together. Brigade Headquarters dug in amongst the gun positions, ammunition dumps were laid out near the vital fighter strip, every shell or bomb that was dropped on the Beachhead was bound to hit something.

The newly arrived soldier, as he lay in his tent in the reception centre and heard the whistle of the shells and the continuous crackle of the ack-ack, sensed the malaise of Anzio long before he came to the front line. The place felt shut in—there was claustrophobia in the evening air and the Germans, upon the Alban Hills, seemed to be able to see straight into the private lives of our soldiers. A tough sergeant from Oklahoma said to his commander, 'General, with them Krauts looking down from the mountains, I feel just like bacteria in a bottle.'

Even the wounded could not be brought out of danger quickly enough. The British Casualty Clearing Station, with its operating theatres, nurses, hospital wards and blood-transfusion units, lay within range of the German guns. The American hospital was sprayed with bombs. The gallant nurses suffered casualties and the whole American hospital area soon gained a grim nickname; the troops called it 'Hell's Half Acre'. General Harmon reported that some of his men had concealed their wounds and stayed forward rather than risk being taken to it.

The Germans may not have deliberately shelled and bombed the hospitals. It is difficult to excuse their sinking of the British hospital ship *St. David*, in the early days of the landing, because the *St. David* was brightly lit according to the International Red Cross code, but the field hospitals lay amongst ammunition depots, near important crossroads and communication centres. Their dark green and khaki tents were difficult to pick out from the hundreds of others which now littered the Anzio landscape. The doctors, orderlies and hospital nurses had to stand in the line of fire with the soldiers.

Those Casualty Clearing Stations at Anzio had a nightmare quality which seemed to have returned from the First World War, yet the devotion of the Medical Service has never been more nobly demonstrated than in the dark days of the battle along the Albano road. The wounded poured in, while outside the weather turned savage and pitiless. The hospital tents stood in mud and it was impossible to dig them into the waterlogged ground for safety. The wounded were sometimes killed as they lay in the wards. One of the medical men at the British Second CCS Major J. A. Rose, wrote down exactly what he saw, and his description can be paralleled from the American hospitals. Here is the ghastly reverse side of modern war—where the anguish becomes almost intolerable. Penicillin and the new sulphur drugs, blood transfusion and every new method of modern medicine, were there at hand, but they could not keep away the anti-personnel bombs or the whine of the diving aircraft. This was the sight in the pre-operation ward at night.

The wounded lay in two rows, mostly British, but some Americans as well, in their sodden filthy clothes; greatcoats, pullovers, battle-dresses, all of the thickest, soaked, caked, buried in mud and blood; with the ghastly pale faces, shuddering, shivering with the cold of the February nights and their great wounds. Some had been already splinted at the RAPs or the field ambulance ADSs; some were brought straight from the battlefield; for the CCS, owing to the shrinkage of the beachhead area, was much closer to the line than in normal circumstances. Most men had their first field dressings or shell dressings on. I grew to hate that combination of yellow pad, bloody, dirty brown bandage, and mud-darkened skin. Many men reached us who would not normally have survived long enough to have reached a CCS at all: some unconscious, these chiefly head wounds, whose loud snoring breathing distinguished them; some (too many; far too many) were carried in dying, with gross combinations of shattered limbs, protrusions of intestines and brains with great holes in their poor frames torn by 88-millimeter shells, mortars and anti-personnel bombs. Some lay quiet and still, with legs drawn up—the penetrating wounds of the abdomen. Some were carried in sitting up on the stretchers, gasping and coughing, shot through the lungs; others, less badly wounded, clutched mounds of equipment, and 'agitated' about pieces of their kit which had gone astray. All were exhausted after being under continuous fire, and after lying in the mud for hours or days.[1]

These were the sights which the nursing sisters had to face when they came to the Beachhead. The Queen Alexandra's Nurses and their American colleagues were an important factor in building up the morale of the wounded. However skilful and friendly a male orderly may be, the wounded man still thinks of him as part of the Army, a reminder of discipline and war. The nurse brings a healing touch of normality to the tented wards. A badly wounded man who had been brought down only a few hours before from the infernos around the Flyover felt, on seeing the nurse coming to attend to him, that he was already starting on his journey back to the sanity of everyday life.

The surgeons at the Casualty Clearing Stations stated that the wounds they had to deal with were as severe as any in their experience. 75 per cent of the wounds received in the Second World War were inflicted by fragmentation missiles —they were the result of bursting mortar bombs and hand grenades, artillery shells and bombs dropped by aircraft. To these should be added the 10 per cent which came from mines and booby-traps. A very much smaller proportion came from bullets and anti-tank shells. The bayonet wound was almost unknown. One surgeon at Anzio said that the only one he saw was caused by the man prodding his friend too enthusiastically during assault practice.

Fragmentation missiles caused cruel gashes, while mines and mortar bombs wrecked the body of the unfortunate soldier with a whole series of multiple wounds. In the confused fighting in the wadis, mines and mortars were major weapons and the wounded came out of the wadi country dreadfully lacerated.

Yet the layman who visited the CCSs at Anzio was continually amazed and inspired by the ability of the doctors and surgeons to make something out of the most hopeless cases. The men of the American and British Medical Services at

[1] J. A. R. (Major J. A. Rose), 'With a Casualty Clearing Station at Anzio'. *Blackwood's Magazine*, 1946.

Anzio made it their proud boast that 'there is no such thing as a corpse until the funeral.'

Against this picture of skill and courage, set now a scene Breughel might have painted. The ground beneath the houses of Nettuno was honeycombed by a maze of passages and cellars excavated in the porous volcanic soil over many centuries. Some were catacombs similar to the more famous ones at Rome, others had been constructed for the maturing of wines, the well-known Vini di Castelli, which are produced on the Alban Hills.

As the Beachhead contracted the civilian population took refuge in these caves. Although the Germans had ordered the evacuation of the houses along the coast the peasant farmers had remained in the *poderi* of the countryside. They had been caught in the net of the Beachhead front lines and inevitably drifted into the towns as the fighting got bitter. Some went reluctantly, and clung with the grim determination of peasants to their land even when the shells and the bombs fell all around them. One old farmer in his seventies told the officer who ordered him out, 'Yes, Mama she may go to the cava when the bombs fall, but I must remain here, for who else will comfort Ferdinanda?' Ferdinanda was the name of his last remaining cow.

General Lucas's first intention when he landed had been to 'freeze' the area and order all civilians to stay in their homes until the fighting had swept past. The fighting, however, had refused to sweep past, but had stayed savagely amongst the farm lands. The peasants cowered in their houses as the shells fell around them and battalions set up command posts in their living rooms. Then at last the families would be swept hurriedly out of the way—the battle was a mere few hundred yards down the road and the bewildered civilians, clutching their bedding and a few battered suitcases, would stumble through the darkness, the noise and the shell-bursts to the dubious safety of the rear.

The Allied Military Government officials grappled manfully with the task of collecting, feeding and sheltering these refugees, but the problem got worse as the Beachhead contracted. The wretched civilians seemed to be under everyone's feet, in the way of all army movements, until it became clear that there was only one sensible thing to do: as many non-combatants as possible had to be hurried out of the

144

Beachhead. In mid-February, as the guns thundered along the Albano road, the first batch of evacuees was gathered into the huge, red-bricked church on the outskirts of Anzio which afterwards became the embarkation centre for all civilians. There they waited until the lorries came to carry them to the LSTs or until the men were marched in hurrying groups to the quayside.

Sometimes the state of the weather delayed sailings and the church became cluttered with anxious families, adrift in a strangely dangerous world. The babies wailed, mothers crossed themselves as the shells came near, children gulped down the soup and bread handed to them by the AMG workers, and the priests moved slowly through the vast, darkened cavern of the church, comforting and reassuring their bewildered flock.

With the dawn the refugees assembled to scramble into lorries which would bump and hurry them to the quayside while the dust-covered passengers looked in amazement at some new alteration wrought by bombs in their old, familiar Anzio. Nearly twenty thousand civilians were eventually taken out of the Beachhead. A small number were left to supply a labour force or to try to look after the livestock.

In the early days of the evacuation the numbers which could be carried in the returning LSTs were bound to be small so that, during the crisis of the Beachhead battle, thousands of civilians were still clustered into Anzio and Nettuno towns, adding to the supply difficulties of the Allies at a time when every ton of shipping was needed for bringing in ammunition and food for the fighting men. Many of these refugees spent their whole time in the cellars. They filled the dark vaults, lit by petrol flares, with the smell of cooking and of stale unwashed, overcrowded humanity, while their babies sprawled amongst the stoves and the piled-up furniture.

Inevitably some of these underground caves became 'speak-easy' dens where the local black-marketeers sold *vino* to the troops. The Military Police placed them 'Off Limits' and kept a strict watch on them, but it was impossible to clean them up altogether. Soldiers found their way past the guards wherever a notice was scrawled on the door which said *Al Ricovero*. True, this simply meant 'To the Air-raid Shelter' in Italian, but the troops assumed that 'Al Ricovero' was the proprietor of the wine-store and a visit to 'Al's place' could procure you a flask of something which might help you to forget the present miseries and dangers of the threatened Beachhead.

The visitor groped his way down a steep flight of worn steps, cut in the slippery rock, to find himself in a huge, murky cavern which reeked of wine, garlic and earthy mould. Enormous vats and barrels lined the walls, and above them in the flickering light the dark roof was seen to be covered with spiders' webs and dripping with moisture. Families lived in squalid discomfort in the narrow space between the vats. 'Al' himself, *il padrone* to his assistants, would usually be found surrounded by his little court of retainers, counting out the greasy *lire* notes of the Military currency and issuing his orders to his minions to fill the big glass flasks with *vino bianco*—always 'the most magnificent *vino* in Italy, *Capitano!*' The wine was drawn from the casks by the simple process of removing a bung at the top, inserting a rubber tube and sucking vigorously. The lucky purchaser carried it off in a big glass container, set in a wicker basket.

No one inquired too closely at the mess where he had got it from for a 'slug of the old *vino*' before going to sleep gave a good many people on the Beachhead enough 'catacomb courage' to face the anguish awaiting them next morning.

The Germans strove to break the morale of the defenders by propaganda as well as by bombs. Every night the air over the Beachhead was filled with the voices of Sally and George, speaking from Radio Roma. Sally had a soft, sexy voice—although when she ultimately fell into our hands her captors were somewhat disappointed to find that the glamorous 'Axis Sally' with the inviting voice was extremely fat and plain. She was the specialist in insidious suggestion, 'What are those smart GIs doing to your English women while you are fighting and getting killed over here? Easy to guess, eh?' Sally spared none of the details when she described the love-affairs of the GIs and the girls back home. Words which were taboo on American and British radio came easily to her lips, for Dr. Goebbels and his experts knew that a little bawdry mixed in amongst the slogans and jazz-records would attract the troops to listen.

George was full of silky menace and a specialist in the grisly tale. 'Have you heard about Private Fox? He went on patrol and stepped on a shoe-mine. Nasty things, shoe-mines.

All his guts were blown away. But he went on living an other twelve hours. You should have heard him yelling. . . .' His voice had a slow, insidious and unnerving quality as he put over his slogan, 'Go easy, boys. There's danger ahead.' The GIs caught his tone and the slogan got repeated around the Beachhead—which was just what George and his masters wanted.

Jerry's Front Line Radio had its peak hour at eleven o'clock at night, when the troops could pick it up on the wireless sets which were used to maintain communication with the forward units. George and Sally did their nightly act for the men crouched in their fox-holes. Jazz tunes, played on old records, blared away, and Sally would talk between the records. Her husky voice would whisper: 'Do you know who we got as a prisoner the other day? Private Konduski. He's got the right idea. He's given himself up. He's finished with fighting. Not badly treated, too. Think it over.' The radio would pick up on music, 'Happy days are here again'. Then George would continue the story: 'Men of the 157th Regiment, remember what your Colonel said, "Fight like hell and then retire. I'll start now because I've got a bunion on my toe." ' Sally's voice would add an ironic chuckle and the snappy jazz disc would scratch its way on again. 'Go easy, boys. There's danger ahead.'

Jerry's Front Line Radio continued long after the German offensive had died away and became a permanent feature of the Beachhead. Sally's efforts were supplemented by pamphlets fired from mortars and guns. The shells exploded over the front-line areas with quiet popping noises, and the pamphlets lay on the ground where the troops could pick them up as they came out of their forward positions. On some mornings the outskirts of places like the Padiglione woodlands looked as if a giant paperchase had been held there.

In the first days of the German counter-attack the pamphlets were obviously 'rush jobs', hurriedly printed to put over the 'facts' about the battle, of which the front-line soldier was presumed to be ignorant. One of the earliest ones said:

British soldiers, you are fighting against an opponent you know very well.

You are not facing Italians but Germans. As gallant soldiers you have had the occasion to become acquainted with the courage and the grit of your German opponent.

You know how well the Germans stood up in battle, although they were always inferior to you in number. But you know well enough what it means when the Germans are numerically equal to your own forces or even superior.

In the face of insurmountable odds a thousand men of crack British Guards surrendered.

If they were forced to do so, then it is not dishonourable for you to lay down arms in case you are facing nothing but certain death.

General Clark certainly played you a dirty Yankee trick! And who has got to bear the consequences?

The other side of the pamphlet harped away at the theme of inefficient American leadership:

WHAT IT MEANS TO BE PUT UNDER AMERICAN COMMAND YOUR FORCES ARE FINDING OUT AT NETTUNO.
The 'accomplishments' of this American leadership are indeed typically American: operations were insufficiently prepared and led to the most dreadful reverses for your troops. Your picked units were carelessly thrown into the battle.
CERTAINLY, THE YANKS PLAYED YOU A NASTY TURN.

Another early pamphlet adopted a more threatening tone. It warned the British soldiers that unless they laid down their arms they would be swept into the sea.

What happened to the British 1st Division on February 4th was only a prelude. The same fate may be in store for you.

Americans and British were included in the same warning on a few occasions.

Remember the Hell of Dunkirk? How great were the hopes of the British expeditionary force and how dreadful was the end! Think of the terrible hours when the German broom swept your fellow soldiers, tanks, guns and lorries off the continent. How many ships were sunk then and how many brave Tommies kicked the bucket!
AND NOW THE HELL OF NETTUNO!
Boy! What a hot reception the American and British forces got this time again!

The beaches at Nettuno are covered in the Dunkirk fashion with debris and dead American and British soldiers crushed by the German military machine.

Overleaf was a crude drawing of a dead soldier, clutching a broken flag and floating in the water amongst sinking ships.

As the propaganda machine got into its stride the pamphlets became more elaborate and better produced. One showed a drawing of a skull neatly fitted into the outline of the Allied front line with the inscription 'Beachhead—Deathshead'. Another depicted a terrified woman screaming during an air raid with the caption, 'London Blitzed Again'. Forms were fired in mortar bombs containing instruction about how to get your name on to Jerry's Front Line Radio when you were captured.

A careful differentiation was made in the type of propaganda fired at the two Allies. The British were treated to variations on the theme that the 'Yanks are lease-lending your women'. One pamphlet announced that 'the Yanks are putting up their tents in Merry Old England. They've got lots of money and loads of time to chase after your women.' The reverse side had the picture of a girl lying on her bed in her 'undies', about to be embraced by an American sergeant. She sighed, 'You Americans are so different!' Another had a drawing of a naked girl pulling on silk stockings as she sat on the edge of a crumpled bed. In the background a smart and smiling Yank knotted his tie, whilst a bottle of wine lay handy on a tray.

The Americans were regaled with a whole series of pictures depicting the adventures of Sam Levy, a cigar-smoking Broadway Jew, who seduced the women (still smoking his cigar) while the 'dough-boy', newly returned from the war as a legless cripple, gazed helpless in the cold outside.

The language used in the leaflets fired at the Americans aimed at tough 'two-fisted man-talk'. They appeared to have been written by men who had hair on their chests and who didn't mind using the language of the fox-holes.

We protest, we—the soldiers on the fighting Anglo-American front—the boys who have to stick their necks out and take it! And we protest like hell against the way some civilian gents back home are carrying on their 'brain war'.

It must be nice to sit at home behind the writing desk

and fight battles in all the four corners of the world—
battles in which the bullets fly only one way and the
Jerries are mown down by the simple stroke of a pen.

It must be nice to carry on the kind of war portrayed
in the revues on upper Broadway; a long-legged, grape-
breasted girl in a cute little uniform squeals 'Bum!'—and
the poor hungry, lousy, demoralized Germans wet their
pants and reach for the sky. When we see stuff like
that, we feel like reaching for something quite different!
Why, it's enough to make a decent guy puke himself
sick, all this mucking revue and newspaper crap.

WE PROTEST AGAINST IT BECAUSE WE HAVE TO PAY THE
BILL.

This propaganda could have no dramatic effect. Guns and
bullets always speak louder than the printed and spoken
word. Anzio became tense because of what the Germans did
and not because of what they said. The slang in the pamphlets seemed false and dated, and no soldier, crouching
against the bursting mortar shells in his shallow trench, both-
ered to follow the dull and stale political arguments. The
soldiers appreciated the nude ladies but not for the reasons
which prompted the Germans to send their pictures over the
front line. They were in demand as 'pin-up' girls—although,
as one sergeant complained, 'they don't look a bit like my
old woman to me.'

The leaflets might make a man whose morale was already
low feel still more listless and depressed, but they could not,
at this stage of the war, appreciably weaken the Allies' determination to continue to fight.

Perhaps the German propagandists were well aware of
this. They did not seriously suppose that British and American soldiers would walk forward through the bullets and the
minefields, waving the surrender forms supplied for Jerry's
Front Line Radio; they were simply aiming at increasing the
general air of anxiety that now hung over the Beachhead. In
this they undoubtedly played some part at a small cost to the
German army.

Rumour behind the Allied lines was even more effective
than German propaganda in building up an atmosphere of
crisis at Anzio. The crews of the LSTs talked to the reinforcements as they came on board—stories circulated on the
Naples waterfront, the headlines in the Press at home were

alarming and copies soon came out to the front. Anzio was 'all hell let loose in a hat-box', the German offensive was rising to a crescendo on the fatal Albano road and what was now left to stem the onslaught?—two mauled and tired divisions. All night the ammunition dumps exploded. Would there be enough shells to keep the next German attack at bay?

The front-line troops, worn as they were by battle, were yet more optimistic than some of the units in the rear, but none could deny that there was an uneasy feeling abroad that the Beachhead was trembling on the verge of disaster. What would happen when the Germans advanced again—as they were certain to do? Anzio now stood to its final defences: the Allies had to 'do or die' around the Flyover bridge.

At this critical moment the Allied High Command cut off all direct transmission of news from the Beachhead. Newspaper and radio correspondents had landed with the first troops ashore and had been at Anzio through the weeks of growing crisis. Most of them were veterans of the Desert, North African and Sicilian campaigns who had received the fullest co-operation from the officers of Sixth Corps in getting their news. Every morning they assembled in Corps Headquarters, which had gone underground in the catacomb of Nettuno, to be briefed by the Corps G-2, Colonel Joe Langevin. The Colonel and the correspondents got on well together, for he had always been frank with them about the difficulties facing the Beachhead while yet striking a note of confidence. At this stage of the war the Army and the Press had come to terms—the Army recognizing that the Press was not just a nuisance to be tolerated, since no democratic country could wage war properly without it, and the Press understanding the difficulties of the Army and its commanders. At the vital moment at Anzio this link of confidence between Press and Army suddenly snapped.

The War Office had become alarmed at the headlines in the newspapers at home and the generals in the field were worried about the morale of their fighting men. Anzio had rapidly acquired the reputation of being the worst shambles of World War II. The people on the spot knew that this was an exaggerated picture, but who was responsible for spreading it? The war correspondents on the Beachhead seemed the obvious source of the trouble.

The generals would have been less than human if they had not felt some irritation with the Press. Here was their Beachhead in mortal danger, with their bright hopes for the landing long since faded. Mistakes had been made—none knew better than the generals what those mistakes were—but in this hour of crisis their duty was to see that their troops were in good heart. How could they possibly nerve their men for the supreme effort when a stream of discouragement came pouring out from the Press? It would be well if the correspondents ceased writing until the danger had passed— or if their writing were subject to a far stricter scrutiny. For a brief and bad moment the Army regretted the alliance it had made with the Press. Everything would have been so much simpler if the war-correspondents had remained safely back at Caserta and Naples writing up the war from the 'handouts' at Army HQ.

But war correspondents could not be corralled as they were in World War I. The modern British soldier would not give of his best unless he knew that the people back home in Britain realized that he was fighting a tough war. The American soldier went farther; he wanted the folks next door to know personally what he was doing, and he was delighted to see the correspondent around, if only to make certain he got his mention in the local newspaper back home.

The British correspondents will remember the meticulous care with which that most human and courageous of reporters, Homar Bigart of *The New York Times*, used to pin-point personal details. They were received by a newly arrived general who was explaining the tasks ahead assigned to his division. He was about to embark on his technical exposition of the position when Homar stopped him, with his gentle and persuasive stammer: 'One minute, General. First things first. What is your home town?'

A British war correspondent's report of an action might begin dramatically with: 'More than a thousand guns roared out in a great barrage before General Mark Clark watched his infantry and tanks move forward over the red poppy fields towards the German ring.' Or else: 'Anzio beachhead was aflame from end to end last night in a great new Allied offensive.'

His American confrère, with his eye on the folks back home three thousand miles from Europe, might be tempted to start: 'At dawn this morning, Sergeant Michael J. O'Dwyer, 357 West Jefferson Street, Des Moines, Iowa, looked at his watch, turned to Private James P. Sanduski, 19-34 49th Street, Great Falls, Montana, and gave the crisp order, "Fire". General Mark Clark's Fifth Army had begun its long awaited breakout from the Beachhead.'

This might seem 'small town' reporting to those who did not realize how hard Americans found it to picture what a war in distant Europe meant. It was, in fact, one of the best ways of conveying the personal involvement of the American people in the battle.

The American correspondent felt it his duty not only to report the deeds of GI Joe but Joe's criticisms of his commanders as well, and the rise and fall in his 'morale'. This was not so popular with the Army authorities.

Not all correspondents lived up to what the Army or the GI expected of them. There were plenty of reporters who were chary about approaching the front, and there were some at Anzio who moved out rapidly when they sensed that the Beachhead was in danger, muttering as they went. 'This is going to be a second Dunkirk.' But this was not true of the majority of them. Most of the alarmist reports in the Press did not come from the Beachhead reporters but from farther back—from Naples and Algiers. The real difficulty arose because the reporting of the War had now become a complicated affair. Army spokesmen 'briefed' correspondents at both Army and Army Group HQ, and the farther the 'briefing' was from the front, the less factual, of necessity, it became. Harassed editors, waiting impatiently in the news-rooms in London or New York, were bound to use the first reports which came to hand.

The Army authorities wanted to take no risks. They withdrew direct transmission facilities from the correspondents on the Beachhead with the result that, for some of the most critical days of the German attack, Naples and Algiers were the source of the news from Anzio. Small wonder that the news continued to be alarming.

On the day before the Germans launched their final all-out offensive General Alexander came to the Beachhead. The 14th of February saw an uneasy lull in the struggle. Everyone knew that in a matter of hours the supreme test would be upon them. General Alexander toured the front and came back to meet the correspondents. They had assembled in a bare room in Sixth Corps Headquarters after passing along the narrow corridor covered with posters of innocent American girls exhorting the GI to 'Come back clean'.

An air-raid warning wailed as the General came in, dressed in his fur-lined jacket which was his characteristic hallmark. For once he was not his urbane self. He spoke to the assembled group with the firm tone of a headmaster disappointed at some misdemeanour in the Upper School. He admitted that the Beachhead landing hadn't gone as he had hoped: 'We wanted a break-through and a complete answer inside a week. But once you are stopped it becomes a question of building up and slogging.' He insisted that it was the people with guts and determination who were going to win when it came to a slogging match. The correspondents listened politely—generals are bound to sound more optimistic than the man in the fox-hole—but when General Alexander went on to say that the reports sent from the Beachhead were causing alarm, there were emphatic protests. General Alexander looked sternly at the protesters. 'Were any of you at Dunkirk?' he asked. 'I was and I know that there is never likely to be a Dunkirk here.'

But the Commander-in-Chief, a reasonable man, felt the strength of the protests and promised that the whole thing should be checked when he returned to Naples.

A strange little scene, a small and trivial affair when compared to the general agony of the Beachhead, one is tempted to say. Yet it might not have been so trivial as it seemed. Could you have imagined it taking place at Kesselring's Headquarters or behind the front of the Red Army? The C-in-C took time in a crisis of the battle to meet the correspondents because he was not certain in his own mind that justice had been done, and although his sympathies must have lain with his commanders he struggled to see the viewpoint of the Press. It was a small part of the democracy that the Western Allies were trying to defend.

The correspondents walked slowly back through the dismal wintry weather to their battered villa on the edge of the sea near Nettuno. For the moment they could not send any news, but hadn't the news almost become too depressing to send? In the British section one of the correspondents sat down at a piano almost as battered as the villa and started to pick out a tune from *La Traviata*. At once the irrepressible old man known to the British Pressmen on the Beachhead as

'Zio' bounded into the room.

Zio, who was approaching his seventieth year but remained still lithe, gaunt and energetic, was a survivor from the days of a settled European civilization. His mind refused to grasp the extent of the catastrophe which had engulfed his beloved Nettuno. To Zio the invasion was a temporary thunderstorm which would pass and leave one thing untouched—Italian music. The Americans had played him jazz, but Zio declared that, like the shelling at night, one could live through it philosophically.

His ageing voice rolled out the choruses as the gunfire crackled outside:

'Ah, what great musicians have come to our Nettuno! My father waited on the great Brahms, who visited us here, and I, when I was very small, saw the even greater Verdi walking through our street. I played his music in our town band when I grew bigger. *Aida! Rigoletto!* while the rich people from Rome sat in the cafés eating or thinking of making love. We were happy in our Nettuno before the war.' (Zio meant the First World War, for the Second was a *'sbaglio'*, an unfortunate mistake and not a serious political affair.)

'But Verdi, he was the man—magnificent, with a noble beard and the people all bowing to him as he walked on proudly and looked neither to the right or to the left. This was the old Italia, *signori.*'

A shell plonked down in the bay outside the window and Zio interrupted his *aria* to shake his fist at the fountain of muddy water staining the sea. '*Ah, questa guerra! E un sbaglio, un cattivo sbaglio!*'

Zio accepted a glass of wine, which he tossed off with the condescension of a Roman emperor.

Dusk was falling on the bay, and the smoke screen began to blot out the ships. The Navy was having its troubles, too, for the civilian masters of the big Liberty ships were refusing to bring them in close enough for the DUKWs to unload them. The crews felt on edge the whole time they lay in the shell-splashed anchorage off Anzio, and even in the American Navy the officers were reporting an abnormal number of cases of severe mental strain. Admiral Lowry stated afterwards that the US Navy suffered more casualties from 'emotional break-down' than from bullets.

Naval gunfire was playing a vital part in holding the German drive, and although the cruisers and destroyers which supplied it were exposed to excessive risks from air-attack and shelling the British and American Navies never withdrew their gunnery support from the Beachhead.

Our warships had little to fear from surface attacks, for the Italian Fleet was now in Allied hands and only a handful of smaller craft was left to those die-hard Fascists who were determined to stand by the Germans to the bitter end. Prince Borghese, whose palace at Anzio was now Beachhead headquarters for the Fifth Army, scraped together enough fast motor torpedo-boats to raid the anchorage on the night of 18 February, but the attack was easily beaten off.

The air remained the big threat to the Allied fleet. The Luftwaffe was now making its greatest effort in Italy since the early days of the Sicilian campaign, and while this effort could not for a moment compare with the weight and power of the Allied air attack, it was enough to cause anxiety to troops and commanders who had come to take their own air supremacy for granted. The temporary air-strip constructed outside Nettuno was under continual shell-fire from the German long-range guns and had to be abandoned. At dusk the fighter cover over the Beachhead had to be withdrawn, and this was the enemy's opportunity. Raid after raid came screaming in over the shipping; the evening sky was filled with the black puffs of bursting ack-ack and the roar of diving aircraft.

The anti-aircraft defences of the port area were formidable. Every ack-ack gun on the Beachhead was controlled from a nerve-centre set up in the old Casino, where the operators brooded over their huge maps of the Beachhead laid out on tables and marked with the zones of defence. They gave their orders calmly and clearly as the hubbub of explosions and gunfire began outside; they were men withdrawn from the battle to play a skilful and deadly game of chess, placing their guns like pawns to check the attackers. But from time to time the most skilful operator could not prevent a German pilot breaking through the screen.

As dusk fell on the evening of 15 February the ships in the anchorage began to change their position in the light smoke haze that drifted out from the shore. The inevitable German reconnaissance plane had already been over, and the fleet therefore carried out its usual drill of altering the lay-out of the anchored vessels so that the raiders who were due at dusk should not have too easy a run onto their targets.

The Liberty ship *Elihu Yale* lay about half a mile off the beach discharging shells into an LCT which had come alongside. The control centre sent out its warning, the ack-ack guns on shore opened up and the tracers from the Bofors on board the ships started to stream up into the sky. A glider-bomb steered its way through the bursting 'flak' and hit the Liberty ship, which exploded with a bang that seemed to shake the waterfront for many miles. The PT boats raced to draw a veil of white smoke around the stricken ship. It flared up in its agony through the smoke, driving an enormous spreading cloud high into the darkening sky. Showers of star-shells, rockets and tracers leapt from the cloud, which rose swiftly until it towered over the whole Beachhead, a pillar of fire by night—or a warning of impending disaster?

Where could the Beachhead now turn for help in its hour of desperate need? All through the dismal days of the retreat down the Albano road General Alexander and General Clark had been rushing as many reinforcements as possible into Anzio, but they were still handicapped by the straight-jacket of LSTs. There was a limit to the number of fresh troops which could be transported to the Beachhead. Moreover, the British, after four years of full mobilization for war, were in the throes of a man-power crisis. Every available citizen had been assigned to his or her war post with a ruthless thoroughness attempted by no other nation in the Second World War, and there was no large untapped pool of man-power on which the British Army could draw such as still existed in the United States. When they met in Italy General Sir Ronald Adam, the British Adjutant-General, told General Clark that replacements were so lacking 'that he was breaking up divisions in the British Army at the rate of one division every two months in order to use the men as replacements for the other units committed to action'. The British divisions in Italy could look to no such constant flow of reinforcements as nurtured the American divisions, yet it was precisely the British units in Anzio which most needed reinforcing.

The 56th (London) Division, under Major-General Gerald Templer, had already begun to arrive, and its 168th Brigade had been immediately rushed into action. Now the second brigade was ashore, and the third was due in by 21 February. But the gallant 56th would have been the first to admit that they were hardly the fresh blood that the Beachhead so urgently required, for they were in need of rest and refreshment themselves. They had been in action for months, in the preliminary advance to the Gustav Line and in the fighting across the Lower Garigliano; they were withdrawn from the frying-pan of the Cassino front, rushed into LSTs and flung into the fire of Anzio. They fought magnificently —the Beachhead would not have held without them—but they were as weak in numbers as the 1st Division and harassed by the same problems of replacing their casualties.

General Clark turned to this southern front which the 56th had just left. Could Cassino, for whose benefit the Anzio adventure had been launched, come to the aid of the Beachhead? There was bitter irony in this: the rescuer was now himself in desperate need of rescue. But the Fifth Army had divided itself into two sections, separated by seventy miles of sea, mountains and determined enemies, and neither section had the strength to help the other.

The Southern Front, goaded once again into attack, did its best, and the Second Battle of Cassino began. It was no more successful than the First. In the very nature of things, this was bound to be so. Fresh troops had been brought across from the Adriatic Front of the Eighth Army including the Indians, British and New Zealanders of General Freyberg's Second New Zealand Corps, but the ground over which they had to advance was the same impossible rocky mountain which had broken the hearts of every division which had fought there since January.

Worse still, the Germans who defended that ground had been elated by their repulse of the Allies; they were confident, well dug in and ready for the next attack behind improved positions. The pill-boxes around Cassino were stronger than in January, the minefields deeper, and the thickets of barbed wire more impenetrable. Over all loomed the Monastery, still unscarred by war, the only structure standing in a waste land that stretched for miles. It had almost a hypnotic influence on the men dying at its feet. As Fred Majdalany put it in his moving book on Cassino:

Because of the extraordinary extent to which the summit of Monte Cassino dominated the valleys: because of the painful constancy with which men were picked off by accurately observed gunfire whenever they were forced to move in daylight within its seemingly inescapable view: because of the obsessive theatrical manner in which it towered over the scene, searching every inch of it, the building set upon that summit had become the embodiment of resistance and its tangible symbol.[1]

The Germans may not have occupied it—all the evidence is that they respected its sacred precincts—but psychologically the Monastery had become the Enemy of the attackers; it was therefore destroyed.

On 15 February it was blasted by a great force of Allied bombers, many of which had flown from distant bases in Sicily and North Africa. Again that baneful tie between Beachhead and Southern Front bedevilled the operation and brought it to naught. Anzio was threatened, the Germans were about to renew their drive down the Albano Road, and everyone knew that, this time, it was the final all-out effort to push General Lucas's force into the sea. Every aircraft that could fly would be wanted in the air over Anzio. The Monastery had to be smashed quickly to free the air effort to help the Beachhead. Therefore on the clear, cold morning of 15 February at 9.30 a.m. the first of the heavy bombers appeared over Monte Cassino and the first bombs crashed down onto the cathedral church and cloisters of the ancient abbey of St. Benedict. All through the morning and into the afternoon the martyrdom of the Monastery continued; the vast building was riven, split to its very heart, and its stones piled in a chaotic heap one on top of the other. But as the dust storm died down it was not the attackers who advanced to occupy the ruins which had now been converted by the bombing into defensive positions. The bitter need of Anzio had brought the bombing forward by a day, but this was an Air Force operation and the authorities forgot to tell the battalion of the Royal Sussex Regiment attached to the 4th Indian Division. As their colonel said, 'They told the enemy and they told the monks, but they didn't tell me!' By the time the men of the Royal Sussex were ready to rush across the narrow neck of mountain to the Monastery the Germans

[1] *Cassino.*

159

were waiting in the ruins, ready to receive them. After that, no one had any confidence that the Second Battle of Cassino, which now began to fester amongst the crags of Monastery Hill and on the outskirts of Cassino Town, would have any effect on Anzio. It had been rather the other way round.

The Beachhead defenders now stood grimly to their guns, in the knowledge that, in the ultimate hour, they must fall back on their own courage, on those secret springs of hope that they had never really lost, on the terrible yet strangely inspiring knowledge that there was now nowhere to which they could retreat.

8

The Crisis

The Big Push, the Supreme Offensive, the All-out Drive! The very words, pregnant with visions of overwhelming masses of field-grey infantry and tanks sweeping forward under a hurricane of shells to tear apart the enemy defences and drive relentlessly to beaches crowded with panic-stricken fugitives, had power to engender a mood of confidence in all ranks of the German army. At last they had the Anglo-Americans where they wanted them—with their backs to the grey, unfriendly sea. The weary days of endless retreat were over. This time, surely, the advantage lay, without any shadow of doubt, with the long-suffering German soldiers.

They had already accomplished so much! They had weathered the storm of the surprise landing and had pushed the enemy back to within sight of his last-ditch defences. They had defied the much vaunted air superiority of the Allies and concentrated more forces by land at the critical point than the Fifth Army could bring in by sea.

All through the recent fighting, the preliminary sparring for position, the Italian night had been restless far behind the line with the sound of great convoys moving down from the North. Supplies and ammunition were piling up in the dumps close to the front. The OKW had released jealously hoarded reserves. The Luftwaffe had reappeared in a strength 'reminiscent of its past glories'. True, the stubborn defence of the Factory by the British 1st Division had imposed an irritating delay, but as Kesselring surveyed his enemy's position on the eve of the final offensive he could not help feeling that victory was not far away.

> I myself was convinced, even taking their powerful naval guns and overwhelming air superiority into consideration, that with the means available we must succeed in throwing the Allies back into the sea. I constantly kept in mind the psychological effects of their situation on the staff and troops of the American 6th Corps. Penned in as they were on the low-lying, notoriously unhealthy coast, it must have been damned unpleasant.[1]

It was only too clear to the Allies where the Germans' final blow would fall; once again they would advance down the Anzio-Albano road. Kesselring and Von Mackensen had rejected any idea of 'unhinging the Beachhead' by flank attacks along the coast. If they had adopted this course they would have had to assemble their attacking forces under the fire of the American and British Navies. The grey ships, laying out to sea ready to pour down their shells on every target that presented itself, were a firm flank guard to the harassed men on shore. The German commanders also looked at the Cisterna front and even made a feint of assembling their armoured reserves behind the ruined town. But this deceived no one. The Anzio-Albano road was as always the destined place for the life-and-death drama of the Beachhead.

Everything conspired to force attention back onto this battered bloodstained highway. Von Mackensen advised Kesselring, and Kesselring agreed, that here alone could a decision be obtained. The Factory was a perfect strong-point for concentrating tanks and the key to a small network of tracks along which the heavy Tigers could move. From Carroceto the road led directly to the sea, and an advance down it of even a few miles would split the Allies in two. The German staff observers wriggled into the narrow tunnels dug into the earth of the Carroceto embankment and carefully swept the ground before them with their binoculars. Straight ahead, lining the eastern side of the road, was a series of

---

[1] *The Memoirs of Field-Marshal Kesselring.*

damp, level fields. The wadi country still made the going difficult for both armies to the west, but here at last lay some miles of flat land over which tanks might pass. The fields stretched as far as the Flyover, and behind this battered bridge the Germans saw something else which gave them brisk satisfaction. They could now look straight at the Padiglione woodlands. In this soggy, tangled area the Allies had concealed the bulk of the artillery supporting this section of the front, but the Germans were not thinking of the guns as they prospected the woods. They were seeing it through the eyes of men trained in the tactics of infiltration—this country was perfect for the job, better even than the wadis. Once in amongst those trees, nothing could stop them; the Beachhead was doomed.

The observers looked closer at the fields immediately in front of them. They were pitted with low mounds of upturned earth, like worm-casts, marking the hurriedly dug slit-trenches where the Allies, newly evicted from the Factory, had struggled to rebuild something resembling a front line. This improvised line did not look strong. There was no natural feature along which Sixth Corps could rally until the Flyover itself. The Germans felt that they were in sight of the Promised Land.

Only three short miles to go! Three miles to the Padiglione woods! And a mere three miles beyond lay the sea. The troops immediately in front of them, the troops who would have to try to stop the onslaught of the German hordes, had already been shaken by ten days of savage fighting or were new and unfamiliar with the line.

Small wonder that the staff of the Fourteenth Army allowed a new note of confidence to creep into their operational orders. Von Mackensen's final plan had a brutal simplicity and a directness of approach which generals can permit themselves only when they are certain that they have their opponent groggy, leaning against the ropes. Now was the time for him to step in and deliver a punch straight to the heart—a direct frontal attack with all the power at his command behind it. In the shelter of Carroceto and the Factory he had assembled the best part of six divisions to be flung forward in the first wave of the assault. Part of the 4th Parachute and the 65th Infantry Divisions under the First Parachute Corps, were to advance through the wadis to the west of the Anzio-Albano road while the 3rd Panzer

Grenadier Division, the 114th Light Infantry and the 715th Infantry Divisions, with elements of the Hermann Goering Panzer Division under Seventy-Sixth Corps were to drive hard over the flat fields to the east of the road. In reserve, ready to race through the gap made by the infantry, Von Mackensen had a powerful armoured force—the 26th Panzers, the 29th Panzer Grenadiers and two battalions of Panther and Tiger tanks. They would fan out in the rear echelons of Sixth Corps as they crunched their way onto the beaches. All that was now required was a swift breakthrough by the infantry. This time the German High Command had supplied more than enough cannon-fodder to be shovelled relentlessly into the furnace they were planning to create on the fields between the Factory and the Flyover, those fields marked on the map at their southern end with the grim name of Campo di Carne—'the Plain of Flesh'.

At his German headquarters, a thousand miles away from the scene of the actual fighting, Hitler inspected the plan. On such important occasions the Führer reserved for himself the final approval of all details and did not hesitate to overrule the men on the spot, altering firmly anything that was not in line with his own ideas on tactics. These ideas were by no means amateur and impractical—Hitler was no fool when it came to the business of war—but not even the greatest military genius can fight a battle by remote control. Hitler and his advisers of the OKW made two vital alterations to the plan proposed by Von Mackensen and Kesselring, neither of which had happy results.

Fourteenth Army had intended to deliver the main blow on a narrow front along the four miles which stretched from Buonriposo Ridge past Carroceto and the Factory to the watercourse of the Spaccasassi Creek near the old tower of the hamlet of Padiglione. Clearly Von Mackensen was prepared to widen the assault if, for example, it met with unexpected success in the wadi country. Hitler made the plan rigidly inflexible—there was to be no spreading, no danger of dissipating German strength in side-issues. The blow must be concentrated, overwhelming, ruthless, a massive demonstration that Germany still had it within her power to strike back with impressive fire.

To the van of the attack, almost as if to symbolize its importance, Hitler sent from Germany a special regiment, the Infantry Lehr Regiment, a demonstration unit composed of approved Nazis. Kesselring accepted them on the assurance of the OKW that this was a unit of high quality. He placed them in the line just to the east of the Factory at a point where he hoped to achieve decisive results on the first day.

The attack would not begin till 0630 hours, for the new units were unfamiliar with the ground and could not be re-lied on to find their way in the dark. The old tactics of infil-tration at night, which had paid the Germans so well, were now to be abandoned on much of the front in favour of the massive infantry advance at dawn, supported by overwhelm-ing artillery fire. The alteration in tactics contained the seeds of danger.

For the moment, however, all seemed well. The Germans had a superiority in heavy artillery, the Luftwaffe reap-peared in the skies to hearten the veterans and the newcom-ers to the Anzio front were subjected to a strong propaganda barrage designed to bring their morale to the highest pitch. They were told that their advance would be supported by new, secret weapons, that the Allies were shattered and ready to re-embark, that this was to be the supreme effort which would make Europe safe from invasion. It is easy to be ironic about some of the orders of the day issued to the German troops before the attack. Propaganda is only justi-fied by success, and some of the Allies' pronouncements just before the original landing did not read so well after we had been a few weeks ashore. The German commanders sent their men into battle in the most confident spirit. Only three miles to the woodlands of Padiglione, and the Beachhead would fall!

After one or two postponements the all-out, final attack on the Beachhead was fixed for 16 February.

Sixth Corps could not be certain of the exact date and time of the German assault, but no one at Anzio doubted that it would not be long before the storm broke on the defenders of the Beachhead's last ditch.

General Lucas struggled to strengthen his line. Fifth Army helped him as best it could—reinforcements, ammuni-tion and supplies were hurried to the Beachhead, but there was a limit to the amount of material which could be brought in. There was never enough shipping to meet all Sixth Corps' demands. Lucas was only too conscious that he had weaknesses in his defences: he looked anxiously to the threatened sector astride the vital Anzio-Albano road.

The British 1st Division, after their long ordeal, were now officially out of the line, but the Divisional Commander knew only too well that he had tired units still fighting: the divisional artillery still remained massed in the woodlands and never went out of action. The sector held by the 1st was now divided between the American 45th Infantry Division under General Eagles and the British 56th Division under General Templer. The 45th took the four miles that stretched from Padiglione to the area astride the Anzio-Albano road, with the 180th Regimental Combat Team out on the right flank, the 179th in the centre in front of the dangerous strong-point of the German-held Factory and the 157th RCT, under Colonel John H. Church, dug in, as best it might, in the wadi country just south of Buonriposo Ridge and across the key road itself.

The 45th was still reasonably fresh; it had not been heavily engaged as yet in the Anzio fighting and although the 179th RCT had been used in the late abortive counter-attack to regain the Factory, the Division as a whole had escaped the savage maulings suffered by the 1st British and the American 3rd. The three RCTs of which it was composed—an RCT is the equivalent of a British brigade—had received adequate reinforcements.

The British 56th Division, which now took over the tangle of wadis stretching westward from the southern end of Buonriposo Ridge towards the sea, had not been so fortunate. We have seen how its brigades had been arriving at the Beachhead at irregular intervals—the 168th had already been flung into the thick of the fighting, the 167th had arrived on the 13th and was immediately hurried up into the wadi country, while the 169th arrived only as the German attack started. The 56th was tired and strained after incessant fighting on the Cassino front. With no pause for rest it was rushed straight into the crisis of Anzio.

On these two divisions—the British 56th and the American 45th—the full weight of the German offensive was about to fall. Behind them General Lucas had only the tired British 1st Division in reserve, and the American 1st Armored as a possible counter-attacking force. The defence of the rest of the Beachhead perimeter—a very wide stretch indeed—demanded the whole of the remaining troops at his command if it was to be safely held. The 3rd Division and the

Special Service Force defended the great curve in front of Cisterna round to the Mussolini Canal and the sea. Lucas could not withdraw anything from this eastern flank to support his centre. He had placed all his available reserves behind the danger-point. He could only pray that his line would hold.

Afterwards men remembered that the hours before the dawn of 16 February had been unusually quiet. Not a sound came from the German lines, not a shot was fired and nothing moved behind the Allied front. These strange, unnerving periods of silence always seemed to prelude the great set-piece attacks of this war. It was as if the house-lights were being lowered in the theatre; the hum of talk died away and the audience held its breath waiting for the quick tap of the conductor's baton. It came—the sharp crack of a field-gun firing from behind the Factory—and then the whole overwhelming orchestra of the German artillery opened up with a crash that seemed to drive in the ear-drums. The light strengthened and the storm of shells increased with it; our own guns joined in and the Germans strove to smash them with counter-battery fire. The front line became covered with clouds of drifting smoke as the German shells burst on our positions. From 0600 to 0630 the thunder of the guns rolled over the Beachhead. From their dug-outs and fox-holes far behind the front, from ruined farms and from the broken, flat-roofed villas of Anzio and Nettuno themselves, men came out and stood to look towards the north, towards the Alban Hills and the great grey cloud rising from fields around the Factory. There was no need to ask anyone what had happened. Not a man on the Beachhead who did not realize that 'This was IT.'

The first reports began to come in. At 0630 attacks had developed all along the perimeter of the Beachhead—there were six against the American 3rd Division alone—but it was soon clear that the main drive was being made, exactly where Sixth Corps felt it would be, down the Anzio-Albano road. The Germans came in closely packed waves with their tanks in support. They took terrific losses, but their sheer weight of numbers told. The tanks, in addition, could use the Factory as cover from which they could sally to pour fire, almost at point-blank range, on the forward American positions and to which they could easily retire to replenish their

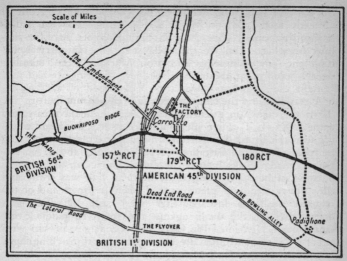

THE BEGINNING OF THE FINAL GERMAN ASSAULT, 16 FEBRUARY 1944

ammunition. The forward defences of the 179th RCT began to crumble. The calls for artillery support became desperate as the morning went on. Men in isolated fox-holes, or surrounded in farm-houses with no hope of escape, called also on their reserves of courage and almost against their own will performed deeds of strange, unexpected valour.

The Beachhead artillery now flung all the weight of its formidable fire-power into the battle. The Germans were advancing in the open and were vulnerable to shell-fire. The Allies, even before the attack, fired ten times the number of rounds that came from the German guns. The enemy infantry, again and again, collapsed under the storm of bursting shells. It was gunfire that, by mid-afternoon of the 16th had destroyed the morale and reputation of the Infantry Lehr unit on which Hitler had set such store. As they struggled forward against the 179th RCT positions south of the Factory they were caught by a devastating concentration of Allied gunfire. Their officers were killed, the men wavered and finally broke, refusing to face the storm and hurrying back in confusion to the rear. Says Kesselring, 'The regiment was thrown back disgracefully.' But what else could have been expected from the 'poor devils' flung into real battle for the first time? The 179th RCT thanked its stars for the short breather given by the collapse of the Infantry Lehr Regiment, but Kesselring and Von Mackensen had reason for disappointment about that first day's fighting. It had not brought the signs for which they had hoped of a crack in the Allied line and the beginnings of a break-through.

The Germans, on the whole, had been held on the sector of the 179th RCT. They met with more success farther west.

The German artillery fire had been particularly heavy on the front of the 2nd Battalion, 157th RCT, astride the Anzio-Albano road. Tanks helped the enemy forward, but after a morning of heavy fighting the American line was still basically intact although platoons had been overrun and some forward positions lost. Farther west still the Germans pushed through the wadis against the 167th Brigade of the British 56th Division. The forward companies of the 8th Royal Fusiliers and the 7th Oxfordshire and Buckinghamshire Light Infantry were overrun. At one point a few companies of Germans taking advantage of the confusion of watercourses that patterned the whole countryside in this complicated area, worked their way southward until they actually reached the lateral road running from the Flyover towards the mouth of the Moletta River. British tanks raced along the road to round up the intruders. Later, a strong counter-attack wiped out the wedge the Germans had driven into the front of the 56th Division.

Again the result of the first day's fighting had been indecisive—the Allies had been subjected to a severe ordeal, the German gunfire had been terrible and the weight of their infantry attacks impressive, but the Beachhead front had not been broken.

Then came the night and with it a swift change for the worse in the fortunes of the Anglo-American forces. Night had always been the Germans' opportunity at Anzio. They had won their earlier successes by infiltration, by skilful penetration of the unoccupied ground left of necessity between the forward companies of battalions forced to defend a wide front with few men. Now the Germans had the men —enough and to spare—to infiltrate in a massive way.

Just before midnight the German 715th Infantry Division launched a strong force which penetrated between the right flank of the 157th RCT and the left companies of the 179th. Throughout the night the Germans closed in on the Americans across the Anzio-Albano road, and, in spite of the desperate attempts of three tanks firing point-blank to hold them off, the enemy decimated the unhappy company defending this vital point. The survivors struggled westward under the cover of smoke to take shelter in the wadis. They had left the road clear for the Germans. When dawn came a dangerous gap was exposed between the 157th and the 179th RCTs. Von Mackensen and Kesselring had at last got that crack in the Beachhead defences for which they had fought so hard the previous day.

They lost no time in exploiting it. Now the Allies learnt with bitterness how serious a loss they had sustained when the 1st Division had been driven out of the Factory and Carroceto, for behind the massive walls of Aprilia and the embankment of Carroceto the German Fourteenth Army could conceal any amount of unpleasant surprises. At 0740 thirty-five aircraft swept low over the forward positions of the 45th Division, bombing and machine-gunning; swift on their heels a powerful force of infantry, backed by tanks—over sixty were used before dusk fell that day—was launched from the firm base of the Factory and Carroceto. One column struck south-east down the dirt track that led towards the Spaccasassi Creek and the hamlet of Padiglione, the other, the most dangerous column, pushed straight down the main road into the vacuum left by the withdrawal of the flank company of the 175th RCT during the night.

The Germans were thrusting a complete brigade into this crack in the American defences, using it as a lever to split apart the whole front across the Anzio-Albano road. If they could widen this gap during the day's fighting they would have obtained room to deploy their armour, now waiting eagerly in reserve for the moment when the infantry would have made an opening big enough for the tanks to pour towards the Flyover and the Padiglione woodlands behind it.

Within an hour the Germans succeeded in both widening and deepening the gap to a startling degree. The forces advancing down the main road swung eastward and caught battalions holding the right section of the 179th RCT front in the flank; a brigade suddenly fell upon one battalion. The 2nd Battalion of the 179th RCT disintegrated, overwhelmed almost before it could do a thing about it. The companies were isolated, smoke blotted out the battlefield, the German tanks seemed everywhere and the tidings of disaster poured in upon the headquarters of 45th Division.

At 0855 this was the unnerving position of the 45th. The remnants of the 2nd Battalion were trying to reform along what was called by the Allies the Dead End Road (a dirt track leading from the main road for some hundred yards eastwards to end in the fields north of the Flyover), while the 3rd Battalion was straining every nerve to keep in touch with the battered 2nd. A huge bulge, two miles wide and two miles deep, had been driven into the heart of the Allies' defences along the vital Anzio-Albano road. For the first time a chill doubt penetrated Sixth Corps Headquarters: if the Germans' advance went on at this speed it would only be a matter of hours before the Flyover and the final defence line were overwhelmed.

General Lucas had, since the beginning of the German attack, clamoured for the strongest possible air support. General Clark had done his best to get him every aircraft available in Italy. This had not been as easy a job as might be imagined—the cries for help from Anzio could be answered only by twisting the Allied air effort in Italy out of its carefully planned shape. The heavy bombers, in particular, had been sent to Italy in order to take part in Operation Pointblank, the long-range bombardment of the big manufacturing centres of Southern Germany, and to the air experts it seemed absurd to divert these aircraft, constructed for a specific purpose, to a job of close-support bombing for which they were not designed or suitable. But the Beachhead was in danger: General Clark was desperate and persuasive. He had already told General Saville, commanding 12th Air Support Command:

> I know that concentrations of enemy troops and material are not conditional targets for the Strategic Air Force, but the fact is that ball-bearing factories and rail junctions in Northern Italy are not going to have any effect on the battle of Anzio for a few days. The German troops are already in Anzio, and their equipment is there and I would like to hit them with everything we've got.[1]

[1] *Calculated Risk.*

The Air Force stifled its misgivings and flung every aircraft at its command into the skies over Anzio. This, incidentally, meant that as far as the Air was concerned the Cassino Front had to be left to take care of itself. On 15 February, the day before the German attack at Anzio, the Monastery had been split apart by the biggest bombing effort yet seen in Italy: two days later not an aircraft could be seen over the hills around Monte Cassino, everything that could fly was swarming over the Beachhead. The heavy B-17 Flying Fortresses and the B-24 Liberators, the Mitchell and Marauders Medium bombers, the armed reconnaissance planes and the Wellingtons, all concentrated on Campoleone and the Albano road: they unloaded the greatest weight of bombs dropped so far in the war in direct support of an army.

The troops, pinned to the ground by enemy fire, had no chance to look up, but they heard the roar of engines overhead and were comforted. One Flying Fortress was hit and limped towards the harbour at Anzio, losing height every mile. Its engines hiccupped as it scraped over the housetops of the villas on the edge of the bay. It came lower and lower; now it was skimming the sea, and as it touched the surface of the water it staggered like a wounded bird trying to alight. Its forward engines hit the sea first and flung up a white fountain of spray. Then for a moment the aircraft lay waterlogged with the men climbing hurriedly out onto the wing. Seven little black dots standing in a row as the wings sank lower and lower; then the tail tipped up and the whole lot were thrown into the sea. Half the boats in Anzio harbour circled around, fishing for the seven black specks.

In cold blood the heavies may not have done vital damage to the Germans forming up on the ground; they were never designed for such a close-support job. The bursting bombs were a terrifying sight, the whole earth below the bombers seemed to be in constant eruption, but somehow or other the advancing Germans still emerged from the smoke. General Ritter von Pohl, Kesselring's anti-aircraft expert, noted:

I personally witnessed the concentrated approach of the Allied bombers to the German positions crowded around Nettuno, executed with minute precision. The density of the hail of bombs on these positions, which even in our opinion were most vulnerable, led us to expect the complete annihilation of the unit under attack. However, on entering such a position immediately after the bombardment, one would find that aside from a few exceptions, the guns, the machine guns and the observation instruments were intact and that even the effect on the men's morale wore off after the initial experience.[1]

Frankly, no one on the Beachhead on that critical morning of 17 February stopped to analyse the precise effect of the bombing: every piece of high explosive flung at the enemy, from whatever quarter, was of value to the hard-pressed defenders.

In addition to the bombers General Clark now sent a telegram to the Beachhead which in the long run seemed to many at Anzio to promise an even more important effect than the Air Force on the fortunes of the Allies. General Truscott, the commander of the American 3rd Division, had turned in early after the fighting on the first day of the great German attack, satisfied that his front was intact and that the main weight of the German blow was not falling on his sector. Just after midnight Colonel Carleton shook him awake, saying, 'Boss, I hate to do this, but you would give us hell if I held this until next morning.' Truscott sat up, rubbed his eyes and read this message from General Clark: '. . . Major-General Truscott relieved from command of 3rd Division and assigned as deputy commander Sixth Corps. Brigadier-General O'Daniels to command 3rd Division. . . .'

The blow that General Lucas had feared, ever since the early days of the landing, was about to fall—this was the first step on the way to his replacement. General Clark, he felt, had yielded to the pressure of General Alexander and the British, who had been opposed from the beginning to the Lucas policy of cautiously building up the Beachhead and who had become increasingly critical of the way he was handling his corps. But Clark had by this time come to agree with Alexander about the need for a change and was prepared to shoulder the responsibility of ultimately removing Lucas from his command. He wrote in his Memoirs:

My own feeling was that Johnny Lucas was ill—tired physically and mentally—from the long responsibilities of command in battle: he died a few years later. I said that I would not in any circumstances do anything to

[1] Article in *US Journal of Military Affairs*, Vol. XVII.

hurt the man who had contributed so greatly to our successes since Salerno and our drive northward to Anzio.[1]

Truscott had no ambition to succeed Lucas: he declared that he was willing to serve him loyally in any subordinate capacity and he was well aware that Lucas felt he was the victim of a British intrigue and that Truscott was being used to 'pull someone else's chestnuts from the fire'. But the Beachhead was in danger, there was no time for argument and Truscott was sure of one thing—he could help to buttress up morale, help to bring much needed confidence into the higher command at Anzio.

For on that early afternoon of 17 February, things looked black to the men at Sixth Corps. Their General was conscious of the veiled disapproval of his superiors, a great bulge had been driven into their front within a matter of hours, German shells had knocked out the fighter strip at Nettuno, and the artillery spotter's planes were being swept out of the sky. No wonder that when the Corps Chief of Staff telephoned 3rd Division to inquire when Truscott would report at Corps HQ he added gloomily that he wasn't at all certain if there would be a HQ to which to report by next morning—they would all have been driven into the sea.

When Truscott did report at about half-past one that afternoon he found that there was ample cause for gloom in every message received from the front: the Germans were preparing to enlarge the bulge, 180th RCT were now under pressure on the eastern jaw of the salient; the 2nd Battalion 159th RCT were almost cut off on the western flank and two German tanks had actually pushed straight down the main road to the Flyover itself before they had been knocked out by our anti-tank guns. Lucas had ordered part of the 1st Division back from the rest they had fondly hoped for in the rear areas and placed them in charge of a last-hope 'stop line' around the Flyover immediately behind the heavily engaged 179th RCT General Penney had, as a matter of fact, already anticipated the order and had notified General Eagles that he was going to move into the area. Someone had indeed to hold it at all costs, for the defences were crumbling rapidly in front of the Flyover. The 1st Loyals tramped stolidly up the road, turned off into the muddy fields and started to dig

[1] *Calculated Risk.*

their slit trenches in the damp ground. The German shells fell around them as they dug and a white smoke-screen drifted across from the wadis. The Loyals went on digging grimly: it would not be long before their trenches would be needed.

Lucas had also ordered a counter-attack: Harmon was to send tanks past the Flyover straight up the road to help the 157th RCT and Eagles was to launch a night-attack to restore the line of the broken battalions of the 179th. At Corps Truscott now felt that he was surrounded by a feeling of hopelessness and desperation, for no news had been received of Harmon, Eagles or Penney for some time and everyone feared the worst. 'No liaison officers had gone up to see,' says Truscott. 'My optimistic assurance that nothing ever looked as bad on the ground as it did on a map at Headquarters did little to dispel the pall-like gloom.'[1] The truth was that, for the moment, General Lucas and some of the high-ups at Sixth Corps, after the prolonged strain of the last few days, had used up their reserves of resilience: they were mentally tired and found it hard to believe that events could ever again take a favourable turn. They had lived for over a fortnight in an atmosphere of frustrated hope, and now the Germans were assailing their last-ditch defences. What was there in the present scene to feel optimistic about?

Throughout the 17th and into the early hours of the 18th February, the tidings of woe continued to pour in. Harmon's tanks did not succeed in getting far; the ground was damp, they had perforce to stay on the main road which was now being remorselessly swept by German gunfire; by the afternoon they were back behind the Flyover. The night counter-attack of the 45th Division fared worse. The battalions which were scheduled to make it had been badly battered during the day, shaken by the German breakthrough and pushed back down the road and over the muddy fields between Carroceto and the Flyover. Now in the darkness they were going to try to fight back over the ground they had lost. The 3rd Battalion of the 179th had already been reduced to 274 men, and the 2nd Battalion was in no better state. The only comparatively fresh unit that was available to General Eagles was the 3rd Battalion of the 157th, which was to attack up the road on the left and try to restore the situation on the left-hand side of the bulge.

[1] Truscott, *Command Missions*.

Any officer who has tried to drive his men forward again after a day of gruelling retreat, to attack an enemy who is rushing up reinforcements, will know exactly what the American infantryman was now up against. There was no question of attacking with confident gusto; this was going to be a dreary slog forward, with no expectation of success, in a darkness full of menace under a leaden sky threatening rain, with no reinforcements to hearten the troops when they reached their objective. They did not reach it. The marvel was that they got as far as they did—a few hundred yards beyond the Dead End Road, the last turning off the main road before the Flyover, and about a thousand yards in front of it.

The Germans were already at the western end of the Dead End Road, preparing for their dawn attack; there were plenty of them, fresh and confident. When the American advance struck them the situation, in the words of the official report, 'became confused'; in other words the night was now a wild mix-up of tracer bullets, bewildered men flopping hurriedly into shell-holes, shouts, the crump of bursting shells, the sudden uprush of flares and the sinister clanking of tanks moving in the darkness. When the dawn came the battalions of the 170th were cut off from communication with their headquarters, they were desperately trying to reorganise themselves in unfavourable positions and the Germans were ready to launch their final all-out effort against Anzio. The supreme crisis—'the moment of truth' for the Beachhead—had arrived.

Early on the morning of that fateful 18th day of February I had crawled to the edge of the woodlands to look out over the Flyover. Everything was smoke and chaos. Tanks were firing amongst the scrub, white clouds from shell-bursts vomited in the soggy fields. The sky was rainy—no hope of heavy air support today, only the light stuff. A roar of aircraft overhead—fighters! A Spitfire plummeted down like a gannet diving. A sickening crash and another life gone. We hunched ourselves close to the ground, as the Focke-Wulfs raced over to send machine-gun bullets hissing around us; then a giant spray of bomb-bursts was ruled in a straight line across the ground ahead. Our guns went on coughing out ginger smoke from their gun-pits amongst the trees. We crawled back and drove in our jeep through the dripping trees towards the headquarters of 45th Division. Our nerves were on edge and it was reassuring to meet the G2, calm, unhurried and smoking his pipe. 'No, sir,' he said, 'we've not got a clear picture. Maybe we won't get one for a bit. Things are a bit confused up at the front this morning. Maybe we'll have to write off the 179th Regiment. Nothing has come in from them for a time.' And he led us across to the map.

There it was, outlined in china pencil on the plastic covering for all to see—the plight of the Beachhead! A huge bulge was strongly marked in the middle of the Allies' defensive perimeter. It stretched down the main road almost to the Flyover and expanded eastwards in a disconcerting manner. At the base of the bulge near the Flyover itself and the lateral road that led across it, the 1st Loyals were marked in position, the back-stop, the last-ditch hope. The remnants of one of the companies of the battered 2nd Battalion 157th RCT were still entrenched just in front of the bridge, with smaller bodies of Americans scattered westward towards the wadis.

The eastern curve of the bulge was held by the 179th RCT, or at least so it was marked on the map. But these tired, broken units could not form a firm line. Here all was uncertainty: no news had come from the regiment for some hours and no one knew how many men had rallied or got back to their battalion.

But the critical points of the bulge, even more important than the base along the Flyover, were the two shoulders—as long as these could be firmly held there was hope. The Germans had got far, but they still needed more space to manoeuvre, a wider penetration of the Allied front to allow the full deployment of their armour and reserves. But on that damp, cold morning of the 18th no one was certain, at the HQ of the 45th Division, that the shoulders could be held. They had been under heavy pressure all night, and the Germans were back at their old game of infiltration. Everything depended upon the steadfastness of the American infantrymen, grimly holding the shoulders of the bulge.

The right or eastern shoulder was being defended by the 2nd Battalion 180th RCT. So far the battalion had beaten off all attacks, but the Germans were obviously going to turn their attention to its liquidation in no uncertain manner. The western shoulder was manned by the 2nd Battalion 157th RCT. It had already suffered losses when the Germans broke through on the 16th. One of the companies of the 157th—

176

the 1st Company—had been driven back down the main road and was dug in precariously almost in front of the Flyover. The rest had been pushed westward from the main road and were now holding out in the wadi country, with headquarters established in a group of small caves, the battalion rolling itself into a ball like a hedgehog, prickles outward. The Germans infiltrated behind 2nd Battalion, communications were cut and again and again the enemy got close enough to shower grenades into the gullies almost on top of the defenders.

But the battalion had a commander, Lieutenant-Colonel Laurence C. Brown, who refused to allow himself to be dismayed. He turned the caves into a fortress, ignoring the fact that he was completely cut off from his base and from his British allies of the 56th Division to the west. He settled down to fight a private war—he was destined to fight it for nearly six days—and to hold the western shoulder at all costs.

On the morning of the 18th no one yet knew of Colonel Brown's determination or could judge his quality: the news or rather the lack of news, from his sector looked ominous. For good measure we now heard that General Penney had been wounded in the night and that General Templer had taken over command of both the 56th and the 1st Divisions. Penney was out of action for four days. The Beachhead had never seemed in such a sorry plight. Soon after dawn the Germans attacked, and the agony of this most desperate of days began.

Kesselring and Von Mackensen had not got the width of penetration they needed, but they had the depth. The Dead End Road area was only a thousand yards or so in front of the Flyover, the Lateral Road and the woodlands. A thousand yards over level ground—and before them a small company of the 157th, the 1st Loyals and the tired, disorganized 179th RCT. Once across that thousand yards and they would be into the woodlands! It seemed to the German High Command that victory was now very near. Their troops had suffered severely in the first two days of the attack, but with one tremendous effort they must surely burst through the bottom of the bulge and split the last defensive line of the Beachhead. There was, it is true, the difficulty of space; the German attacking troops were penned into a narrow area and

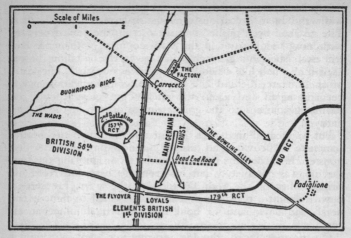

THE CRISIS ON THE ALBANO ROAD, 18 FEBRUARY 1944

the Allied guns were being presented with remarkable targets, but given enough weight behind the attack the Flyover must fall. Fourteenth Army packed everything it had into this final punch straight down the Anzio-Albano road. They were ready to be thrown into the cauldron, as the day wore on, the whole of the 721st, 741st and 735th Infantry Regiments, the 309th and 29th Panzer Grenadier Regiments, and, later on, in the crisis of the battle, they used their final reserve—hoarded for the exploitation of the break-through —elements of the 26th Panzer and the 29th Panzer Grenadier Divisions.

The morning went badly for the defenders. The first German attacks cut through the disorganized 179th RCT. Tanks moved down the Bowling Alley on the left flank and came on in strength down the main road. The German big guns registered onto the Flyover bridge and blew huge craters out of the swampy ground. The enemy got within a swift rush of the bridge and surged around the 1st Company, in its isolated defensive ring before the Flyover, attacking in hundreds. Some got as far as the Loyals manning their last-ditch line on the Lateral Road.

Out on the shoulders the 2nd Battalion 157th RCT had to

beat off the most determined attack yet made on its position, while the 180th on the eastern shoulder was pushed half a mile towards the east. Company G received no orders to withdraw, and stayed fighting where it was. The enemy had still not succeeded in driving in the shoulders of the bulge.

And all the while the Allied artillery poured its hurricane of shells into the area of the German attack. Never had it been presented with such a target. The ground was level, the enemy had no cover under which to form up such as he had enjoyed in the wadis or near the Factory. The last thousand yards to victory were the hardest and bitterest part of the journey. For every shell fired by the Germans the Allied guns could reply with fifteen or twenty. As the day wore on the battle seemed to be reducing itself to one simple proposition—would the German infantry have enough strength to push through the shell storm and swamp the Allied defenders? Could the German command keep shovelling its men remorselessly forward—into the mincing-machine of the Allied artillery? Until the late afternoon of 18 February it seemed as if the German will to victory would carry them through. Now the field-grey tide had surged up to the Flyover and the Lateral Road itself. The Loyals were fighting hand to hand in their slit trenches, and behind them the men of the RASC and REME had dropped stretchers and spanners and were looking along their rifle sights preparing for the worst.

As their men fought, the generals debated. Crisis was upon them and they still differed over what was to be done. That morning, as the Germans drove their spearheads over the fields before the Flyover, General Truscott and General Lucas argued on the keypoint of Allied defences—was this the time to throw in the last Corps reserves in a counter-attack? Truscott, vigorous, still confident and determined on action, pressed the need for a counter-attack as soon as possible. There were still resources left on the Beachhead to mount one—Harmon had his 6th Armored Infantry and his tanks, the British 169th Infantry Brigade of 56th Division was due to disembark at Anzio Harbour that very morning, Truscott had withdrawn the 30th Infantry Regiment from 3rd Division before he himself had joined Corps and Eagles still had a battalion of the 157th Infantry in Divisional reserve. There was also the tired remains of 1st Division, which were yet game to the last. This all added up to a worth-while force. Why not use it, backed with the weight of the Allied artillery?

Lucas still hesitated. He stuck to the theme that had haunted him ever since the German advance began—there was worse to come. He clung to the insurance of his 1st Armored, and feared to risk his last powerful striking force. Truscott pressed him hard. If this was not the time to risk everything, when was it? If we did not strike now there would soon be no Beachhead to save.

General Clark joined the group and listened to the debate. He asked first what Sixth Corps had left with which to counter-attack and how soon it could be organized. Truscott firmly stated, 'Tomorrow morning.' 'General Clark,' reports Truscott, 'placed his fingers on the shoulder of the salient on the map which lay before us. Then in a somewhat pontifical manner reminiscent of an instructor at a service school, he remarked, "You should hold these shoulders firmly and then counter-attack against the flanks of the salient." '[1]

It is always a little irritating to hard-pressed soldiers who have been harassed by a problem day after day to be given a glimpse of the obvious by their superior. Truscott and Lucas would have been delighted to have been able to hold the shoulders of their salient firmly—but at the moment the 2nd Battalion 157th RCT was lost from view, surrounded by Germans. Sixth Corps could only hope and pray that this shoulder would hold long enough for them to mount the attack under discussion.

Clark, however, gave his support to the idea, and reluctantly Lucas agreed. The plan was simple. Force T, under General Templer, was to strike north from the Flyover to establish contact once again with 2nd Battalion 157th RCT. This column would be made up of the 169th Brigade, which, as the 168th and the 167th had done before them, would thus go into action as soon as it landed. Force H, under Harmon, would have the 30th Infantry, the 6th Armored Infantry and the 1st Armored Division Tanks. This would strike up the Bowling Alley towards the end of the Dead End Road. General Clark promised the biggest air effort he could organize. Harmon and Templer set off immediately to begin their planning, and Clark drove with Truscott to General

[1] *Command Missions.*

Eagles's headquarters.

It was then that Clark broke the news to Truscott that, in a few days' time, he was to succeed to the command of Sixth Corps. Truscott did not relish the news; he was not blind to Lucas's faults, but he felt that he was in a good position as Deputy to advise and guide his Corps Commander and wondered if a change at this critical time, with the Beachhead on the verge of disaster in the eyes of some waverers, was a good thing for morale. Clark replied that he appreciated Truscott's reactions and that he did not wish to hurt Lucas; the change would wait until the crisis was over. All Truscott had to do was to make certain he had a Beachhead to command when the change came!

In every battle there comes a turning-point, a critical hour when victory hesitates to declare itself, when it seems as if even the smallest extra effort will turn the scales for one side or the other. So it seemed to the Germans towards the end of that savage 18 February. One final punch and they would be through the Sixth Corps defence line. They brought up their reserves and committed tanks of their armoured force in support.

The tanks drove straight down the Bowling Alley until they were stopped by a blown bridge near Carroceto. But they blasted away at the men of the 180th RCT holding the vital shoulder of the salient, and the infantry sought to find a way around the defenders. They were held with difficulty. But the fiercest drive came once again down the Anzio-Albano road, the main axis of the German attack. They flung wave after wave of infantry supported by tanks against the 1st Loyals and the 1st Battalion 179th RCT, which held the line to the right of the Loyals. It was now a battle against time. Could the Germans break through before the Allies mounted their counter-attack?

Darkness fell and still the issue was not decided. The Allied artillery fired relentlessly into the small patch of bombed and churned-up earth between the Dead End Road and the Flyover and its Lateral Road—never in the history of the Beachhead had there been such a concentration of shelling put down on such a small area. But again and again the Germans succeeded in forming up and advancing to the attack. There was hand-to-hand fighting around the actual bridge of the Flyover.

Farther back, behind the Lateral Road, the officers of the 179th RCT were rallying all stragglers, bringing them back into the line, while over the whole Beachhead small mobile groups were patrolling the main roads in the back areas—parachutists might be dropped, so our Intelligence warned Sixth Corps—to give the final touch of confusion to the Allied defences.

For a moment in the darkness the German tide ebbed at the Flyover; then at 0400 hours, in that chill unnerving time before the dawn, they came again. They overran a company of the Loyals and for a moment seemed to be about to split the battalion apart. 2nd Brigade ordered all men who could fire a weapon to be hurried forward: storemen, cooks, and drivers grasped their rifles and grenades, men of the Docks Operating Companies left their derricks and came up the Anzio road.

And then, quite suddenly, the German attack cracked. The grey-green waves did not come on: the German infantrymen, after a display of incredible endurance in the face of our artillery fire, had reached the point when flesh and blood could not stand it any more and the German command had no more reserves to shovel forward. In the dawn light the Loyals, worn but with a pride in their hearts, saw a sight which they had hardly dared to hope they might see on the Beachhead—their enemies were retreating, falling back across the bloodstained fields, falling back from the Flyover and from the last-ditch defences of the Allies, while away to their right, striking at the flank of the bulge, the American tanks were beginning to move forward under a dense smoke-screen. Our counter-attack had begun.

The fighting was, of course, by no means over. The North Staffs had now to help the Loyals clear the Germans out of the ruined farms near the Flyover in which they had fortified themselves as they retired, and this was a tough and costly business. Harmon's counter-attack had to advance without help from Task Force T, German planes had mined the harbour at Anzio, and the vital equipment needed by 167th Brigade could not be got ashore. But these difficulties seemed small beside the one great overriding fact—the Allies were counter-attacking and the Germans had ceased to advance!

The counter-attack was launched with drama and tension still in the air. The 30th Infantry marched five miles in the darkness to their jumping-off point at the shoulder of the salient: they were to advance on the right-hand flank of the Bowling Alley with the 6th Armored Infantry's 1st Battalion. The 3rd Battalion of the 6th was to push forward on the left side of the road. The tanks would rumble up the track itself. Infantry and tanks were also to swing more directly northwards on the flat ground that stretched along the Ficiocca Creek, to give a flanking support to the main thrust.

A tremendous concentration of artillery was laid on to Force H. Eight British field-artillery regiments co-ordinated their fire to sweep the ground in front of the advance, and eight battalions of Corps artillery plastered the area as well —a 'ladder barrage' Harmon's Chief of Staff christened the huge artillery effort, a storm of shells which was to pour up and down the Bowling Alley as the Task Force prepared to move.

In the mud and cold, following their guides or waiting in the darkness until hooded lights flashed them forward, the columns of tanks and infantry formed up around the ruined farms of Padiglione hamlet. The night was alive with that chaos of sounds which are inseparable from the tricky business of getting troops into the order carefully planned for zero hour. Tanks skidded awkwardly off the track, lorries revved up in muddy fields and the dark files of sweating men —each man carrying 120 rounds of ammunition and his gun —stumbling through the blackout. Away to the southward, almost, so it seemed in the darkness, directly behind them, the night sky was being split apart by the continuous flashing of the guns and the shells bursting round the Flyover. The din was endless and overpowering. The Germans were making their final effort to break the Beachhead line.

The telephone rang urgently in Harmon's headquarters. Corps were on the line: the Germans were almost over the Lateral Road, our final defensive position was about to be swamped. Harmon's men were desperately needed as soon as possible back at the Flyover. Harmon protested vigorously. He could not possibly get back in time to affect the battle, and his infantry had already marched miles through the mud and darkness to get to their jumping-off point at Padiglione. What sense was there now in sending them marching off again in a new direction? Corps must stick to the plan and take the risk that the Loyals and the 179th RCT would hold at the base of the salient while Harmon struck boldly at the

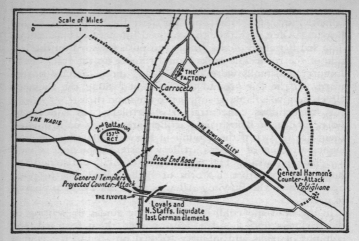

THE ALLIED COUNTER-ATTACK, 19-20 FEBRUARY 1944

shoulder. Boldness pays in danger. Corps agreed, and Harmon went on with his preparations.

Then, just before zero hour, he was confronted with the need to make another agonizing decision. In the general uncertainty that now surrounded the Beachhead no one could be confident that the exact position of every American unit had been correctly marked on the map. The Germans were swarming everywhere and communications had been cut again and again. Harmon received reports that an American battalion—later messages said a company—still lay somewhere out along the Bowling Alley, fighting desperately in the darkness, surrounded by hordes of Germans. The lost Americans were reported to be directly in the line of the 'ladder barrage' about to begin in support of Force H.

Harmon had to decide at once—stop the barrage and wreck his counter-attack or let it begin and kill hundreds of hard-pressed men. He was in great anguish of mind; it would be terrible for his own men to see the barrage going down ahead of them, killing their comrades to aid their advance. And yet the Beachhead was in danger. If Harmon delayed his counter-attack the last defences, away to the south-west around the Flyover, might crack and let the Germans

184

through. Enemy tanks would be fanning out onto the harbour and beaches, German infantry would be swarming through the Padiglione woodlands and around the Allied guns. Harmon did not hesitate. He gave the order, 'Fire on time'.

The concentration of shell-fire went down along the Bowling Alley with a tremendous howl and shriek of explosions that erupted smoke and flame over the whole landscape ahead. The attacking infantry followed. They made steady progress for a mile up the road—and, to their intense relief, found that the Americans reported in their path had in fact retired before the barrage began. But they also found the Germans in strength. There was a mass of units still in the salient or forming up to try to advance again towards the Flyover. But there was no question that the Germans were disorganized. They had taken such punishment during the last day and night that they were mixed up, uncertain of themselves and not steady on the ground. Harmon's men pushed them swiftly back.

A blown bridge on the Bowling Alley delayed the tanks until the engineers rushed up to repair it under fire; but the Americans' blood was up, they were attacking again at last, striking back in strength. Nothing could stop them.

By late afternoon Harmon's men had reached the area of the Dead End Road from the east, and his tanks had pushed ahead in the flat lands along the Spaccasassi Creek. The Germans were shaken and disorganized. Two hundred prisoners had already come in through the American lines. Away to the south the Loyals and North Staffs prepared to assault the last pocket of German resistance in a ruined farmhouse just north of the Lateral Road in front of the Flyover. A white flag was suddenly hoisted over the ruins, and then one or two Germans staggered across the road to surrender. In a moment a group ran forward to follow their comrades; and then, before anyone realized what had happened, hundreds of Germans were crawling out of the rubble and stumbling blindly forward to give themselves up. They had reached the limit of human endurance.

Harmon could not continue his advance without exposing himself to counter-attack, since Force T had been unable to launch its projected attack up the Anzio-Albano road to join him. That night Force H also withdrew slowly to strong positions on the eastern flank of the salient. But it had done its work well and thrown the Germans into confusion. On the evening of 19 February it seemed to the weary defenders of the Beachhead that a miracle had occurred.

Small wonder that Colonel Langevin 'felt chipper' as he met the correspondents at Corps briefing. 'We've made him worried,' he said, 'up in those draws of his'—the British were worried, too, until they realized 'draws' were wadis in American!—'I reckon we caught those Heinies and just smeared them over the landscape.' General Lucas sent off his message of congratulation to the troops, 'Swell work today—keep after them.'

Brigadier Pasley, in charge of the 1st Division's artillery, sent a glowing message to his men:

> I can assure you that the infantry of this Division have complete and utter confidence in you to a degree that I personally have never seen before. You in your gun-pits never see them and they never see you. But they know you are always there. They see the worst side of war, and they need something to depend on, something to lean against. They one and all lean against you, because you have saved them over and over again—and they know you will go on doing so.[1]

Modern victories—and the defeat of the great German attack on the final Corps Defence Line was a victory in every sense of the word—usually have a sour aftermath, some small flaw in the perfection of success which prevents the victors from rejoicing with wholehearted fervour. The enemy never again attacked in decisive strength across the bloody ground before the Flyover; the bridge, battered, holed, bedraggled and with its steel entrails dangling obscenely below the girders, stood amid the bursting shells as the Beachhead's symbol of its unbroken will to resist. In Anzio it had now acquired the same sort of aura that surrounded the Menin Gate at Ypres or Fort Douaumont at Verdun during the First World War. The defenders looked up at it from their slit-trenches and vowed, 'While it's there, we are there, too!'

But out on the western flank of the salient, amongst the miserable, infuriating wadis, there was still danger and death for the Allies. Somewhere ahead of the Beachhead Defence Line, in a sort of lost no-man's-land of deep-cut watercourses

---

[1] Quoted from his personal papers.

continually plastered by high explosive, the remnants of the 157th Regiment fought on. They had been shattered and brushed aside in the first German onrush towards the Flyover, yet their commander, Colonel Brown, had not lost heart for a moment. Again and again the Germans got behind them, cutting their slender communications with the rear, plastering the muddy hollows in which the Americans crouched with a deluge of mortar shells. Again and again the Allied artillery put down fearful walls of fire to stop the Germans rushing in and overwhelming the defenders. As long as the 2nd Battalion held the western flank of the salient the enemy could not sweep in strength through the wadis to infiltrate towards the Lateral Road.

Some wounded had been dragged out during the diversion caused by the counter-attack of 19 February, then the battalion was cut off again. Looking out in the darkness from the Flyover the anxious observers could see a Very light soar up and hear the occasional rattle of machine-guns. Colonel Brown and his men were still resisting somewhere out in no-man's land, still holding out after five days and five nights of continuous battle. They had to be relieved at all costs.

The British 56th Division was now manning the line to the west of the Flyover, since Sixth Corps were trying to tidy their front after the German drive to the sea and to disentangle the units mixed in the chaos of battle. General Templer was therefore entrusted with the formidable task of breaking through to the 2nd Battalion, bringing out the survivors and putting in fresh troops to hold the vital strongpoint of the caves.

No one doubted that the caves had to be held. The British were only too well aware of the dangers that threatened the Beachhead from this tangled area: there had been moments during the great German counter-attack when their commanders had sighed with relief to find that the enemy had reverted to the tactics of the mass assault over open ground instead of continuing his infiltration through the impenetrable cover of the wadis. They shuddered to think what might have happened if Kesselring had decided to push in overwhelming strength through the wadi country.

General Templer selected the 2/7th Battalion the Queen's Royal Regiment (West Surrey) to make the relief attempt. The unfortunate Queen's met with ill luck as soon as they started to push their way forward in the noisy darkness of the night of 21 February. They bumped into strong forces of Germans who were creeping up to try to seal off, once and for all, the beleaguered Americans. In this confusing landscape no one could be certain of path or direction: the Queen's were heavily shelled, swept by machine-gun fire from unexpected quarters. Tanks tried to help them, but when the battalion eventually struggled into the caves they found themselves without supplies, ammunition and supporting weapons.

The relief force now needed relief itself. All next day the Germans swarmed around the caves: British and Americans fought side by side to hold them off, the Americans naturally anxious to get away and the British equally anxious to be reinforced.

Next night the Americans were ordered to make a break for it. They split into small groups and tried to get back through the wadis to the main defence line. Anyone who has tried to crawl around rough country on a pitch dark night, stumbling and falling over rocks and into brambles, will know the physical anguish which awaited the Americans: to the sheer torture of weary men, plodding through mud and rain, was added the nerve-racking crash of shells, the cries of pain somewhere in the darkness and the sudden shouts to surrender as the GIs bumped into the waiting Germans.

Out of eight hundred men at the beginning of the week's fighting the 2nd Battalion 157th Regiment succeeded in mustering only two hundred after their retreat from the caves. Out of this remnant a hundred were battle casualties. But they were proud men. They had held the western flank of the salient against enormous odds and fought one of the most memorable infantry battles in the annals of the American Army. The men stumbled out of action deafened by high explosives and unable to sleep, with their eyes bloodshot and their hands scarred by burns. They looked more like scarecrows than soldiers, but they had earned with their battered bodies the right of their unit to the rare honour of a Presidential citation.

The 2/7th Queen's now struggled to hold the caves in their place. There was no glory left—only mud, misery and misgivings that the place could be held any longer. Their sister battalion, the 2/6th Queen's, tried to break through to them but failed. Bad weather wiped out all hope of dropping supplies by air, the Germans overran the forward companies and there was nothing for it but to order the survivors to get back as best they could. Again a handful of sorely tried men alone got back. As he limped at last into safety, one of the Queen's turned to look out over the dark shell-torn country and muttered, 'A bastard of a place'.

Yes, 'a bastard of a place'! The wadis remained so until the bitter end. Companies, whole battalions had disappeared into their labyrinths. After the battle of the caves the British generals knew that, even if the main German drive to the sea had now spent its force, they had been presented with a running sore on their front which would fester away, sapping their strength, until at last we broke out of the Beachhead.

As the tide of the German attack ebbed, one man on the Allied side watched it go with mixed feelings. General Lucas had now become aware that General Clark was only waiting for this moment to make a change in the command of Sixth Corps; General Truscott was at his side to remind him that he had lost the confidence of his superiors. Truscott was loyal, tactful and sincere in his desire not to step into Lucas's shoes. He was happy to stay where he was, helping and advising Sixth Corps: but he, too, knew that Clark and Alexander had now marked Lucas for removal.

On 22 February, a month after the landing, Clark broke the news to Lucas that Truscott was to take over Sixth Corps immediately. He took it bitterly. He felt deeply that his policy of consolidating on the beaches had been sound and, in the end, justified by the repulse of the great German assault. British influence, he was sure, was behind his dismissal, Mr. Churchill's in particular. Back in London the Prime Minister was still harping away at his 'wild cat versus whale' simile—'I thought we were landing a wild cat that would tear out the bowels of the Boche. Instead we have stranded a vast whale with its tail flopping about in the water.'[1] There was a moment when he wanted to send Alexander himself to take personal charge at the Beachhead, and in the event the British General Evelegh did arrive to smooth Anglo-American relations.

But no reshuffling of the command could meet the major difficulty—rightly or wrongly, Lucas had lost the confidence of the British units at Anzio and of some of the Americans

[1] Churchill, *The Second World War.*

as well. When that happens the Higher Command has no option: an operation of radical surgery is necessary to cut out the sore point in the military body. The operation was painful both to Clark and Lucas, and Lucas never forgave the commander of the Fifth Army, who, he felt, had sacrificed him to British intrigue.

Lucas has been heavily criticized—and in these pages as well as elsewhere—but it is impossible to withhold sympathy for a man who, at the summit of his military career, finds himself in a position from which he is removed under a cloud of professional disapproval.

Yet this is the hazard under which all have to labour who are called upon to exercise important command in war. Generals are judged by more exacting standards than other men, with success as the only criterion. Lucas had not led Sixth Corps to the expected success, and that was all that counted; he left the Beachhead and Truscott took command.

The new commander spoke to the correspondents who remained at Anzio soon after his appointment. I made a note of the conference in my diary:

We've got a new head at Anzio, tough, Barrymore-profiled General Truscott, husky-voiced and with slightly greying hair. But he looks—as we hope every general should look—like a two-fisted fighter and not like a tired business man. He was honest, outspoken and completely realist. 'No,' he said, 'I don't reckon that everything is for the best, we're going to have a tough time here for months to come. But, gentlemen, we're going to hold this Beachhead come what may.' And he stuck out his jaw in a way that convinced you that any German attack would bounce off it.

A new commander cannot change a military situation overnight, he needs time to make his influence felt, but the knowledge that Truscott was at the helm had a heartening effect on the men holding responsible positions on the Beachhead. Orders were now positive, staff officers moved more often around the front line and there was an air of confidence blowing through the underground corridors of Sixth Corps.

General Evelegh, who understood the Americans as well as Truscott understood the British, became Deputy Corps Commander with the result that the old irritations quickly disappeared. Anzio had survived the biggest punch that the Germans could throw against it, and Truscott arrived at the right time to consolidate the new feeling of hope and achievement. Over his desk in his above-ground office in Nettuno he hung one of Bill Mauldin's most successful cartoons. It showed two GIs, damp and unshaven, resting in water-filled holes in Anzio, while one says to the other, 'The hell if this isn't the best hole in the world. I'm in it!'

Truscott's first task was to ready the Beachhead for the next German attack, for it was impossible to doubt that they would attack again. Hitler had personally approved of the first all-out assault, supervising its preparation down to the smallest detail; it was impossible for him to accept the check before the Flyover as final. Kesselring and Von Mackensen knew in their hearts—and their professional judgment approved their instinctive feelings—that the attack on 19 February was the high-water mark of German offensive power in Italy. They also knew why it had failed; apart from the disappointing performances of certain units the attack had been made on too narrow a front and in too rigid a pattern. The Germans had abandoned their infiltration tactics and offered themselves, Verdun-wise, as cannon fodder to the terrible Allied artillery on the killing ground in front of the Flyover. Hitler and his advisers in their far-distant headquarters in Germany, had by their insistence on the narrow-front advance knocked the heart out of the men of the Fourteenth Army.

But how would Hitler react if his generals in Italy insisted that he abandon his attempt to sweep the Allies into the sea? In North Africa and in Russia he had always refused to admit defeat. 'Never retreat! Fight on until you are overwhelmed!' was his military creed, to which, at Anzio, could be added, 'Attack until you haven't a single man left who will get out of his trenches and go forward.' Hitler, in those desperate days of early 1944, was in the mood of Napoleon talking to Metternich, the Austrian Ambassador, after the disasters of the Russian campaign of 1812. He could see the dangers ahead, yet not for a moment could he contemplate making peace or negotiating with his enemies. 'A man such as I', declared Napoleon, 'cares little for the lives of a million men.' 'Sire,' replied Metternich, 'you are lost. I felt it when I came, and now I go, I am certain.'

There was no one who dared to talk to Hitler in 1944 as Metternich had talked to Napoleon in 1813. The Führer demanded an immediate resumption of the attack in spite of the misgivings of his commanders on the spot. Let them prepare a new offensive immediately, since it was clear from Berchtesgaden that the Allies were tottering, broken, reeling; one final effort and the day was won.

Easy for the Leader, far distant from the fighting, to talk of one supreme effort; Kesselring knew that the supreme effort had already been made. Yet he did not dare admit to Hitler that he would not attack again. He comforted himself with the thought that, even if a new offensive could not break through to the sea, it might yet make another big bulge in the Allied line which would allow the Germans to keep the Beachhead under continuous medium artillery fire and thus make it untenable.

The weary German divisions were reshuffled and withdrawn from the unlucky front along the Albano road. Swiftly they were concentrated in the easterly sector of the Beachhead, around Cisterna.

Truscott had a shrewd idea what was coming, and like a cunning boxer shifted his guard as swiftly as the Germans shifted their reserves. He was ready for them when the enemy swept forward again on 29 February. The attack was fierce, bad weather helped the enemy to bring up his tanks unmolested by the air, and the German infantry again did its best, droves of shouting men plunging forward following a furious artillery concentration. The infantry knew nothing of Kesselring's feelings. Once again they thought they were going to sweep the Allies into the sea. Luckily for them they also knew nothing of Truscott's feelings, which even included a sense of relief that the attack was being delivered against his trusted 3rd Division, now back to strength after its ordeal in the early days of the Beachhead, and not against the worn, exhausted 56th and 45th Divisions in the wadi country.

This attack of 29 February, the last serious attempt of the Germans against the Anzio Beachhead, has an air of anticlimax, a Higher Command project which had no inner conviction behind it. The men who struggled bravely forward over the muddy ground in driving rainstorms that hid the battlefield from time to time had already given of their best in the assault before the Flyover; they could dent the 3rd

Division's position but had no real hope of splitting it. They made gains of a few hundred yards, then on 2 March the skies cleared and the full weight of the Allied air bombardment fell on the unhappy Germans.

Two hundred and forty-one Liberators, 100 Fortresses, 113 Lightnings and 63 Thunderbolts swarmed into the skies. Cisterna, Velletri, Carroceto—there was hardly a moment when the earth around these places was not shaking with the demoralizing thud of exploding bombs. The Allies unloaded an even greater weight of high explosives than on 17 February, during the crisis of the Beachhead.

Those of us who watched the attacks, lying behind the broken farmhouses of Isola Bella, were ourselves continually shaken and deafened by the unbroken drumroll of the heavy explosions. Overhead the sky was filled with the glitter of the winter sun. The great flight of aircraft looked strangely beautiful, remote, and efficient as they came up from the south in an endless stream, jettisoned their load of death with a clinical detachment and swung back for more. For hour after hour the procession continued in the clear sky.

As the last of the bombers disappeared over the Pontine Marshes to the south, their fuselage glittering in the bright morning sun, the huge fountains of dust and smoke raised by their bombs fell slowly back to the torn, upheaved earth. The air around the Beachhead became very calm and still. The birds, stirred by the crash of the high explosive, started to sing, hurriedly at first, then boldly as the silence crept over the craters and the chaos of broken brick and twisted wire that now marked the German forward positions.

In the anguish of the long weeks of fighting, pinned to their fox-holes and thinking only of the menace of the tank advancing from the burning farmhouses or the grenade flung from the gully ten yards away, the front-line soldiers had hardly been aware of the battle high above their heads. Now they could look up into the clear sky, and see the full air might of the Allies smashing down in awe-inspiring weight and power on their enemies. They almost felt a sympathy for the Jerries under that merciless rain of explosions. They knew only too well what that downpour meant. For a brief moment the foe with whom they had been locked in their death struggle for so long came closer to them than those of their own side who, living in the safety of a Southern Italy which seemed infinitely remote from the Beachhead, had not shared the anguish of Anzio.

'Christ, General,' Truscott's aide murmured to him as they watched the smoke drift away from the German lines, 'That's hitting a guy when he's down.'

9

What We Have We Hold

In every period of furious and intensive action there comes a moment which all taking part in that action suddenly recognize as marking the end of their effort, a signal that, for good or ill, it is not humanly possible to go on struggling any more. The crisis at the Beachhead had passed on the morning of 19 February, when the high tide of the German advance had flooded up to the Flyover, but the real end of the battle came with the great air attack of 2 March.

Naturally the fighting did not end dramatically as the sound of the bombers died in the distance, for a big offensive cannot finish abruptly like a football match to the sound of the referee's whistle. After that moment of stunned silence, the guns on both sides began to fire again and the German tanks crawled forward to try one more push down the road to Isola Bella. There was fierce fighting here and there on 3 March when the Americans launched a strong counter-attack and flung the Germans back at Ponte Rotto. But already the German High Command, looking down on the stubborn Beachhead from the Alban Hills, felt the chill of defeat creeping over them. They had committed everything they had to breaking through at Anzio—their carefully hoarded reserves of men and material, their military reputation and their hopes for the future. Never again would they be able to send their soldiers to the attack buoyed up with confidence in ultimate victory. After the collapse of their drive at the Beachhead the professionals at the head of the German Army knew that, whatever Hitler and his advisers might say, there was now more than a possibility that the shining weapon of the Wehrmacht, which they had forged with such pride and skill, would one day break in their hands.

194

Three thousand five hundred Germans were dead, wounded or missing since the last punch had begun, 30 tanks which could ill be spared were now lying as smoking and battered wrecks on the level marshy land south of Cisterna. The Allied lines were intact everywhere.

Field-Marshal Kesselring sensed by the afternoon of 1 March, even before the big air raid hit his troops, that the final gamble had failed. As dusk fell on that eventful day he ordered the assault in force against the 3rd Division to be brought to a halt. At a German High Command conference on 3 March it was decided to abandon for the time being all plans for offensive action on the Anzio front.

General Clark and General Truscott did, however, plan another round within a week after the ending of the German attack.

In their own agony the men fighting on the Anzio Beachhead had long forgotten that they were part of the Fifth Army and that their operation was closely linked, in the minds of the Higher Command, with the battles around Cassino. They heard news of the bombing of a monastery and of some disaster on a stream called the Rapido, but these were far-off, remote events to the troops battling on the Albano Road. All they knew was that, somehow or other, the Army in the south which was supposed to join them on the Alban Hills had never 'got rollin'; it was stuck as firmly in front of Cassino as they were stuck on the Beachhead. They expected little from it except bad news.

Operation Panther—a pincers attack to reduce the salient that the Germans had driven into the Beachhead perimeter during the great battles of the last month—was designed to chime in with the third battle for Cassino on 19 March. Once again the Cassino drive died against the rubble of Monastery Hill. It was clear that neither in the south nor on the Beachhead was there much prospect of advance for a long time to come, for the plain truth was that the Allies were as exhausted as the Germans, the fighter had no strength left to come out of his corner. He must be left to recuperate and build up his punching power before his managers could enter him for another fight.

One man alone refused to accept this faltering in the tempo of the battle.

Withdrawn from all contact with the actual fighting, Adolf Hitler brooded over his maps in his mountain-top eyrie at Berchtesgaden, issuing orders which were increasingly out of touch with reality. He was still the terrifying, all-powerful driving force behind the German war effort, the man in whose presence field-marshals trembled. Who would dare break the grim news to him that the attack he had personally planned and ordered had failed, and that Army Group South had neither the strength nor the will to renew the effort? Written reports made no impression on the Führer: he had started to enter a world of dream fantasies, in which he still saw himself, by the aid of secret weapons, of daring combinations of yet untapped reserves, dramatically turning the tables on his enemies. He was compensating himself on the maps at his HQ for the failure of his armies in the field. Any suggestion that the Anzio counter-attack should now be abandoned was bound to produce an explosion. It was essential that the messenger bearing the bad news should see Hitler face to face. General Westphal undertook the thankless and dangerous task.

He reached Berchtesgaden early in March, a day after the fighting had died down on the Beachhead.

His account of his visit gives us a vivid glimpse of the strange atmosphere of Wagnerian doom which now surrounded Hitler. Westphal was reporting at the Court of an Oriental despot who still had power to make heads roll. General Jodl, Chief of Operations Staff, begged him urgently to stay out of the Presence until he himself had spoken to the Führer. Hitler received Jodl's news with a violent outburst of rage—'Where,' he demanded, 'was the man who had been slandering his troops?' Then he ordered that twenty men should be immediately flown to him from the Italian front so that he could question them about the state of affairs—the only occasion when he took such a course throughout the whole of the war! 'He would have done better', comments Westphal dryly, 'to visit the front himself.'

At last, on the evening of 6 March, Westphal was shown into the room in the luxurious 'hide-out' high above Berchtesgaden, where Hitler waited to receive him. The General pleaded his case for three hours, constantly interrupted by Hitler's outbursts. But the desperate condition of the Italian front made Westphal desperate himself, and he stuck firmly to the points he had to make. Army Group could not mount another major attack on the Beachhead. Slowly, reluctantly, Hitler seemed to realize that what Westphal was telling him was the truth. 'At the end, with obvious emotion he said that he knew how great was the war-weariness which afflicted the people and the Wehrmacht and he would do his best to bring about a speedy solution.' Then the old illusions returned—'all he needed to solve the present problem was a victory!'[1]

He was still hoping for it, by some unexpected miracle, when the Allies were closing in for the kill over a year later. Anzio had not destroyed his strange dream-picture of the working out of his destiny and the ultimate triumph of his Thousand-Year Reich!

As Westphal left Berchtesgaden to return to Italy, Field-Marshal Keitel came to say good-bye. 'You're lucky,' he said with feeling. 'If we fools had said half as much, the Führer would have had us hanged.'

Far away from Hitler's mountain retreat the spring sun slowly began to warm the sodden earth of the Beachhead and the first primroses appeared in the Padiglione woodlands. Anzio settled down to a long wait. 'We'll be here until they come and rescue us from the Second Front,' was the quip that went the rounds of the British sector.

For the next three months the front line of the Beachhead retained the form imprinted upon it by the battle for survival in February. Minor adjustments were made here and there, especially in the wadi country on the British sector; these were concerned at the most with abandoning a ruined farm which gave no observation, capturing a few yards of shell-torn gully, to obtain more easily held, forward positions, and to achieve a little more defence in depth. The great salient that the Germans had driven into the Beachhead perimeter remained as a perpetual reminder of how near they had come to success.

As the months passed this front line took on all the character of the Somme or Ypres in 1916. For the first and the only time in World War II the soldiers had to think in terms of communicating trenches, barbed wire in no-man's-land and the rest of the grim paraphernalia of *All Quiet on the Western Front*.

'You're here to stay,' one British brigadier insisted to his men. 'You've just got to dig, dig, dig your way to safety.'

[1] Westphal, *The German Army in the West*.

There was nothing the American or the British soldier hated more in the last war than an order to 'dig-in'. He had been trained for offensive action, or for at least a war of movement, and his whole being revolted against a *Sitzkrieg*, as he called it. The German was a far better 'digger' than the Tommy or the GI, for he regarded it from the point of view of a man whose ideal in life has always been to become a sound, professional soldier. To him digging was part of the technique of fighting, so he got on with the job like a good professional.

But there was no help for it, the British and Americans had to dig too. The Beachhead was still under fire and 'Anzio Annie' rumbled overhead at regular intervals to remind the man who didn't use his spade that he was in constant danger. Grumbling, but spurred on by necessity, the Allies began to go underground, and as generally happens when the soldiers of a democracy have been taught by disaster, they began to outstrip their enemies. From the air Anzio seemed a field ravaged by a vast army of industrious moles.

As the ground dried with the approach of the warmer weather the men were able to dig deeper without the danger of water seeping into their pits. Dug-outs became more ingenious and elaborate, constructed out of doors from ruined farms, piles of broken ammunition boxes and even, in some cases, from the huge wine vats left in the cellars of Anzio and Nettuno. Everything went underground or at least as far below the surface as possible. Bulldozers flung up huge banks of dirt around the munition dumps to dampen the effects of explosions, the gun-pits were surrounded with solidly built walls of rubble and timber, the hospital tents sank between closely packed mounds of earth and clay. The German guns fired into the Beachhead during the whole period of its existence, there were nightly air-raids and no area was safe from its occasional sprinkle of 'butterfly bombs'—small but dangerous anti-personnel bombs, sprayed out from a canister dropped by aircraft. They lay hidden in the undergrowth amongst the woodlands and could blow a foot or a hand off if you stumbled on them unawares.

But the digging undoubtedly made the Beachhead tenable. Considering the amount of high explosive emptied onto this small area day and night, the actual casualties suffered by the troops in this static period were comparatively small. It was rather the uncertainty of life, the sudden eruption of shattering noise on a quiet morning, the whistle of shells going overhead when you least expected it and above all the knowledge that you could never get out of range of the enemy's gunfire that made the Beachhead a place apart from the rest of the fighting world.

The February battle had given it an aura of danger, a reputation for death and destruction which never left it even when the fighting had died down. Reinforcements shuddered when they learnt that they had been drafted to Anzio. They expected to approach the port through a curtain of shellfire and be rushed to a front in constant danger of being driven in. It took them some days before they realized that all the stories they had heard at Naples and elsewhere could not possibly be true and that the actual front at Anzio was no worse than the front at Cassino or along the Moro River.

What gave Anzio its peculiar atmosphere, however, was the absence of any 'rear areas'; there was nowhere you could retire to in the absolute certainty that, for a day or two, you would be able to get out of the war to laze and relax in the sun. In Anzio no one was out of the war: the hospitals were shelled, the supply dumps were set on fire, the Negro drivers of the invaluable DUKWs, on their way out to the Liberty ships anchored in 'Bomb Bay', were constantly glancing over their shoulders to spot the sneak-raider planes that came skimming wave-high at dusk.

Yet in the perverse way of soldiers much tried in battle the old Anzio hands began to take a strange pride in the place; for them it was THE Beachhead, their private war which a stranger could never understand, but one which would set the 'Anzionian' apart from other men. They had accomplished a great feat of arms in stopping the German drive to the sea and they were understandably proud of what they had done.

They also knew that they had done it together; Americans and British had stood shoulder to shoulder, units mixed up, American guns supporting British troops, British tanks firing behind hard-pressed American companies. At Anzio, Allied co-operation which was so uncertain at first eventually went far deeper than the levels of Army and Corps at which it usually stopped. Common misfortune does not always bring allies together, but Anzio was too small a place not to fuse those who took part in it into a firm, strongly welded group.

For the Beachhead in its final form was astonishingly small as a base from which to wage a modern war. It stretched for about sixteen miles along the coast from the Moletta River in the north-west to the banks of the Mussolini Canal in the south-east, but it was a mere seven miles inland along the Albano road before you reached the British forward positions, nine miles inland from Nettuno before you got to the American front line facing Cisterna. The greatest part of the Beachhead area, however, lay within three and four miles from the front—no distance at all by the standards of modern gunnery.

Yet no one who was at Anzio from beginning to end will be content to dwell only on the slaughter and destruction without remembering another Anzio, of comradeship, high courage and even of gaiety and laughter. If this second Anzio had not existed, the grim Beachhead of dirt, sudden woundings and anguish, would not have been endurable. In the long months of waiting it was possible to trace the growth of a distinct 'Beachhead spirit' and men felt a sense of purpose there that they did not feel in many other fronts. There is nothing new in this; it happened at Gallipoli and even on the old Western Front where men looked back, in peace time, to 'the spirit of the trenches' and sighed to see it absent from the civil life to which they returned.

There is no point in over-sentimentalizing this spirit. Its presence does not justify war in any shape or form; it was simply a tribute to the astonishing resilience of quite ordinary men in times of danger and stress. So it was that many visitors, who came to the Beachhead expecting to find it enveloped in an atmosphere of gloom and despondency, departed surprised and even uplifted. Anzio, in the months of waiting, was always dangerous—it was never totally depressing.

To begin with it was a densely packed place. As the months went by seven divisions and a whole mass of extra Corps and Army units were crammed into an area which had seemed intolerably crowded even in the days of the first landing. Newcomers had to bargain for space with the skill of land agents in London or New York, and the generals when offered more troops began to reply, 'Fine, but where the hell do we put them?'

Yet it was because they had to live so close together that

the men developed an easy tolerance which smoothed away the smaller difficulties and irritations that plague the mind when danger is not present. When you know that you can get blown up at any minute you do not become too critical of your neighbour who can get blown up with you.

Because of its crowded life the Beachhead always seemed an intensely busy place, especially in the section around Anzio and Nettuno. There was no moment without movement. All through the day the DUKWs came streaming ashore from the great fleet of supply vessels which filled the seaward horizon, lorries plastered the broken trees of the waterfront with clouds of dust, signallers festooned yet another cable amongst the endless miles of wire that now covered the broken villas of the towns with a spider's web of communications. Bull-dozers were everywhere throwing up new mounds of rubble and obliterating vineyards and gardens to stamp a new geography on the unresisting Anzio landscape.

This zone of intense activity extended for some miles back from the coast. As you drove farther inland, however, a subtle change seemed to come over the countryside. The traffic faded away, the road became suspiciously quiet. At a certain point at the side of the road large notices in flaring red paint gave the warning: 'Danger. Shelling. Make no dust.' Farther along this warning became more emphatic: 'No traffic in daylight past this point.' Ahead lay the dead country where for hours on end nothing moved and hardly a sound broke the unnatural silence, but where, without warning, shells could come hissing overhead, bullets crackle across the bare earth and a shower of red-hot tracers shoot swiftly into the menacing, brooding distance. This was the land where every living thing had to go to ground under penalty of ceasing to live. Tens of thousands of men were somewhere out there in this wilderness, not one of them visible, not one of them daring to lift his head. It was as if a whole countryside was holding its breath, waiting.

As night fell a strange reversal of atmosphere took place —the rear areas became quiet, the front leapt into busy, dangerous life. The convoys with supplies came up the roads, columns of sweating men, like porters on an Everest Expedition, staggering slowly forward towards the communication trenches; there was gunfire and Very lights hung in the sky for long enough to give the whole scene a swift unwanted,

unreal illumination with the shadows lengthened and pointing the wrong way. The light would fade and the febrile
movement towards the front start again. No one in the front
or in the rear areas thought of night as friendly, at Anzio.

The Beachhead perimeter had remained static so long that
by the end of the fourth month of waiting every yard of it
had acquired its own character and history. As soon as the
last German attacks had died away, General Truscott carried out a complete reorganization of his front line and tidied
its administrative lay-out by grouping together, under their
own divisional commanders, those American and British
units which had got inextricably mingled at the height of the
battle.

The British sector—the smaller of the two—now lay from
the Albano road westward. The front near the coast was
held by the British 5th Division, which had been sent to the
Beachhead in March to replace the much-tried 56th. The 5th
had already been in action on the Garigliano and had seen
heavy fighting in Sicily and Southern Italy; it was a most
experienced and efficient division, but the men were hardly
the fresh reinforcements needed by the British sector. They,
like the men of the 56th, could have done with a long spell
in rest camps rather than in the trenches of Anzio. But they
had in General Gregson-Ellis an outstanding divisional commander who could impress his personality on his own men
and on his American colleagues. Truscott had known him
in England and records his vivid impression of Gregson-Ellis
in action at Anzio: 'He was fearless. His gaunt figure clad in
shorts, his hawklike features topped by a rather silly-looking
(on him) tin hat, stalking about the front lines with a long
staff reminiscent of a shepherd's crook in hand, always
brought Ichabod Crane to my mind.'[1]

Gregson-Ellis found that his section of the line had a split
personality; it was at once deceptively quiet in places and in-
fernally noisy in others. Along the lower reaches of the
Moletta stream, where it reached the sea, the front was comparatively calm and soldiers transferred there from areas
more frequently shelled were tempted to call it the 'Rest
Camp'. Farther inland, however, the 5th found itself involved in a part of the infuriating wadi country, fighting a
minor war of patrols and trench raids in the tangled water-

[1] Truscott, *Command Missions*.

202

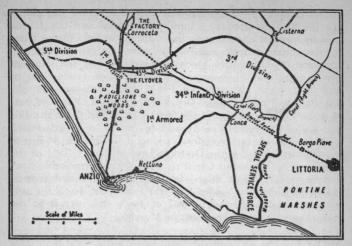

THE STATIC BEACHHEAD

courses of the upper Moletta. This section of the line was always dreaded by newcomers and helped to maintain the reputation of the Beachhead as the worst battlefront in Italy.

The 1st Division, with General Penney back in command, held the rest of the wadis and the flat country around the Flyover. The 1st had been on the Beachhead so long and had suffered so much there that its staff had almost forgotten that any war existed other than the one which they had fought for months around the few square miles of broken ground between the Factory and the Flyover. They had been 'officially relieved' on several occasions, but in actual fact there had never been a moment when some units of the 1st were not in contact with the enemy.

The Americans defended the perimeter from near the Flyover eastwards. The 45th Division under General Eagles held the front before Padiglione and, like their comrades of the British 1st Division, felt that this section of the front was a landscape they knew only too well. They had suffered severe losses in the February battles but as the American always had more men available for reinforcements than the British the 45th was, in fighting power, soon back to what it was before the landing.

203

The rest of the line, stretching eastwards from Padiglione in a great swelling curve around to the Mussolini Canal, was held by various units during the waiting period. The American parachute troops and the Rangers left Anzio, and the American 34th Infantry Division came in. The 3rd Division and the 1st Armored came out of the line from time to time and went into reserve for special training—General Truscott had the eventual break-out in mind from the moment he took command of the Sixth Corps. His place as commander of the 3rd Division had been taken by a very tough and resilient character indeed, General O'Daniels, who was quickly nicknamed in the Division 'Iron Mike'.

Along the Mussolini Canal to the sea the remarkable Special Service Force, a mixed force of highly trained Americans and Canadians under General Frederick, fought a private and highly successful war of raids and patrols in the waterlogged levels of the Pontine Marshes.

This was the shape of the front line on the great maps that covered the walls of Corps Headquarters, the position of each unit carefully marked by china-clay pencil on the transparent trace which covered the printed maps. The visitor could look at the complex but orderly pattern made by the elaborate symbols for Corps troops, divisional headquarters, signal units and the rest; he would see at a glance that the Beachhead was now a highly organized and efficient machine, gearing itself for action in the future. But no map could convey to him the actual feel of life in that neatly marked front line—the smell, the tension, the grotesque humour of it all.

Perhaps the best way to bring it vividly back to mind is by reading some of the diaries kept by men who fought through the Anzio campaign. The Beachhead was a natural inspirer of diaries—for days time hung heavily on the soldiers' hands and they scribbled industriously once they were out of the line.

Here are recorded the 'trivia', the small-talk, the grumbling, the rumours and the local jokes that bulked far larger in the minds of the ordinary soldiers than the 'Big Picture' of the rest of the war in Italy. General Alexander might be busy moving over his divisions from the Eighth Army to the Fifth Army front, General Truscott preparing four different plans for the coming assault on Cisterna, but the diarists of the

British 5th Division were unconcerned—their minds were on the absorbing new sport of beetle-racing which swept the British sector in April.

The rules were simple. You first caught your beetle by digging a small slit-trench, and in an hour the bottom of the trench would be black with beetles, all struggling to get out. From the numerous runners you made careful tests to select the fastest mover: certain beetles gained fame on the Beachhead and changed ownership at high prices, the champion being sold for over three thousand lire. The lira stood at 50s. or $10 to the thousand, so this insect can claim to be one of the most expensive black beetles on record.

Colours were painted on the beetles' backs, and they were paraded around the ring in jam-jars. When the bets were placed the jam-jar was dumped in the centre of a circle six feet square, the beetles came under 'starter's orders', the starter lifted the jar and the beetles made for the edge of the ring. The first to cross the circle was the winner.

The Anzio 'bookies' brought off their smartest *coup* when they bought up the beetle which was far too consistent a winner at Divisional Headquarters races—and promptly stamped on it!

Rumours were as plentiful on the Beachhead as racing beetles and equally unreliable; Hitler had been assassinated, the Second Front had begun, the Germans had landed parachutists at Anzio harbour, and always that pathetic piece of wishful thinking—the battalion was to be withdrawn and sent to Sorrento for a rest.

Minor characters emerge from the diaries, men who made a vivid impression on their small circle, and who gave colour to life on the Beachhead. There was, for example, the cheerful Swazi Pioneer, known to the whole British sector as 'Shoe-shine', who dashed around the football field in an enormous beret and with a grin that matched his headgear. At one time he could draw more enthusiastic crowds than most first-class professionals. He also got credited with a curious power—if 'Shoe-shine' was playing, the football pitch would never be shelled!

In the American sector Sammy Goldstein was the symbol of determined Mark Tapley-like cheerfulness. Sammy was small, wiry, and Jewish, with an accent that proclaimed his origin in the Bronx. He was an official photographer who roared around the Beachhead on his motor-bike, always game to crawl into the front line to get a shot of Private Joe Doak in action if he thought it would make the local paper. He had the news photographer's chirpy irreverence for forms and protocol: 'Hold that, Colonel—sorry, I mean General, I've got ya out of focus!' as General Mark Clark indicated a line of advance on the map. And he meant no disrespect, but simply demonstrated his keenness to do a good job when he interrupted a mass baptism on the Beachhead with the cry, 'Duck 'em again, Padre, once for God and twice for Sammy.'

Sammy made a striking contrast to the tall, bluff, distinguished-looking British Conducting Officer whom the Americans voted 'Typical Englishman No. 1'. He, again, possessed that quality of imperturbable courage which was intensely valued on the Beachhead. Most soldiers can steel themselves for their first ordeal by battle, but their resistance to danger gets progressively weaker as the ordeal continues; they need to draw on the reserves of courage still retained by certain exceptional men around them. The gallant captain was one such reservoir of strength, and his clipped English and stylized public-school attitude to every situation helped to create the legend that nothing could 'rattle' him. It was impossible to believe that an exploding shell held any menace when the captain remarked in his quiet drawl, 'Gad, that one landed only a mashie-shot away.'

He had the Englishman's conviction that he could speak good Italian. 'Not bad chaps, these natives,' he used to boom in a kindly way. *Come sta? Sempre dormire, eh?*'

'These monks,' he inquired of the Catholic Padre, 'good types, I suppose?' It was a convincing demonstration of the power of Anzio to cement Anglo-American friendship when the captain, who on first meeting the GIs had characterized them as 'shockers, can't rely on soldiers who don't shave before battle', declared in the end that the Yanks were also 'damned good types'.

The Americans retained an affectionate picture of 'Typical Englishman No. 1' trying to lure them on a tour of a particularly sticky section of the British front with the irresistible inducement that 'the violets are out already along the whole of the Wadi Battaccia. Got to get up to see these, you know!'

As the BBC Correspondent on the Beachhead, I also kept a diary and made a tour of the forward positions during the first few weeks in April. These notes jotted down hurriedly on the spot or immediately after returning from the front to the battered Press villa on the water's edge near Nettuno may help to recreate the strange atmosphere of danger, boredom, dirt, courage and humour which never left the Beach-head perimeter.

Here is a night spent at the mouth of the Moletta stream, which marked the extreme north-west position of the British sector, held in late April by a battalion of the Wiltshire Regiment.

This strangely calm sector at the mouth of the Moletta is a blessed relief to troops who come to it direct from a spell in the wadis. In spring the wild flowers are scattered in thousands amongst the sand dunes while the sea looks invitingly near—though death to bathe in. The Boche wants no trouble here: the American combat engineers told the British as they left, 'You leave that guy alone and he won't get mad at you.' The men camp in dug-outs amongst the dunes and on a warm night a single nightingale pours its heart out somewhere in the sweet-smelling bushes.

The forward platoon of the Wiltshires lived within fifty yards of the enemy, and I went on hands and knees down a shallow crawl trench to visit them. Their position was just a series of sand-bagged holes sunk amongst a tangle of shrubs and small trees, but by peering cautiously through a slit between two of the sand-bags I could see the wire in front of the German line: it seemed so close that there was no need of the warning to talk in whispers.

A youngster of nineteen murmured quietly to me, 'Come and see our German.' I wriggled farther forward still, crawled beside him into his look-out post and immediately sensed a foul reek, sickly sweet, like a pile of rancid butter left too long in the sun—the unmistakable, clinging smell of an unburied corpse. There he lay right under our noses, for it was impossible to get out to bury him; all the Wiltshires could do was to sprinkle creosote over the body at night and try to get used to the stench. Few people could get it out of their nostrils and out of their memory. 'Two more out there amongst the minefields.'

I crawled back into the next sap. 'Listen,' said the sergeant, and in the quiet of the evening with no gun firing for miles around I heard a hoarse cough and a shuffle of feet. 'It's old Ted,' said the sergeant. (Ted, from the Italian *Tedeschi*, is the new term for the 'Jerries' out here.) An eerie business to hear your enemy, the man you are supposed to kill, scuffling around in a slit-trench as cramped as your own, feeling as you do the evening nip in the air, thinking as you are thinking of the chance of getting leave and escaping from it all. It's easy to feel venomous about Old Ted when he comes charging towards you with a gun in his hand, but when he coughs and scuffles, unaware that he's been over-heard, he becomes suddenly human, a fellow man caught in the same predicament as yourself.

Maybe this is why the sergeant suddenly turned to me and whispered, 'You ought to have been here on Hitler's birthday: they had a high old time, singing *Lilli Marlene* and yelling their heads off—plumb crazy or just bomb happy. It takes you that way sometimes when you've been having a real basin-full up in the wadis.' Then the sergeant had his brainwave; 'Tell you what. Put your mike up here on the parapet and tonight the bastard will come out wiring—I'll guarantee you a winner. He cusses something horrible, bangs away at the old wiring posts and whistles; proper Blackpool it is out there sometimes. If we don't open up on him you'll get the recording of a lifetime.'

Carried away by the sergeant's enthusiasm I placed the mike on the parapet, crawled back along the trench with the mike-lead and joined Bob Wade, our engineer, in a small dug-out where he crouched over his recording gear. We waited like hunters in their 'hide' by a water-hole in the African bush, for our victims to come out within mike-range.

The strange, inconsequential sounds of the Anzio night were all around us. A sudden chattering from a Spandau began somewhere ahead of us in the darkness and ceased as pointlessly as it began. The dirty blanket that served as the dug-out door was carefully pushed aside and the sergeant squeezed in with two cups of cocoa, thick and sugary but consoling in their warmth, as we gulped the scalding liquid down, and then thawed out our numb fingers around the cup. The sergeant checked on his watch—'They're putting down the big stonk on the Germans north of the "Boot" in a few minutes, come and watch.'

We followed the sergeant out into the trench and looked towards the north-east; the night was very clear and full of stars.

There was a swift flash from somewhere away along the sea-coast, then another and another until the whole sky seemed lit by sheet-lightning which, after a few seconds' interval, was followed by the overwhelming thunder of the guns. The noise seemed to roll in on top of us —an awe-inspiring rumpus of cracks, crashes, thumps and then the muffled thuds of the shells exploding out in the distant German lines. Over five hundred guns are now crowded into the Beachhead, and our artillery fire is so perfectly synchronized that, in the central sectors, every single gun can be brought to bear on one selected target and send five hundred shells smashing down on it in a matter of seconds. Flare after flare went up from the Germans side of the line to the north. The barrage ceased as suddenly as it had begun.

'What are they firing at?' I asked the sergeant.

'Who knows? Some poor bastard's copping it.'

Our war is confined to the few yards of soil around the mouth of the Moletta, and the most cosmic-seeming events can be taking place a few miles away and we still neither know nor care. But in the silence that follows the barrage the nightingales began to sing, a lone bird at first, then a whole chorus of them until the air seemed to throb softly with their trillings and flutings.

A young sentry standing muffled beside us said, 'Lovely, bloody little birds, the more guns there are the more they sing. I can tell 'em—they sing like that near Horsham where I come from.'

The sergeant would have none of this. 'Wait till you've heard 'em every mucking night, the bloody sound they make will get into your bones. We had a lad with us who let them get on his nerves so much that he loosed off with his rifle every time he heard them sing—he was "bird-happy," if ever I saw a man.'

Is it the racking contrast between the nightingale, singing free above the earth, and the muddy, crawling life the soldier has to lead below, that makes this bird song so difficult to bear? We went back into the dug-out, listened on our headphones, dozing and yawning . . . until a grey half-light crept past the curtain. Dawn was at hand and still we had no message from the sergeant. I could stand it no longer and crawled forward again to the line of pits where we had left the mike. I found the sergeant and his men in a state of restrained fury.

'He never came out, Old Ted didn't; the beggar's let me down, that's what he's done, proper let me down. I'll never forgive him for this; he's got no right to do this to me. I'm really disappointed in Old Ted, I really am."

'Should have sent him a contract!' came the laconic mutter from one of the men.

From the mouth of the Moletta the front line followed the valley to the point where it split into a maze of minor watercourses—the wadi country.

We have seen how fatal a part it had played during the great German offensive in February; how the enemy had used the deep gullies to infiltrate his attacking troops, and how whole companies had been swallowed up in the complex warren created by the stream beds and the broken ground in between. When the battle died away the two sides still found themselves enmeshed in the wadis, with a front line that was hopelessly tangled and untidy. The forward positions were simply enlargements of the shallow pits and holes into which the exhausted troops had dropped after all impetus to attack and counter-attack had gone.

The Germans still had the higher ground and could look down the slope into the British positions. The slope was hardly visible to a man standing upright, but for four months no man dared stand upright by day in this country; he would have been scythed down in a matter of seconds by a burst of machine-gun fire. The battle in the wadis was fought by men who had perforce to move over the ground on their stomachs or on all-fours and to whom a slope of a few feet the wrong way was a matter of life and death. This possession of the slope by the Germans was vital; it gave them an infuriating geographical advantage which the British could counter only by active patrolling and general aggressiveness.

But how does a divisional commander keep his men aggressive for months on end in such dismal surroundings? He knows that the natural tendency of the man in the slit-trench during a quiet period is to try to let things slide. The front-line soldier is never tormented with an imperative desire for action—he simply hopes to survive his spell of duty in the mud and then to get back to the rest area as soon as possible. Yet the general has to goad his troops into activity under penalty of getting no information about his enemies and of finding his forward defences gradually whittled away.

The Germans were past masters in the tactics of silent infiltration, and from time to time they would even slip across the Lateral Road behind the British front, which was used to bring up supplies in the night. By day it was swept by machine-gun fire and, on the 5th Division front, an unwritten agreement between the British and the German Parachute Division opposite them allowed safe passage once or twice a day for a Red Cross jeep to drive along the road to a forward First Aid Post. When a casualty had to be moved the men in the post raised a Red Cross flag on a twelve-foot-high pole and the firing ceased on both sides.

But the Germans eventually began to have doubts about the wisdom of permitting this strange jeep to be the only thing that could move above ground in the wadi country and nurtured unfounded suspicions that the British were not playing fair with them. One night the jeep driver, while driving up the road in the darkness, was stopped by a wire stretched across the road and found himself surrounded by Germans. The young officer in charge spoke perfect English and after his men had searched the jeep said to the driver, 'I am letting you go, but tell your CO that an officer and his men from the German Parachute Division have been watching your ambulance for the last two days and have seen ammunition, supplies and personnel taken up in it. I do not wish to see this again. If I do I shall blow the ambulance off the road and shoot the people whether they are wearing Red Cross bands or no.' The Germans slipped away in the darkness.

The Germans were not above suspicion themselves, and the King's Own Yorkshire Light Infantry rounded up four men who approached our lines with a Red Cross flag under cover of burying the dead, but who carried hand-grenades in their pockets. The German general in command of the 4th Paratroop Division fired mortar shells with a demand enclosed in the shells for the return of the men under the Geneva Convention. General Gregson-Ellis promptly replied, via 25-pounder, that men who prowl around front lines with hand-grenades are hardly genuine Red Cross men. This ended a strange diplomatic conversation conducted with the aid of high explosives.

Such incidents were by no means rare, for General Penney and General Templer had also to tackle this problem of the misuse of the Red Cross, but they were bound to make the commanders anxious about the stability of their front line. The troops might grumble, but the Generals had, for their own safety, continually to lay on trench raids and minor attacks to push the Germans back from certain key-points.

Whichever way the raids went they were dreaded by those who took part in them, and loathed by those who received them. The wadi country remained vicious and disheartening to the very end.

Every wadi had now been christened with a name usually derived from its shape on the Divisional map. The Fortress and the Boot were the unenvied possessions of the 5th Division, while the 1st languished in the Starfish, the Culvert, and the North and South Lobster Claw. Some of them, especially the Fortress and the Boot, lay so close to the enemy forward positions that new arrivals could hardly believe that life could go on in the narrow pits on the side of the gullies; the Germans seemed almost to breathe down their necks.

It was the ever-present squalor and boredom of the life in the wadis, as much as the danger of it, which eventually 'got men down'. The commanders were right to force their soldiers to fight against it, for they knew that, as in the previous war, there are limits to the combat efficiency of a man in the front line. A good man might stay on the top of his form for a few months, during which he would crawl out on patrol and fight off any raiding party with the coolness of a veteran. Then something happened: a near miss from a mortar or a few of his pals blown up on hidden mines and he began to go downhill. He counted his chances, took fewer risks and tended to lurk at the back of the dug-out like a wounded bird.

At this point he should have been relieved from the line for rest if he was to remain a good soldier, but at Anzio there was nowhere to go for rest and there were far too few replacements for the British divisions. Men stayed too long in the wadis.

General Gregson-Ellis summed it up quickly as soon as his division took its position in the line when he made the entry into his diary, 'A nauseating bit of country to fight in'.

After a tour of the wadis the visitor to the front line came to the battered bridge of the Flyover with the relief of a man coming out of prison. The Flyover was the most prominent landmark on the British sector, the one point which was lifted a few feet above the general level, and which could give our men observation over the German positions. The gunners had tunnelled an observation post in the soft earth of the embankment and lined the tunnel with wood. Here the officer on duty would crouch over his binoculars and sweep every yard of the broken landscape before him—from this snug hide-out alone could you get a glimpse of the full-scale destruction which had befallen the Anzio landscape. It was a bleak vision of broken farmhouses, churned earth, rusting wire and abandoned tanks.

One young officer with a taste for statistics tried to while away the hours of waiting in the OP by calculating the cost of the wreckage before him, and of the weight of bombs and shells which caused it. He abandoned the calculation when he had reached the sum of twelve million pounds per acre.

The Flyover was constantly deluged with shells during the so-called 'Quiet Period' of Anzio, and on one occasion the wooden lining of one of the OP tunnels was set on fire. The observation party had to jump out onto the German side of the embankment in full view of the enemy and then scuttle hurriedly back under the bridge to shelter. Not a shot was fired at them.

It was one of those strange suspensions of the will to kill which, quite irrationally, would overwhelm the men on both sides for a brief moment. For days they would be mortaring each other, calling down artillery fire on the slightest movement and sniping at every head that dared show itself a few inches above ground. Then something absurdly normal or pointless would happen—a German would hang out the washing at a bend in the wadis or, fed up with crouching in his fox-hole, would stand up on the skyline and stretch his legs. No one would have the heart to fire a shot at him.

So, too, the Germans dealt kindly with the slightly intoxicated GI who had found an Italian top-hat in one of the shell-torn villas, put it on and staggered across the mine-fields of no-man's-land into the enemy lines. The Germans put his silk hat straight, turned him round to the proper point of the compass and sent him back to his comrades with their compliments. Later that day both sides were hard at it trying to wipe each other off the face of the earth with high explosive.

The Flyover produced an unexpected piece of treasure trove after the German counter-attack had faded away. A

British Engineer officer, crawling to inspect the minefields in the darkness of the no-man's-land that now stretched from the battered bridge towards the German lines, came across a strange, intriguing object, a sort of squat metal box furnished with small tank tracks. A broken cable dangled from one end. The box seemed to contain high explosive.

Colonel O'Gorman, of the British 1st Divisional REME, determined to drag the mysterious object back inside our lines. He staged a remarkable fishing operation in which he hauled his prize into the safety of the embankment, playing it like a salmon at the end of five hundred yards of balloon wire wound onto a winch mounted on a big Scammell truck. He and his men made two daring attempts before they landed their queer fish. The object skidded off into shell-holes, the wire broke and twanged back with a noise that brought down a fierce German concentration of shells, while the Scammell truck seemed to be impossible to hide behind the embankment.

But on the night of 20 April the REME engineers had got the mystery object safely inside the Beachhead lines, and it immediately became the sensation of Anzio.

It turned out to be one of the secret weapons with which the German High Command had striven to hearten their men during the great all-out assault on the Allied line in February: a radio-controlled miniature tank. In theory the tank crawled forward and deposited a powerful explosive charge in the middle of the enemy defences, which was then exploded by remote control. Thirteen of these tanks were sent against the Allied line at the opening of the German offensive and not one reached its objective. They foundered in shell-holes or were knocked out by gunfire.

The Germans had far more effective weapons than this simple device in active preparation; and the Allies could count themselves lucky that the V1 and V2 were not ready in time to be used against the Beachhead.

From these British positions around the Flyover the American sector swung in a great arc eastwards and then down to the sea. It was slowly becoming the most crowded of the sectors as more ammunition, supplies and reinforcements were poured into the Beachhead during the last month of the siege. General Truscott, with his mind on the eventual breakout, was driving his troops through an intensive course of training, and the back areas of the American sector echoed with the crackle of guns on the ranges near the coast, while smoke-screens blanketed the areas where the tanks conducted special exercises.

The long period of waiting at Anzio was particularly frustrating for the men of the American 1st Armored Division. Tankers are trained to the tempo of mobile warfare and it is galling to them to have to dig mounds of earth around their tanks or let them sink out of sight in holes in the ground. The very shape of the tank seems to protest against this static role. General Ernie Harmon, that tough, resolute plain-spoken Vermonter, made a point of setting his men a constant series of defence tasks, sending out his tanks in small groups to fire into the German lines at night or using them to give close support to trench raids.

The main concentration area of the 1st Armored lay in the Padiglione woodlands to the right of the Anzio-Albano road, and of this the Germans were well aware. Axis Sally would gloat, 'We'll be bombing and shelling the Armored boys today so have a happy time.' The woodlands would be well and truly plastered and that evening Sally would purr over the air, 'Well, boys, how did you enjoy that blasting you got today?' There was one occasion when the 1st Armored did not enjoy it at all.

On Easter Sunday morning the soldiers assembled for service round the 'Church-in-the-Wildwood', built from trees felled by enemy shelling. The bugler blew the church call, and in the early morning light the men streamed through the woodlands to worship. The Germans spotted the assembly and later in the day were ready with their artillery fire. As the Catholic and Protestant service began the German guns opened up and plastered the whole area. The services were interrupted, but when the firing ceased the men noted that most of the shells had dropped on the lines and dugouts they would have occupied if they had not been attending service.

As April brightened into May the Division concentrated on its training for the eventual breakout, and General Harmon urged his commanders to put forward every idea that American ingenuity could devise for overcoming the obstacles that the Germans had been given four months to prepare. The conditions of warfare at Anzio were such that there was always a premium on ingenuity. If you could think up

215

a trick that would surprise your enemy, a new way of projecting explosive into the deep wadis or a method of crashing through barbed wire, you were bound to reap a quick reward. The lines were so close together that the capture of a hundred yards by unorthodox methods could decide a battle. General Gregson-Ellis, on the British sector, devised a catapult for throwing bombs into the wadis, and General O'Daniels of the American 3rd Infantry Division came forward with a battle sledge on which an infantryman could be towed across minefields in the wake of a tank.

The 1st Armored produced three major tricks. They invented a bridge which could be pushed forward from an armoured vehicle and which would help the engineers to cross ditches under fire.

They experimented with a grapnel which could be fired from an advancing tank so that it fell on the far side of any mass of barbed wire ahead. The tanker could winch the grapnel back, thus tearing a path through the wire for the following infantry.

But the most impressive new trick was undoubtedly the 'Snake'. This curious somewhat two-edged weapon did not originate on the Beachhead, but the 1st Armored Engineers adapted it to suit their purpose. The Snake was a 300-foot tube of steel packed with TNT up to about fifty feet from the tank, which first towed the tube into battle and then swung around and pushed it out over a minefield. The crew braced themselves against concussion and exploded the TNT by fire from their machine-guns. A shattering explosion followed, which detonated all the mines over an area of about 200 to 300 yards. It was the most effective method devised during the war for beating the mine menace, but while it was a godsend for the infantry it involved serious risks for the tankers who had to tow it into battle. The Germans could also fire machine-guns at the Snake while the crew struggled to place it into position: as General Harmon remarked grimly, 'TNT doesn't choose up sides!'

Away on the right flank of the Beachhead, the 1st Special Service Force had been holding the line since the days of the first landing. For months they had fought a private war which differed completely in character from the rest of the Beachhead battle—an affair of bold night patrols, sudden raids on enemy strong-points, and a nerve-racking tussle of wits to set or avoid traps for the other side. The 1st SSF had a long front to hold, but they were helped by good defensive ground—the Mussolini Canal was wide with high banks and made a perfect tank trap.

The force was a picked one on the lines of the British Commandos and one-third of the men were Canadian. When they sailed for Anzio, after a hard time in the mountains before Cassino, they were at combat strength; 68 officers and 1,165 other ranks, but by no means too large a force for the mission assigned to them by General Lucas. When every man was needed along the Anzio-Albano road and in the front before Cisterna, Lucas could not afford to spare many units to guard his eastern flank. It is true that the Germans were not likely to make a major attack in this sector—the Canal was a formidable obstacle and the country around was dead flat, a maze of irrigation ditches peppered with small farmhouses. But in the crisis of Anzio no one could be certain that the Germans might not try a surprise in a sector where the Allies least expected it. Lucas needed aggressive troops on his eastern flank who would carry out a policy of vigorous raids and give the Germans an impression of strength which was not really there. The 1st SSF were the ideal men for the job.

Night after night they raided deep into the enemy's territory. They became a legend to the Germans, who, at one point, reported that the Americans were using 'ferocious coloured troops'—the SSF men usually blackened their faces before going into action. At first all the raids were carried out at night, but later, when armoured support became available, combined tank and infantry attacks were launched, and towards the end of the siege the Germans had been driven back in some places almost four miles from the Mussolini Canal.

The Special Service men were a cocky, confident bunch, imbued with that pride which comes to men when they realize that they are an *élite;* picked soldiers entrusted only with the toughest of tasks. They carried stickers, which they affixed at night on the walls of German-occupied houses; either the Red Arrow, their own regimental crest, or cheerfully sinister threats with an air of schoolboy challenge about them—'BEWARE! THE SS WILL GET YOU NEXT.' These notices were surprisingly effective.

The Germans began to worry about the security of this

sector and from time to time struck back with SSF methods. They discovered the path near the Mussolini Canal along which the American raiders crawled at night and sowed it with *Schu* mines—those vicious, light-weight, anti-personnel mines, cased in plastic to make them safe from the Allied mine-detection apparatus. The SSF men were caught in the snare and when the German ambush opened fire thirty-two Americans lost their legs or feet in the trap.

But this was a private war in which such reverses of fortune had to be accepted, and the SSF never lost the command of their long sector of the line. A Special Service unit depends more than any other on the personality of its commander. He must set the tone and give direct leadership of a kind that has become rare in modern war. The great infantry and tank battles of World War II were mounted by men who had the gift of organization, and the leaders, at moments, almost had the air of being Big Businessmen of War. In the Commandos, the Airborne units and the Special Service Forces we seem to be back in the atmosphere of an older, even a Homeric period of battle, when men took pride in their prowess in personal, hand-to-hand combat and where they looked to their leader to be in the forefront of the fight.

The leader of the 1st SSF, General R. T. Frederick, fulfilled this requirement to the letter. Repeatedly wounded and awarded the Distinguished Service Cross four times, he was idolized by his men as the Bravest Man on the Beachhead. No one looked less like the great Achilles or even like the conventional idea of the modern Man of War. He was a slight, pale-faced man with a dapper black moustache which gave him the air of a bank clerk in a small branch office in the country, and the visitor to his dug-out headquarters near the Mussolini Canal would wonder if this was, indeed, the legendary Frederick, the outstanding battle leader of popular repute—until he began to talk!

Frederick talked swiftly and to the point. I remember sitting with him one April evening waiting for the SSF to go out on a raid when the General fired me with the vigour of his gestures and the common sense of his attitude to the American soldier at war.

You've got to tell the GI the reason for a job before he'll do it, and you've got to show him you can do it as

218

well as he can. When I get up to the front, of course I'm scared, scared to hell, but I know I mustn't show it. I light a cigarette, coolly as I can, and then the boys say, 'Hell, if the General goes there, damn it, we can.' The American soldier made a mess of things at first because he didn't know what he was getting into. Sure, some of them ran away on their first fight, they just hadn't been given the right leadership. But we learnt fast, faster than you British, I think, and if the Kraut had anything good we grabbed the idea quick, like the Flak-wagons and our tank-destroyers. Everything the Kraut can do we can do better.'

The SSF waded into battle with a two-fisted spirit and dominated the eastern flank throughout the length of the Beachhead siege.

Slowly the long months of waiting at Anzio wore away. Spring turned to early summer, and the wadis on the Upper Moletta and the battered ground around Ponte Rotto and Isola Bella became covered with wide carpets of flowers. The Alban Hills and jagged peaks of the Colli Lepini seemed very blue and close at hand, and the watchers on the Beachhead could pick up the familiar landmarks, the broken railway viaduct near Albano, the dark dots which marked the tunnels suspected of hiding the notorious railway guns and the observatory on the summit of the hills above Rocca di Papa.

Out of the line, the men bathed on carefully designated beaches, ignoring the occasional shells that sent up fountains of spray as they dropped into the water. There were sports meetings and amateur concert companies and film shows in the bigger underground shelters. The 5th Division pipers created a sensation on their tour of the American sector, where a big demand grew up for bagpipe music by 'those guys in skirts'.

In the pine woods along the coast the British organized sniping competitions, and it was a favourite spot for those informal talks with which the Army Bureau of Current Affairs strove valiantly to meet the British soldier's need to discuss what goes on in the rest of the world and his preoccupation with the post-war conditions in Britain. One of the big problems of the Beachhead was the sense of being 'cut off' which overcame even the most stalwart of men, the feeling that they had been forgotten in a lost corner of Europe. ABCA was good for morale even if all that came out of some of the talks was an airing of grievances and a tendency by the grumblers in the units to mutter, 'What about Russia?'

All through the history of the Beachhead the actual port of Anzio was never out of the front line. It was constantly under the fire of the long-range guns until the final day, when as a parting salvo 'Anzio Annie' and her sister guns up on the Alban Hills came out of their railway tunnels and fired off all the shells they could in a final outburst of fury. One British observer at Navy House had the heart to count each shell as it fell into the harbour area and made the total 609 for 29 May. For days on end the harbour area seemed swathed in a light mist as the smoke generators, manned by cheerful coloured troops, tried to blot out observation and protect the shipping from sneak raiders. On bright moonlight nights huge white clouds of smoke went billowing up into the quiet sky from the generators, which hissed amongst the palms and broken houses of the waterfront like escaping gas mains.

A walk amongst these generators at night had its own charm, for the operators were not sticklers for military etiquette. An officer carrying out a night inspection was suddenly startled by a deep voice growling in the darkness, 'Whoa, boss!' 'Don't you know how to challenge? Weren't you going to challenge me?' inquired the officer. 'No, boss,' said the Negro soldier with a disarming grin, 'I wasn't goin' to challenge. I was goin' to shoot!'

The enemy tried to break through the smoke-screen by laying two powerful searchlight beams into the harbour area from vantage-points outside the Beachhead perimeter, but he had no success with this experiment. He also tried to close the shipping lane up from Naples by laying mines at night, but the Allied naval minesweepers worked so well that after the initial landing there were no further losses from German mines.

Even in the so-called quiet period of Anzio the Germans never abandoned their attempt to cut the Allies' supply route or to drive the shipping away from the Beachhead anchorage.

Soon after midnight on 21 April an American patrol-boat on a course six miles south of Anzio lighthouse made a mysterious radio contact which was followed half an hour later by an equally mysterious underwater explosion dead astern. Just after dawn another patrol boat, PC-591, was on duty in the same area and the look-out spotted a strange object bobbing through the water on the starboard bow, leaving a small wake behind it. As the patrol boat dashed into the attack the men on the bridge were astonished to see ahead of them a small glass dome about 24 inches in diameter projecting about a foot above the water: the alarm was immediately flashed to the defences, 'Midget submarines attacking anchorage.'

The patrol boats raced zig-zagging across the calm water in a flurry of white wakes and exploding depth-charges. The midgets did not survive long. Patrol-boat PC-591 quickly blew up the submarine ahead of it and fished out of the water a shaken Oberleutnant of the German Navy. A few minutes later two more midgets were detected and destroyed. The surprise had failed, for it was launched too soon, the submarines betrayed their presence too easily and were extremely vulnerable to depth-charges with shallow settings.

It must have been a desperate venture to pilot one of these contraptions into battle. The pilot, in diving dress, sat on one torpedo travelling on the surface with another live torpedo slung underneath. As soon as he reached his target the pilot could release the lower torpedo and then slowly and obviously turn for home—so slowly in fact that the attacker was inevitably spotted and destroyed or else compelled, as in one case, to run ashore for safety on the beach.

Submarines, mines, gunfire, air-raids—nothing could now stop the steady flow of supplies into the Beachhead, so that by 23 May Anzio had, in addition to its normal ten-day reserve, a month's additional reserve of supplies. The LSTs and the Liberty ships sailed on a well-established schedule with an average despatch of six LSTs a day and the arrival and clearing of four big Liberty ships every ten days. In all over 500,000 tons of supplies were unloaded at Anzio, with a peak day of 7,828 tons on 29 March and a second record of 7,015 tons on 27 May. There was a moment when this Italian fishing port ranked seventh among the great ports of the world, and all this in spite of the handicaps of a small shallow harbour and open beaches which were heavily battered by surf as soon as the wind blew directly from the west.

A pleasant exchange of Navy signals took place as the men

on the spot proudly reported to Naples that they had achieved a record unloading at Anzio. Back came the reminder from Headquarters that no matter what tonnage they had landed on the Beachhead their efforts were being surpassed at the moment by the volcano Vesuvius in full and spectacular eruption: 'The Naples group of ports is now discharging at the rate of 12 million tons a year, while Vesuvius is estimated to be doing 30 million a day. We cannot but admire this gesture of the gods.'

10

Break-out

So, through the long months of siege, the Beachhead lived its strange, self-contained life. The old 'Anzio hands' had almost forgotten that any other life existed. They had been cut off from the rest of the military world so long that they had ceased to think of relief or of a link-up with the Fifth Army. Here they were in Anzio and here they would stay for the rest of the war.

Then, as April turned into May, as the fresh green of the springing corn began to soften the harsh, bomb-smashed landscape of the Flyover and the nightingales sang with redoubled power along the Moletta, rumours began to circulate on the Beachhead. Somewhere in that distant, unattainable land of Southern Italy, more remote than London or New York to the men at Anzio, the High Command was apparently preparing for an event which seemed to be beyond the bounds of possibility. Sixth Corps had been ordered to get its plans ready for 'The Break-out'!

Soon even the most hardened of Beachhead cynics were compelled to admit that there was something in it. More and more visitors appeared from the Outside, ammunition and stores started to overflow in the dumps, reinforcements poured in until the Beachhead seemed to bulge at the seams. Could it be true that we were going to see the end of all the long, weary months of waiting and frustration? Was the Beachhead agony about to justify itself at long last?

While the Beachhead had been living its life apart, great events had been in preparation in the outside world. The summer of 1944 was to be the summer of decision for the Allies. The British and Americans were getting ready to launch the greatest sea-borne invasion of all time against the coast of Normandy while the Red armies surged forward again in distant Russia. Italy, which had brought so much disappointment to the Allies, must now show a dividend. General Alexander's armies were to begin the grand assault, now about to be flung from all three quarters of Europe against Hitler's Fortress. To them was given the honour of being the curtain-raisers on the strange and terrible drama that was to be enacted on the soil of Europe.

More than ever was it important that the German divisions in Italy should be pinned there and prevented from arriving in Normandy when our invasion moved to the attack over the waters of the English Channel. But General Alexander now felt that he could think in far wider terms than mere holding attacks. For the first time he had enough men, ammunition and supplies to plan a full-scale battle which would break the Gustav Line and smash the German armies in Italy.

Rome, too, a welcome and glittering prize, would fall into his hands, but this was not his first aim. The real, worthwhile prize was the breaking of Kesselring's front with all that this implied for the future. Alexander felt he had it in his power to win a decisive victory in Italy.

His plan for the great offensive looked simple—all successful military plans have this air of deceptive simplicity after the event has justified them. But successful simplicity is hard to achieve and is the hall-mark of the true masters of war. General Alexander's Italian attack in May was one of the outstanding achievements of World War II in this most difficult art of generalship.

Briefly he decided to transfer as much of his strength as possible from his eastern to his western front, to reinforce his position along the Garigliano and before Cassino so strongly that he would have the requisite overwhelming superiority in men and weapons at this decisive point and thus make his break-through certain. He could not conceal from so astute an opponent as Kesselring that such a movement was in progress from his eastern front on the Adriatic coast, but he could try to deceive him as to where the troops were going. An elaborate cover plan was devised to ensure that the Germans should think that another sea landing was in preparation with its destination at Civitavecchia, on the coast north of Rome.

The Canadian Corps sent wireless detachments to open an elaborate signals net near Salerno. The air filled with message traffic and procedure signals until the Germans were convinced that at least three divisions were getting ready to embark for the new invasion. Meanwhile new divisions were being quickly moved towards the Cassino front, the Poles massed before the fateful Monastery, and the French took over the crossings of the Garigliano. The French held a trump card in their hands, for they had brought from North Africa those formidable mountaineers from the Atlas, the Goumiers.

One of the puzzling things about the Italian campaign had been the absence, on the Allied side, of large bodies of troops specially trained for mountain warfare. The battle had raged amongst savage hills, but most of the men who fought across Monte Cassino and the Aurunci Mountains had never seen such country in their lives before. The cliffs looked twice as steep as they really were, and the mountain paths seemed endless to farmers from Lincolnshire and mechanics from Detroit. A fully trained division of mountaineers might have been of real value in the central spine of the Apennines, where the German defences were perforce not as densely placed as around Monastery Hill and Cassino.

Now, at last, the French were going to put in the line men who looked on mountains as opportunities and not obstacles. When the time came for them to attack, the Goumiers astonished friends and foes by the speed with which they moved over the wild mountain barrier of the Aurunci at night. This skill and speed was one of the major surprises produced by General Alexander's forces.

All through April the regrouping of the Allied armies went steadily forward, and still the Germans did not tumble to the blow that Alexander was preparing for them. By the first week of May he had most of the divisions of General Oliver Leese's Eighth Army concentrated before Cassino and the entrance to the Liri valley, while General Mark Clark's Fifth Army, with the French Expeditionary Force and one American division, was ready along the Garigliano to the sea. Alexander had one other asset which he now had to consider how to use to the best advantage.

Far behind the German lines, seventy miles beyond Cassino and the southern front, lay the Beachhead. At last it was

224

coming into its own. There it was, like a huge land-mine, packed with the high explosive of its highly trained and experienced divisions and its formidable artillery, ready to be detonated with shattering effect whenever the Army Group commander might decide.

When should Alexander press the button: early on in the fighting to help break the deadlock on the Gustav Line, by drawing the German reserves north, or after the breakthrough to turn the retreat into a decisive rout? Alexander looked at the overwhelming force he had concentrated on his main front—surely this time he was bound to crack the Gustav Line! The Germans would be in full retreat down the Liri valley and Route Six. What would be the effect of Sixth Corps breaking out of its Beachhead to throw itself across the main lines of communication of the Germans as they struggled to get back to the north of Rome?

Here was a chance of smashing Kesselring's armies so decisively that they would never be able to rally until they reached the curve of the Northern Apennines two hundred miles to the north. Alexander decided that this was to be the way in which he would use the Beachhead, and with this strategy in his mind he went up to see Truscott at Anzio early in May.

Truscott had, of course, been fully informed of the plans for the coming offensive and had been hard at work preparing his own scheme for the Break-out. He had already discussed four alternative plans with General Clark, one for each eventuality. They rejoiced in a weird collection of codenames—Grasshopper, Buffalo, Turtle, and Crawdad. There were plans to outflank the Alban Hills via Carroceto and the south-west in case the Germans fell back onto the new defence line they were reported to be constructing in the hills; plans to push southward through the marshes in case the southern front never got 'rolling'; and plans to smash the German beachhead ring at Cisterna, and push through the Velletri gap to get across Route Six. Truscott showed them all to Alexander with some pride since they represented hours of intricate staff-work. He was prepared to mount any one of them with forty-eight hours' notice.

Alexander immediately told Truscott there was only one of these plans that interested him, Buffalo, the break-out to the Velletri Gap and Valmontone. This would place Sixth Corps squarely across the line of retreat of the beaten Ger-

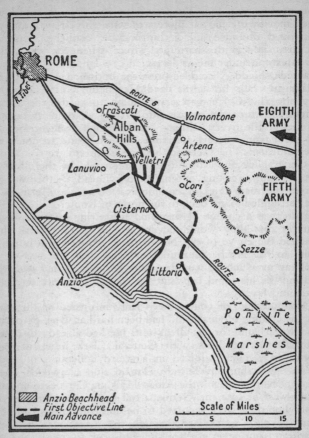

THE BREAKOUT PLANS, 23 MAY 1944

mans. 'This is the plan I want and I reserve for myself the decision as to the time of launching it,' said Alexander. Buffalo would make the break-out a real knock-out. Truscott concentrated on preparing it.

But now came a most puzzling and bewildering development. General Clark arrived at the Beachhead next day. He admits that he was irritated at what he felt was General Alexander's interference in the American chain of command, and even more worried that there was some sort of plan afoot to deprive the Fifth Army of the glory of capturing Rome. At all costs Clark was determined to be first in. He soon called up Alexander on the telephone and told him firmly that he wanted all orders to his subordinates issued through him, Clark; he wasn't going to have Alexander 'move in and run my army'. Truscott had prepared his four alternative plans under Clark's orders, and the Fifth Army Commander wanted to feel free to move in any direction that the development of the battle demanded—above all, one feels as one reads General Clark's account of the incident, into Rome.

General Alexander withdrew gracefully and assured General Clark that he had no intention of interfering. A curious picture, surely, of the Supreme Commander, with his plan set for dealing a decisive blow at the enemy, refusing to insist that his subordinate should carry out the most important part of that plan! Clark may have been right, no one could be certain how the attack might develop but in the chain of command in an Army Group, who has the last word?

Thus, even before it was launched, a shadow lay over Operation Buffalo, and General Clark held himself ready to alter the direction of its charge.

Meanwhile Truscott pushed ahead with his preparations for mounting it. He had decided to make the Break-out mainly an American affair. The British divisions had fought a fearful battle in the early days of Anzio and had never been as fully reinforced as the Americans.

The plan called for the capture of Cisterna, the breaking of the German defence line based upon this strong-point and the railway embankment that ran north-west from it, followed by an advance into the gap between the Alban Hills and the Colli Lepini. In the first phase the 1st Armored Division would push around Cisterna to the west, the 3rd Division would assault the ruined town itself and Frederick's Special Service Force would advance on the eastern flank to cut Route Seven. The 45th Division would make a limited advance in the area of Carano while the British would mount diversionary attacks to hold the Germans on the western perimeter of the Beachhead.

The Break-out would not be easy. The Germans had five and a half divisions containing Sixth Corps at Anzio, and in addition Von Mackensen could call on the 26th Panzers and the 29th Panzer Grenadier Division, which Kesselring had withdrawn into Army Group reserve and placed just south of Rome. They could be flung at short notice against Truscott as soon as Buffalo showed signs of breaking the Beachhead ring. But the Allies could count on overwhelming air supremacy and their immensely powerful and efficient artillery.

They possessed a further advantage: Truscott had imbued Sixth Corps with his strong, confident attacking spirit. All that was now wanted was the word 'GO'.

Away to the south among the mountains of Cassino the night of 11 May was starlit and clear with promise of a helpful moon later on. At eleven o'clock over fifteen hundred guns opened fire on the front between Cassino and the sea. The Germans were taken by surprise—they had been told that they need not worry about any move by British and American Armies until 24 May. Now in a storm of shell-fire more violent than anything they had imagined or encountered in the bloody earlier battles in Italy, their enemies were upon them.

There could be no swift break-through: Alexander's men were going up against long-prepared positions which the Germans had already successfully defended through the long winter months and fortified with every ingenious defensive trick at their command. The battle would perforce take on the classic form of all the great set-piece attacks of the war. First a terrible slogging match, a remorseless pounding in which the German reserves would be dragged to the danger-point and pinned until they were exhausted; then the decisive blow at another part of the line and, at last, the break-out.

This had been the pattern at Alamein and was to be repeated on the beachhead at Normandy. So it was in Italy in May.

At Anzio men looked to the south and waited anxiously for news. Sixth Corps was an actor, ready off-stage and tensed with anticipation as he listened for his cue.

Day by day the situation reports poured into the Nettuno headquarters of General Truscott, and the rumours flew around the Beachhead. Thirteenth Corps of the Eighth Army were over the Rapido, the French had started to race through the Aurunci Mountains, the Americans were held on the coast and the Poles were nerving themselves for their final, searing battle ordeal against the Monastery itself.

The days passed, the grinding struggle rose to its climax, and still, to those who waited at Anzio, the break-through seemed as far off as ever. Then the signs started to multiply that it could not be long delayed. Intelligence brought news of the first importance to Sixth Corps; the two German reserve divisions south of Rome had set off post-haste for the Gustav Line. Kesselring, in spite of Von Mackensen's protests, was thinning out his ring around the Beachhead to bolster up his creaking front around Cassino.

Then, after over a week of bloodthirsty slogging, there could no longer be any doubt: the Germans began to pull out. The Poles, heroic and triumphant, stood at last amidst the ruins of the Monastery, the Americans were driving forward hard long the coast, the Eighth Army had fought its way into the Liri valley and the astonishing Goumiers, disdaining all problems of logistics, air support and artillery fire plans and all the complexities of mechanized war as practised in the 1940s, had taken to the mountains and penetrated deep into the German positions beyond the Garigliano. Soon the Hitler Line, a series of positions prepared behind the Gustav Line as a last stop, found its name being hurriedly changed to the Dora Line—the Führer's prestige could not be jeopardized. By 20 May it was clear that Kesselring would have to cut his losses and make a bolt for safety north of Rome.

Was this the moment to detonate the Anzio land-mine in his rear? And should Buffalo now charge towards the Valmontone-Velletri gap and cut Kesselring's escape route to the north? General Alexander thought so and directed Sixth Corps to be ready to break-out on 21 May in the direction of Cori and Valmontone. This timing was in fact premature since the Eighth Army was still finding difficulties in the Liri valley, but Alexander remained determined that when the break-out came, it should drive straight through the Velletri gap to cut Route Six.

Again General Mark Clark violently disagreed. His reasons are on record in his book, *Calculated Risk*.

I was shocked that Alexander made this decision without reference to me. I should point out at this time that the Fifth Army had had an extremely difficult time through the whole campaign . . . we were keyed up, and in the heat of battle there were almost certain to be clashes of personalities and ideas over this all-out drive. We not only wanted the honour of capturing Rome, but we felt we more than deserved it, that it would make up to a certain extent for the buffeting and the frustration we had undergone in keeping up the winter pressure against the Germans. . . . Not only did we intend to become the first army in fifteen centuries to seize Rome from the south, but we intended to see that the people at home knew that it was the Fifth Army that did the job, and knew the price that had been paid for it.

The Fifth Army Commander was a good soldier, a fine organizer and could advance sound military reasons for keeping the direction of Buffalo fluid until the last moment, but it certainly seems as if Rome was colouring his thinking about the Break-out. Nobody, in the words he used later, 'would get in on the act' if he could help it. General Alexander comments: 'I always assured General Clark in conversation that Rome would be entered by his army, and I can only assume that publicity rather than military considerations dictated his decision.'[1]

But Rome had still to be fought for; the Germans might yet cause the Allies grievous losses before they entered the sought-for city. It was high time that Anzio played its part in the battle.

For now the southern front really was 'rolling', the French were tearing through the mountains and the American Second Corps had thrust along the coast and were to hammer at Terracina. Soon the American vanguards would be out onto the Pontine marshes.

General Clark had already embarked the 36th Division for the Beachhead; fresh and eager, it would be used to pass through the 3rd Division after the capture of Cisterna and become the spearhead of the Buffalo charge. Clark now set out himself for Anzio, to establish the advanced HQ of Fifth Army in the Villa Borghese. The Break-out was fixed for dawn on 23 May 1944.

The pattern of the great set-piece assaults of World War II never varied. Always we felt the strange silence creeping over the dark landscape as zero hour approached, then the violent shock of the guns tearing the silence ruthlessly apart,

[1] From an article in the *Sunday Times*.

followed by the slow, insect-like crawl forward of the tanks with the small, huddled figures of the infantrymen bobbing amongst the shell-holes! The dense pall of smoke blots out the front, the crackle of machine-guns erupts from somewhere inside it, the crump of bombs and shells echoes in the heart of the smoke cloud, and the watchers wait, with fear and anxiety in their hearts, for the first news back. Success? Or have all our long preparations, all the careful staff-work, the minute analysis of intelligence reports and the cunningly devised cover-plans gone for naught in the first half-hour of battle?

We knew the routine by heart, and yet who could have the heart to stay away? Even those who had no business there, from high-up generals to war correspondents, went as far forward as they could in the early hours of 23 May. We huddled against the walls of a ruined farmhouse near Isola Bella. Away to the westward the flashing of gunfire on the skyline marked the British holding attacks on the Moletta: they were a vital part of our assault plan and convinced the enemy that we were going to make our break-out along the old battle-fields of the Albano road. Von Mackensen kept his main strength around the Factory and Carroceto until it was too late to save Cisterna.

The dawn was strengthening, dull and with a threat of rain, but we still spoke in whispers, afraid to break the silence around us. Over 160,000 men were close at hand, waiting, watching and, maybe, wishing desperately that the minute-hand would at last mark zero hour and that they were out of the tension of fearful anticipation.

Few men carried small books of verse in their pockets in this war as they did in the last. *The Shropshire Lad* seemed to have no place in the world of the Nazis, but some words of Milton's, learnt at school, persisted in running through my head:

> Oh, how comely it is and how reviving
> To the Spirits of just men long opprest,
> When God into the hands of their deliverer
> Puts invincible might. . . .

The GIs getting ready for the advance had other things on their minds than apt quotations from the poets.

Then at 0546 hours the Beachhead guns crashed into action. For three-quarters of an hour they poured down a concentration of awe-inspiring violence upon the German forward positions. The orchestral drum-roll of the bombardment stopped, as if at the wave of a conductor's baton, and the lighter orchestra of machine-guns, mortars and anti-tank guns took up the theme. The advancing infantry got up from their fox-holes, gritted their teeth and went forward into the smoke and dust under a leaden sky.

They did not have a 'walk-over': no advance against Germans in well-prepared positions ever was, even after the enemy had been surprised and shaken by bombardment. The 1st Armored Division, pushing westward of Cisterna, had driven five hundred yards beyond the Embankment by the end of the day. One of its Combat Units, pinning its faith in the Snake, had pushed four of these dangerous double-edged weapons into the German minefields. They exploded with appalling violence and not only blew paths through the mines but stunned the German defenders in distant strong-points. The triumphant Americans swept over the railway embankment, which they had expected to be a major obstacle, with surprising ease.

Boldness pays. The Second Combat Command of the 1st American Armored feared the Snake and suffered heavily in the minefields. They did not reach the embankment until darkness was falling.

Meantime General Frederick's Special Service Force had also outflanked Cisterna on the east and had cut Highway Seven. 3rd Division were still fighting fiercely in the outskirts of the town.

But when he looked at the situation at the end of the first day's battle, Truscott had reason to feel pleased. His men were onto their objective, he was well placed for the renewal of the attack next morning and the German defences were cracking. Fifteen hundred prisoners were being hustled back to the cages at Anzio and Nettuno.

Next morning the advance went on. The 45th Division, acting as a shield to the western flank of the attack, held off a series of counter-attacks by the anxious Von Mackensen. He had been caught on the wrong foot, 'off balance' in Montgomery's parlance, and he could not get his reserves across to the danger-point at Cisterna. Harmon's tanks swept on towards Velletri, and although the German gar-

232

rison held out stubbornly in the ruins of Cisterna, 3rd Division infantrymen were already on the move far behind it, onto the road that climbed through the vineyards towards the hill village of Cori. Truscott knew that he had now broken through the main German defences.

His men had taken losses. I crouched with the GIs who were still trying to get into the reeking ruins of Cisterna. Clearly there was nothing for it but to take the place rubbish heap after rubbish heap, cave by cave, and accept the casualties which come with street-fighting. Clearing Cisterna took two days. The Americans flung their grenades into the cellar gratings, risking the rush into the fetid darkness where automatics might be waiting to cut them down, their fire trained on the patch of light which marked the cellar enrance.

So they fought their way slowly into the centre of the town until, at last, they reached the pile of rubble which marked the *palazzo* in the main square. The two hundred men of the final garrison came shambling out of hiding, hands up and covered with white dust from broken stonework. When we went down into the great cellar below the palace, in which they had endured the Allied bombardment, we found it a stinking heap of dead and wounded, strewn over with filth and dirty clothing.

In the clearer atmosphere of the hills towards Cori their comrades who got away fared worse. Our aircraft were soon to catch their crowded columns on the narrow, hilly roads and turn them into a shambles that was to become a classic horror demonstration of the power of air attack.

There was another cause of satisfaction reserved for those of us who followed the fortunes of battle in these first few days of the break-out. Truscott was proving himself an outstanding commander. This was his first big operation, but clearly he had taken in his stride that difficult jump from Divisional to Corps Commander and from Corps to Army as well! Some excellent divisional generals, quick, courageous and competent, can never make the crossing. They have not got that inner detachment which allows a commander to judge coolly between the capabilities of men—of his friends as well as his enemies.

Truscott had straight away demonstrated his gifts for high command and it is well to bear this in mind as we reach the crucial point in the Battle of the Break-out.

Now was the time, on the second day of the offensive, with Cisterna encircled and Harmon's tanks moving towards the low gap in the hills which led to Valmontone, for the generals to remember the central point of the operation, the justification for the whole business of the Beachhead—General Alexander's plan for cutting the German retreat. Again and again Alexander had emphasized that the capture of Rome was only incidental to the grand object that he had in view when he launched his May attack. This was the smashing of Kesselring's armies beyond immediate recovery. The place where they could finally be smashed was Valmontone.

Late in the afternoon of the second day General Clark met Truscott and discussed the progress of the attack. He raised again the question of its direction. Had Truscott, he asked, now thought of the possibility of swinging it away from Valmontone north-east into the Alban Hills? Truscott replied that he had indeed given some thought to this; there was a danger that too obvious an advance through the Velletri gap towards Valmontone would put the Germans on their guard. Elements of the Hermann Goering Division were reported to be arriving in the Valmontone valley, after hurriedly unloading from the transports which were to have taken them to France. Truscott, as a prudent general, was immediately preparing a plan for a switch to the north-west if it should be forced on him. Clark told him, before he left, to keep this plan up-to-date.

But next day, 25 May, came heartening news. This was the morning which saw the great air attack on the German columns retreating along the Cori road; fourteen Tiger tanks lay burning and smashed amid miles of broken lorries and dead horses in as grim a scene of destruction as the Italian campaign could show.

The road into the Velletri gap was opening fast. Harmon's tanks had, in part, been held before Velletri itself, but his mediums and some of the men of his infantry units were now working their way up through the vineyards which covered this countryside towards the little village of Giulianello, at the lowest point of the gap. General Frederick had also got his Special Service Force crossing the rough hillsides of the Colli Lepini beyond Cori. Behind the tanks the 3rd Divisional infantry was also on its way up into the gap.

The hill-township of Artena lies on the eastern side of the

Velletri gap. It is a most picturesque huddle of medieval houses, embellished by a steep terrace added in the heyday of the Renaissance. From the terrace you can look out over the valley to the east which held Valmontone and the vital highway of Route Six leading to Rome. It was one of these highly dramatic views which were the speciality of the Italian campaign, where, as on no other battlefield, you could see every position and strategic possibility at a glance.

Valmontone, bombed and broken, was a mere three miles away. Behind it was the chaos of mountains marking the Central Apennines. Any army in retreat from the south would not find easy passage here; Route Six was the essential escape-route, dictated by the cruel facts of Italian geography.

Not that we were given any time to contemplate the view. Whistles and whines filled the air followed by the cracks of shell-bursts in the fields around Artena. The town was unapproachable, since the first elements of the Goering Division were in the valley below and hurrying into position to repel the advancing Americans. As we crouched in a ditch well below the skyline and tried to see where the enemy was firing from, a distracted woman ran along a path through the vines, clutching a six-months-old child and dragging a frightened girl. She brushed past us, shouting, 'Why did you come if you cannot frighten the Tedeschi away? You mustn't bring the war with you. . . . You must take your war away . . .'

Had we but known it, this was just what was about to happen.

Late in the afternoon Truscott had returned to his command post from a look at his front, feeling, as he confesses, rather jubilant. He had now assessed the position and knew that he could pour his full strength into the Velletri gap, capture Artena and cut Route Six. By the morning of 26 May he was confident that he would be firmly across the German line of retreat. He could swiftly brush aside the light reconnaissance units of the Hermann Goering Division which had got into Valmontone: he had his chance of bringing the Italian campaign to a magnificent fulfilment.

At his command post he was met by General Don Brann, of the Fifth Army's operational staff, who told him, 'The Boss wants you to leave the 3rd Infantry Division and the Special Force to block Highway Six and mount that assault you discussed with him to the north-west as soon as you can.'

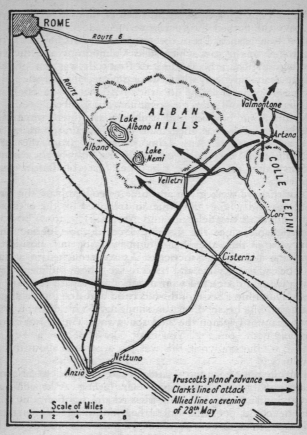

SWITCHING THE BREAK-OUT, 28 MAY 1944

Truscott was profoundly shaken and at first would not believe the order. He insisted that he would not obey until he talked to General Clark in person. The Germans were still in strength on the western slopes of the Alban Hills; they had prepared Switch-line Caesar to which they were falling back, while the road through the gap was for the moment wide open. But Clark could not be reached by telephone, Truscott could not argue his case and had no option but to obey. He gave the necessary orders and turned the main drive of Sixth Corps into the steep vineyards, the thickets and the fortified towns of the Alban Hills. Next day the Hermann Goering Division occupied Valmontone in strength and firmly held open the escape route of the German Tenth Army.

Thus, at the very end of its existence, the Beachhead was bedevilled by that same ironic spirit of frustration which had brooded over its beginnings. Or so it seemed to us at the time, as we halted before Valmontone and started the hard, bitter fight through the Alban Hills. The foregoing account of the switch of plan is based on Truscott's memoirs, written after the event. The Sixth Corps War Room journal, however, records that at 3.55 p.m. on 25 May General Brann radioed Clark that Truscott was 'entirely in accord' with the Army commander's ideas.

Stranger still, General Clark did not let Alexander know of his swing away from Valmontone until twenty-four hours after he had given his orders to Truscott—and then he left his tactful Chief of Staff, General Gruenther, to break the news. General Alexander, whatever he may have thought privately, had no option but gracefully to accept Gruenther's assurance that he could depend on Clark to 'execute a vigorous plan with all the push in the world!' But which plan? Certainly not General Alexander's!

Reluctantly Sixth Corps turned away from the gap. The commanders made the complicated alterations to their time-tables, their artillery support plans, their command-post locations and their supply routes forced on them by this sudden change in the axis of their advance. The infantry and armour began to push along the western slopes of the Alban Hills; they left the wide prospect of the descent into the Valmontone valley for the close, bitter fighting amongst the gardens, the steep gullies and the farmhouses around Lanuvio and Campoleone village. They lost tanks and men. Above all they lost time.

As Sixth Corps now battered at the front door of the German defences in the hills the remains of Kesselring's forces were creeping northwards to safety around the back.

When, at last, the American infantry climbed the highest points of the Hills and the enemy gave way, it was too late. The German Tenth Army had taken heavy losses, it was in full retreat with the Cassino Line broken behind it and the rest of the American Fifth Army hot on its heels —but it was still an army in being and not the mauled, disorganized force that General Alexander hoped it would be. On the morning of 4 June 1944 the first tanks of General Harmon's Armored Division entered the city of Rome. The wildest Roman holiday of the last hundred years began to erupt around them as the citizens poured in hundreds of thousands into the streets. At last the men of the Beachhead—and the men of the Cassino Front—saw the outward show of victory. The outward show only, for their real prize had, once again, escaped them. The Beachhead stayed treacherous to the bitter end.

But the story of the fall of Rome and the subsequent campaign up through Italy is no longer the story of the Beachhead. On the morning of 26 May—the very day on which General Mark Clark gave his orders to General Truscott to switch his attack—the Beachhead had officially ceased to exist.

As it became clear, on the morning of 24 May, that the advanced elements of the American Eleventh Corps must be pushing up through the still flooded Pontine Marshes, a small force, called Brett Force after its commander who was Colonel of the Reconnaissance Regiment of the British 1st Division, set out from the eastern flank of the Beachhead. It consisted of men from the Recce Regiment and the American 36th Engineers. They pushed forward carefully during the night, removing mines and negotiating the shell-holes blown in the coast road. Then at 0730 next morning a Recce sergeant, crossing one of these demolitions on foot, looked up to see a group of strangers waiting for him on the other side. They wore the insignia of the American Eleventh Corps. He looked at them and knew that the adventure of Anzio was over.

Later that morning General Clark, accompanied by every war correspondent who could get into a jeep, drove to the spot. On that lonely road near Borgo Grappa, with the level marshes all around and the sound of the battle drifting to us from Cisterna, we took our photographs, slapped each other on the back, exchanged cigarettes and then drove slowly back into Anzio.

Those of us who remembered the four months' siege would not have been human if we hadn't come to think of it as 'Our Anzio'. In the perverse way of men who never know when they are happy we almost regretted our freedom. . . .

11

Epilogue

Anzio today bears few traces of the terrible scars inflicted in 1944. Some battlefields never lose their air of menace, their threat of death and destruction. The broken forts that moulder on the bare chalk downs around Verdun still seem to be waiting for the terrifying thunder of the German bombardment to begin, while the Monastery of Monte Cassino, looming high on its rock above the Liri valley, looks as unaproachable today as it did to the Allied troops marching towards it through the sleet and rain of the Italian campaign. But Anzio has returned so completely to the normality of everyday life that it is impossible to believe, as you see it in the warm sun of early May, that this was a place where men suffered and died in their thousands.

The harbour is charming and peaceful. Every bombed building is rebuilt or restored. The fishing-boats swing at anchor on the clear waters and the tourists eat their *zuppa di pesce* in the restaurants on the quayside. The old fort and walled town of Nettuno look romantic and untouched across the curve of the bay. In the background are the blue hills and the gently swelling slopes of the Colli Laziali and the sharper, wilder outlines of the Colli Lepini. From the mole of Anzio harbour Monte Circeo seems a lonely island rising from the heart of a tranquil, waveless sea. The music sounds in the little cafés and the children play on the Riviera di Levante or watch the waterskiers twisting and turning on the blue waters of what used to be 'Bomb Bay'.

Inland the battlefield has been even more thoroughly brushed and combed; the industrious Italian peasant has tidied the whole landscape, filling in the bomb craters and ploughing and sowing the fields which were once covered with dug-outs and artillery dumps. The trenches in the wadis have fallen in, and a dense growth of brambles and bushes covers the Fortress, the Lobster Claw and the rest of the insanitary gullies in which the British troops spent the weary months of the siege. The woodlands of Padiglione have been largely cut down, the pine woods behind the landing beaches are littered with building lots and Lidos, and a big soap factory has been built near Padiglione station.

Aprilia—the Factory of the Beachhead battles—has grown into a small town with houses everywhere. 'The Bowling Alley' is the new main road from Rome to the south, busy with heavy traffic hurtling at sixty miles an hour along the track where the American 1st Armored Division sent its tanks slowly forward to the counter-attack. Every farm has been rebuilt, every field restored to the carefully tended vines and the green, springing corn.

In the midst of this careful restoration one spot has been left untouched. The Flyover Bridge is still there—broken, scarred and pitted by gunfire. Here is a place for memories. The returned soldier can climb the grass-covered embankment and feel the atmosphere of the old Beachhead return with irresistible force. He can recognize the old landmarks. Even the remains of the old observation tunnel are still there and the ditch below it where an abandoned tank lay silent and askew for the four months of the battle. He can look across the road where a new house stands on the edge of a small, carefully tilled field. The peasants are at work in the sun tending the orderly rows of the young vines. Can this really be the scene of the crisis of the enemy counter-attack, the 'killing ground' of the February struggles? The Flyover seems to be the only place in modern Anzio where the old soldier can ask himself these questions. The Flyover—and the military cemeteries.

The American cemetery has been built on the outskirts of Nettuno. It is a place of great beauty, where lie not only the men who fell in the Anzio landing, but also those killed in the Sicilian and Cassino campaigns and whose bodies were not taken back to the United States for burial. The Stars and Stripes wave in front of an impressive memorial, but inevitably the eye turns from the statues, the marble columns and the inscriptions to the endless rows of white crosses that curve across the green lawns. There are so many of them and the men they commemorate seem to have come so very far to rest at last in this quiet corner of Italy. Texas, Nebraska, Brooklyn, Miami, Chicago—no matter how remote the state or how crowded the city one of its sons is here in a soil thousands of miles from home. No one who walks through these orderly ranks dares question again the disinterestedness of the American sacrifice.

The main British cemetery is smaller, containing only the Anzio dead, but it makes an equally moving impression. It lies on the Albano road at the point where the new reinforcements spent their first nerve-testing hours, waiting to go into the line.

Again the ranks of the headstones are set in careful rows on the trim, green turf. The Italian gardeners have placed daffodils before each stone. On the edge of the cemetery stands a wood of dark umbrella pines. The quick green lizards sun themselves on the stones or dart in amongst the flowers as visitors walk slowly along the line of the graves.

Sometimes the visitors are relatives who write their few halting words of thanks in the book placed at a desk near the gate; or else they feel bound to add a comment such as 'God bless them, for they saved the free world.' Or else 'Beautifully kept, but *we* must not forget.'

From the rows of quiet graves the visitor looks beyond the spreading pines to the north-east. On most days of the year the Alban Hills are clear: in the warm air they seem astonishingly close to Anzio. You can pick out the details of the farms and vineyards, the small white-walled towns and the masts of the observatory on the highest summit. The scene has the bright, translucent quality of the background in a painting by an early Italian master.

The Alban Hills seem so near, a mere half-hour in a car, that once again the question forces itself into the visitor's mind—the nagging, insistent question that will always haunt those who fought on the Beachhead—why did not the Allies take the hills when they were to be had for the asking? What would have happened if Sixth Corps had gone boldly for them?

So for the last time, before we turn away from the Anzio scene, we hear the argument that has raged, and will continue to rage, over the operation.

On one side is the voice of Mr. Churchill, still eloquent in spite of the failure of his pet plan, and tireless in using the example of the Anzio landing as a lesson for 'Overlord'. His theme might be stated thus: Boldness pays.

Surprise was complete, and surprise is half the battle in war. If only the force we had flung ashore with such trouble had raced swiftly for the hills and got across the German lines of communication and acted with resolution, Kesselring's reaction might have been very different. Nothing is gained by not taking risks—and the prizes at stake at Anzio were worth every risk.

This Churchillian view is strongly backed by General Alexander. He has placed his considered opinion on record.

> The commander of the assault corps, the American General Lucas, missed his opportunity by being too slow and cautious. He failed to realise the great advantage that surprise had given him. He allowed Time to beat him.[1]

Now that the years have passed and we know both the Allied and the German story, which picture of Anzio is right?

Lucas—and he was not without influential supporters in this—could point out that his landing had started with one overwhelming handicap. It was not made in enough strength. Two divisions were not enough for the task assigned to them. Kesselring said, after the war, 'It would have been the Anglo-American doom to over-extend themselves. The landing force was initially weak. . . . It was a half-way measure as an offensive that was your basic error.'[2]

But the weakness in the landing force was not the fault of Mr. Churchill. In their higher planning of the war the Americans had no real faith in the value of the Italian campaign. To them it was no 'Second Front' and they starved the theatre of the vital landing craft which could have made this campaign a sure success. As it was, the Anzio plan became not a certainty but an adventure and adventures need bold leaders.

This is just what the Anzio landing did not get. General Lucas admitted that he had no faith in the plan; he wrote in his diary, 'In fact, there is no military reason for Shingle.' He

---

[1] In an article in the *Sunday Times*.
[2] In an interview published in *Saturday Evening Post*.

went ashore determined not to advance to the hills and never communicated his intentions to his British subordinates. If Churchill was over-bold and optimistic Lucas was surely too cautious and pessimistic.

Even granted that the Alban Hills were out of reach owing to his lack of strength, was there not more that he could have done? And would that extra have saved the Beachhead much of its anguish? The answer must be 'Yes'.

Lucas was presented with complete surprise. He could have seized Campoleone and Cisterna with ease on the first day. Would this not have given him firmer beachhead? If he had risked some thrusting patrols farther into the hills he would certainly have puzzled his opponent. At the least he would have delayed Kesselring's concentration against him. He might even have created an uncertainty in his enemy's mind which might have effected his decision to hold firm on the Gustav Line.

Battles are not won entirely by logistics, vitally important though they are. There are always the imponderables—surprise, daring, bluff, imaginative leadership. Who can say how they would have effected the position at Anzio? What would have happened if a General Patton had been in command of Sixth Corps?

So the nagging doubts persist. Those who survive from the beachhead can still see, in their mind, the picture as dawn broke on 22 January 1944—the troops pouring unmolested ashore, the quiet, empty countryside, the white road free of all sign of the enemy leading straight towards the beckoning Alban Hills.

In the end, even though at the top leadership was lacking, the Anzio adventure did not fail. The courage and endurance of the ordinary American and British soldier saved the Beachhead and held it to play its vital part in General Alexander's May advance on Rome. Without the breakout from Anzio the Italian campaign of 1944 would have remained a costly, frustrating slog through the mountains.

Perhaps the greatest victory of the men of the Beachhead was not won at Anzio after all. After the war Kesselring admitted, 'If you had not pitted your strength against us at Anzio-Nettuno you would never have landed in Northern France'. The lessons of Anzio were learnt and applied to the Normandy landing. As the greatest and most successful in-

vasion of modern times swept ashore at Arromanches and
the smoke-shrouded beaches near it, the assault troops owed
more than they knew to those men who had gone ashore
over four months before on the sands of Anzio a thousand
miles to the south.

The Beachhead had, at last, paid off.

Bibliography

I have consulted many personal, regimental and formation records, but the following main sources have been indispensable:

Report by the Supreme Allied Commander Mediterranean to the Combined Chiefs of Staff on the Italian Campaign, 8 January 1944 to 10 May 1944 (London. HMSO).

The Second World War, Vol. V: "Closing the Ring," Winston S. Churchill (Houghton Mifflin).

History of the Second World War, Vol. V: "Grand Strategy," John Ehrman (HMSO).

History of United States Naval Operations in World War II. Vol. IX: Sicily—Salerno—Anzio, January 1943-June 1944, Samuel Eliot Morison (Oxford University Press).

Command Decisions. Ed. K. R. Greenfield (Methuen).

Anzio Beachhead. American Forces in Action Series (Historical Division, Department of the Army, Washington).

The Campaign in Italy. Eric Linklater (HMSO).

Calculated Risk. General Mark Clark (Harper & Brothers).

Command Missions. Lt.-General Lucien K. Truscott, Jnr. (E. P. Dutton & Co., Inc., New York).

Cassino, Portrait of a Battle. Fred Majdalany (Longmans, Green).

The Royal Artillery Commemoration Book 1939-1945 (Bell).

The Royal Air Force 1939-1946, Vol. II: "The Fight Avails" (HMSO).

The Memoirs of Field-Marshal Kesselring (William Morrow & Co., Inc.).

The German Army in the West. General Siegfried Westphal (Cassell).

Il Mio Diario di Anzio. Alberto Tarchiani (Mondadori).

Index

249

BUY YOUR COPY NOW

60¢
M2000

TO KILL A
MOCKINGBIRD

The triumphant bestseller that the
New York Times calls "The best of
the year... exciting... marvelous"

a novel by HARPER LEE

**THE
PULITZER
PRIZE
WINNER**

POPULAR ⬢ LIBRARY

WINNER OF THE 1962
NATIONAL BOOK AWARD
FOR FICTION

The Moviegoer

By WALKER PERCY

"WHAT A MARVELOUS NOVEL!...
A CATCHER IN THE RYE FOR ADULTS ONLY"
—WARREN MILLER

"A NATURAL WRITER, A RARE TALENT..."
—TIME MAGAZINE